# Shorthand, Typewriting, and Secretarial Training

By ABRAHAM EPSTEIN
and MORRIS WHITE

A GD/PERIGEE BOOK

*Perigee Books*
*are published by*
*The Putnam Publishing Group*
*200 Madison Avenue*
*New York, New York 10016*

*ISBN 0-399-50814-7*

*First Perigee printing, 1982*
*Three previous Grosset & Dunlap printings*
*Printed in the United States of America*

# Contents

## Shorthand, Typewriting, and Secretarial Skills

## Business English and Effective Speaking

## How to Write Good Business Letters

*Contents*

# Useful Business Facts and Figures

# Shorthand, Typewriting, and Secretarial Skills

---

THIS SECTION commences with concise presentations of the Shorthand systems of Pitman, Gregg, and Speedwriting. This is followed by a course of Typewriting Lessons for Home Study. The section concludes with additional Clerical Skills which we take up under the headings Helpful Hints for Secretaries, Filing Equipment and Systems, and Business Machines and Their Use.

## Basic Shorthand Methods for Home Study

Shorthand is any method or system of writing rapidly, using special signs or symbols to represent letters, sounds, words, and phrases.

### EARLY BEGINNINGS

It is interesting to note that shorthand has at various times been known by such names as Stenography, Polygraphy, Brachygraphy, Tachygraphy, Cryptography, Phonography, Facilography. The origin of shorthand writing has been credited at different times to the Egyptians, the Greeks, and the Romans. The first organized system of stenography dates from the year 63 B.C. Marcus Tullius Tiro, a freedman and friend of Cicero, is said to have invented a scheme for reporting speeches during a period of great eloquence in the Roman Senate. The scribes (penmen) or stenographers of those days were called *notarii*. In taking down a Roman Senator's speech, a number of scribes worked together in relays. This was necessary because the Tironian system of shorthand was rather crude and not particularly fast and accurate. Each scribe, according to his stenographic ability, was responsible for a part of a long sentence. This method of rotation was necessary and helpful in the recording of the large volume of forensic oratory which existed at that time. After the scribes had made transcriptions of their shorthand notes, they were able to "piece together" a fairly accurate and verbatim account of the entire speech. This Tironian system of shorthand, practiced by the Romans, was used for many centuries after the fall of the Roman Empire.

During the Middle Ages very little advance, if any, was made in the art of shorthand writing. Occasional examples of the use of shorthand notations are extant on historical documents. Fragmentary samples of shorthand are confined to a few waxen tablets ranging from the fourth to the eighth century.

In the later history of shorthand three world-wide movements stimulated its use and development. First there was the need to record rapidly the utterances of the religious leaders. Next it became urgent to report accurately the political debates and proceedings of legislative assemblies. Then the trend toward universal education brought about the further development of shorthand. The beginning of this development in England was marked by the publication of a new system of shorthand by Dr. Timothy Bright in 1588. His system was cumbersome, and there was much room for improvement.

In 1602 John Willis introduced a shorthand method based on the alphabet. It was called orthographic because it depended on the spelling of words, though silent letters were omitted. In 1638 Thomas Shelton issued another system which was used in recording the famous diary of Samuel Pepys. In 1720 Dr. John Byrom published a shorthand system called the "Universal English Shorthand." His contribution was greater linability and the representation of vowels by dots near consonants. In 1786 Samuel Taylor isued his system called "An Essay Intended to Establish a Standard for a Universal System of Stenography." It contained many simplifications over previous systems. Arbitrary signs were eliminated, and each letter was given one sign.

About 1750 William Tiffin first published a system using a phonetic base with symbols representing sounds. Many similar phonetic systems followed.

### MODERN SYSTEMS

In 1837 Isaac Pitman published a phonetic system of shorthand. He was the first to classify sounds scientifically, and introduced simple abbreviating devices that made for rapidity. The *Pitman system* was brought to the United States in 1844. Soon thereafter a number of modifications appeared under various names; however, only the *Isaac Pitman* system is in general use today.

Critical of the then-existing shorthand methods, and finding certain weaknesses in their structure, John Robert Gregg published in 1888 his simplified system called "Light-Line Phonography," now known as *Gregg Shorthand.*

According to Dr. Gregg, the following is a résumé of the leading features of his system.

1. The shorthand outlines may be written either light or heavy as in ordinary writing.
2. The writing of the outlines follows the manual movement of ordinary writing.
3. The outlines, which may be written on plain or ruled paper, follow a straight line as in ordinary writing.
4. Vowels and consonants are joined, and follow each other in natural order as in ordinary writing.
5. Curved outlines predominate as in ordinary writing. Angular outlines are rare.

*Speedwriting*, of comparatively recent origin, employs only the letters of the alphabet as used in longhand, and a few characters such as the apostrophe, comma, hyphen, semicolon, and an oblique line.

The presentations of the Pitman and the Gregg systems are printed by special arrangement with the Pitman Publishing Corporation and the Gregg Publishing Company, respectively. Permission for the presentation of Speedwriting has been given by the Speedwriting Institute.

We now take up these three systems in turn.

## THE PITMAN SYSTEM

The Pitman System of shorthand is phonetic. You write only what you hear. The words *know, pay, age* would therefore be written as if they were spelled *no, pa, aj*. Pitman shorthand has a sign for every sound in the English language, as follows:

| LETTER | SIGN | NAME | AS IN |
|---|---|---|---|
| P | | pee | pay |
| B | | bee | be |
| T | | tee | ate |
| D | | dee | aid |
| CH | | chay | chair |
| J | | jay | edge |
| F | | ef | safe |
| V | | vee | save |
| TH | | ith | thin |
| TH | | thee | them |
| S | | ess | us |
| Z | | zee | zeal |
| SH | | ish | wish |
| ZH | | zhee | azure |
| K | | kay | make |
| G | | gay | game |
| M | | em | seem |
| N | | en | no |
| NG | | ing | sing |
| L | | el | lake |
| W | | way | wave |
| Y | | yay | yellow |
| R | (upward) | ray | raw |
| R | (downward) | ar | car |
| H | (upward) | hay | hotel |
| H | (downward) | hay | he |

It will be noted that the consonants form pairs: *p* and *b*, *t* and *d*, *ch* and *j*, and so on.

The light sound is expressed by a *light* stroke, and the corresponding heavy sound by a *heavy* stroke.

The direction of all the strokes is downward except for the signs of *k, g, m, n,* and *ng*, which are written horizontally from left to right. The signs for *ray, w, y, h* (as in hotel), and *l* are written upward.

2

In certain joinings, as in phrasing, the usual writing motion for *l* and *sh* is reversed; also, extra signs are given for *r* and *h* for ease in special joinings.

## Vowels

The twelve vowels in the language are expressed by dots and dashes. These twelve vowel sounds can be arranged schematically in two short sentences:

Pa,    may    we    all    go    too?

That    pen    is    not    much    good.

In the first sentence, a *heavy dot* represents the first three vowel sounds, and a *heavy dash* represents the last three vowel sounds. In the second sentence, a *light dot* represents the first three vowel sounds, and a *light dash* represents the last three vowel sounds.

The vowel signs are written near the consonant strokes. When the vowel comes before the consonant, it is placed before the stroke; when a vowel comes after a consonant, it is placed after the stroke. The consonants are always written first, and then the vowel signs are indicated. Vowel signs may be written at the beginning, middle, or end of consonant strokes. This results in what is known as first, second, or third place positions. The first vowel of a word determines the position. In first position, the first downstroke or upstroke of an outline is written above the line; in second position, it is on the line; in third position, it is written through the line. In the two illustrative sentences above, the sounds of the vowels are in the following positions:

1st position—as in *pa, all, that, not*
2nd position—as in *may, go, pen, much*
3rd position—as in *we, too, is, good*

Notice the placement of the vowel sounds (light or heavy dots and dashes), and the positions of the words in the following illustrations:

| | 1ST POSITION | 2ND POSITION | 3RD POSITION |
|---|---|---|---|
| *heavy dots* | pa | may | see |
| *heavy dashes* | jaw | dough | chew |
| *light dots* | path | etch | live |
| *light dashes* | top | cup | book |

## Diphthongs

The four diphthongs in the English language are *i, oi, ow,* and *u*, as heard in the sentence, "I enjoy Gow's music." The diphthongs, in the order in which they appear in the sentence, are represented by ........ The first two diphthongs are written in the first vowel place, and the last two are written in the third vowel place. For example:

pie    buy    time

joy    toy    toil

cow    couch    outlay

beauty    endure    occupy

## Punctuation Marks

Certain punctuation marks used in Pitman Shorthand are different from those used in longhand. These are:

Period    Question mark

Dash    Hyphen

Capital letters are indicated by two short slanting lines under the word to be capitalized.

## Short Forms

Short Forms for common words are very often expressed by a single symbol. The Pitman System has a total of 259 Short Forms that must be memorized and practiced until they can be written legibly and rapidly.

Some of the simpler and more common Short Forms are:

be          it
to          two, too
do          which
the         but
who         are

Other Short Forms for frequently used words are expressed by outlines composed of two or more signs. For example:

govern          government

immediate          member

...┭.... nevertheless    ...⌐... organization     ...⤳... knows    ....⌐.... air

...⌐... practice    ..⌐⌐.. representative     ...⌐.... bills    ...⌐.... leaves

......⌐... interest    .....⌐.... knowledge     ...⌐... absence    ...⌐... business

**Some Short Forms have two or more meanings:**

....⌐..... different   difference    ....⌐..... special   specially     ..⌐... receiving    ......⌐... message

.... ⌐... object   objected    ..⌐.... improve   improved   improvement

The *s* circle is made with a left or counter-clock-wise movement when joined to straight strokes.

....⌐.... pays    ...⌐..... choose

.....⌐.... said    .....⌐.... such

...⌐... ladies    .....⌐.... days

....⌐..... sets    .....⌐.... cities

## Phrasing

Many Short Forms can be joined in one outline to form a simple phrase. For example, by placing a small tick at the end of a word for *the*, the following simple phrases can be formed:

The *s* circle is joined to Short Forms for the plural of words and in the formation of phrases:

...⌐.... to-the    ........ of-the

...⌐.... be-the    ....⌐.. for-the

...⌐.... do-the

......⌐... your    .....⌐... yours

.....⌐.... think    ....⌐.... thinks

.....⌐... wish    .....⌐.... wishes

Other phrases formed by combining Short Forms are:

....⌐... do you    ..⌐.. you may be

.......... I will    .......... I will be

....⌐... I hope    ...⌐. I hope you will be

.⌐. we hope you will be

..⌐... I think you will be

.....⌐.... our    ....⌐.... ours

...⌐.... show–us    ..⌐.... give–us

....⌐..... is-the    ....⌐.... he–is–the

When the sound *ses* occurs, except at the beginning of an outline, it is expressed by a large circle:

## The *S* Circle

The sound of *s* may sometimes be expressed by a small circle. This facilitates joining it to other strokes. When joined to curved characters, the *s* circle is written inside.

...⌐.... pace    ...⌐.... paces

...⌐... piece    ...⌐... pieces

.......... cause    .......... causes

...⌐... use    ...⌐... uses

....⌐.... face    ...⌐.... safe

...⌐... sense    ...⌐... seems

....⌐.... suppose    ...⌐... supposes

The large circle may also be written in the middle of words, thus:

..... necessary

..... successive

..... successfully

At the beginning of a word the large circle represents *sw*:

..... sweep

..... swing

..... swim

The *sw* circle is used for *as we* in phrases:

..... as–we–have

..... as–we–think

..... as–we–wish

## Two Forms for *R* and *H*

When a word begins with *r* (or ends with *r* followed by a vowel sound) the upward form is used:

... red       ... road

..... dairy       ..... memory

When a vowel precedes *r* (or ends a word) the downward form is used:

..... air       ..... army

..... door       ..... chair

The downward form of *h* is used when it is the only stroke in the word or followed by letter *k* or *g*:

..... hay       ..... high

..... hug       ..... highway

The upward form of *h* is used in other cases:

..... happy       ..... hope

..... hotel

In the middle or at the end of a phrase a tick . ( .. is used for the word *he*:

..... if–he       ..... if–he–should

The tick for *h* is also used before *m*, *l*, and downward *r*:

..... home       ..... whom

..... hall       ..... health

..... harm       ..... here

..... herself

When used in phrases, the word *hope* is expressed by *p*:

..... I–hope–you–will

..... I–hope–you–are

## Upward and Downward *L*

The letter *l*, though keeping its form, may be written in an upward or downward direction, depending on the ease of joining it to other strokes. The upward form of *l* is generally used at the beginning, middle, or end of a word:

..... lady       ..... luck

..... envelope       ..... railroad

..... goal       ..... mail

For convenience, the stroke *l* is written downward after *n* or *ng*:

..... only       ..... unless

..... analysis       ..... exceedingly

The stroke *l* is also written downward when an initial vowel comes before it, and when the *l* is followed by a forward stroke:

..... alone       ..... along

..... Ellen       ..... alike

5

*l* is written downward after *f*, *v*, *sk*, or a straight upstroke not followed by a vowel:

fail

veal

skill

successful

rail

useful

When a vowel sound ends the word, *l* is written upward:

folly

usefully

successfully

lovely

fellow

rely

*l* is written downward or upward by following the direction of the *s* circle:

vessel

cancel

lesson

muscle

council

## The *ST* and *STR* Loops

The small circle for *s* is turned into a small loop to express the sound of *st*, and into a large loop to express the sound of *str*:

*st* post     fast     must

*str* poster     faster     muster

(Loop for *str* is never used at beginning of words.)

Plurals are formed as follows:

posts     posters

## Use of Hooks—Double Consonants

A convenient abbreviating device in Pitman Shorthand is obtained by adding hooks to consonants. Such strokes are known as Double Consonants. A small hook written at the beginning and to the left of straight downstrokes and under horizontal strokes automatically adds the letter *r* (though *r* is not actually written). A small hook written at the end of such consonants represents the letter *n*.

pray     brain

tray     train

grow     grown

price     prices

cream     crowd

April     progress

A small initial hook written on the right side of downstrokes or above horizontal strokes automatically adds the letter *l* (though *l* is not written). At the end of these strokes, the hook expresses the letter *f* or *v*. For example:

play     pave

place     brave

places     replace

blow     claim

glow     glove

## Double Consonant Curves

A small hook may be written at the beginning of curves for the double consonants *fr*, *vr*, etc. A large beginning hook is used in forming *fl*, *vl*, etc.

Friday     average

dinner     farmers

fly     evil

arrival     final

The double consonants *fr*, *vr*, *thr*, *ther*, are also written in reverse form occasionally to provide more easily written outlines:

free     through

three     leather

discover

## SHL, SHR; NG-KR, NG-GR

The double consonant *shl* is always written upward and *shr* is always written downward:

........ official      ...... . shelf

.. ...... essential      ........ washer

........ pressure      ..... Fisher

The heavy sign .. ....... expresses *ng-kr, ng-gr*.

........ banker      ....... finger

........ stronger

### The N Hook

A small final hook on the inside of curves adds *n*:

........ fine      ...... shown

...... zone      ........ than

...... even      ...... known

### Vowel Indication

In rapid writing the insertion of vowels is not necessary. Three methods are used to indicate the presence or absence of a vowel:

1. When letters have two forms, the use of one form generally indicates the absence of a vowel.
2. Placement above, on, or through the line, indicates a first, second, or third place vowel.
3. The third method involves the use of the full consonant stroke instead of its abbreviated form, as in the sign for *s* and the *s circle*:

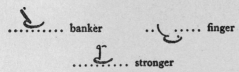

........ assume,    but ...... ... sum;

...... escape,    but ...... ... scope;

........ car,    but ........ carry;

...... lake,    but ........ alike.

The outlines are perfectly legible when the vowel signs are omitted as a result of using these three methods.

### The *SHUN* Hook

The sound of *shun*, no matter how it is spelled, is represented by a large hook which may be written on either side of a straight stroke, thus giving "balance" to the outline:

...... passion      ...... petition

........ occasion      ...... station

When used with curved letters, the *shun* hook is always on the inside of the curved stroke:

........ fashion      ...... motion

...... nation      ...... profession

The *s* circle may be added, thus:

........ fashions      ...... motions

...... relations

### Halving and Doubling

When a stroke is written half its size, it indicates the addition of *t* or *d*, thus:

...... play   ...... plate   ...... plated

...... gray   ...... grade   ...... graded

...... pain   ...... paint   ...... painted

...... love   ...... loved

...... ask   ...... asked

...... label   ...... labeled

When a stroke is written double its size, it indicates the addition of the syllables *ter, der,* or *ther,* thus:

...... pore      ...... porter

........ track      ........ tractor

...... after      ...... father

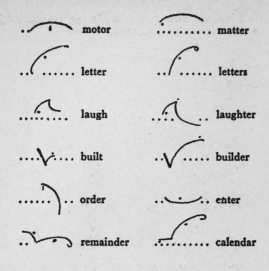

motor    matter

letter    letters

laugh    laughter

built    builder

order    enter

remainder    calendar

## Compound Consonants

There are six compound consonants:

| LETTER | SIGN | NAME | AS IN | SHORTHAND OUTLINE |
|---|---|---|---|---|
| KW | | kwa | quick | |
| GW | | gwa | linguist | |
| | | | camp | |
| MP or MB | | emp emb | embody | |
| LR | | ler | scholar | |
| RR | | rer | poorer | |
| WH | | hwa | where | |

### The Letter *W*

The stroke of *w* is abbreviated at the beginning of *k, g, m,* and both forms of *r*:

week    walk

walked    wig

womanly    worry

work

## Note the following special forms:

which were

they were

we were

When *w* is combined with a vowel in the middle of a word, it is expressed by a small semi-circle (either direction):

twelve    goodwill

guesswork    somewhat

### Upward *SH*

In certain joinings it is better to write *sh* upward.

finish    shave    brush

appreciate    shoulder

## Prefixes and Suffixes

Some valuable abbreviations for long words are obtained by the use of well-selected prefixes and suffixes. The prefixes *con-, com-, cog-,* are expressed by a dot:

condition    conduct

confident    confidence

communication    community

comply    complaint

When these prefixes occur in the middle of a word or in a phrase, they are expressed by writing the strokes of the word or phrase close together:

misconduct    disconnect

uncommon    discomfort

recognize

You will be compelled

I am confident

8

The prefix *accom-* is expressed by *k, intro-* by *ntr, magna-* by disjoined *m,* as follows:

..... accommodate ...... introduced

.......... magnitude

The prefix *self-* is expressed by disjoining the circle *s*:

... self-defense .... self-contained

... self-control

The prefix *trans-* is expressed by the double consonant *tr*:

.......... translate ... transcribe

The suffix *-ing* is expressed by .... ng. However, this form is not used when it is easier to use a dot for *ng*, as follows:

.... requesting ..... ordering

.... meeting .... hearing

When the sign for *mnt* .... cannot be joined easily, the suffix *-ment* is expressed by *nt*:

.......... achievement .......... consignment

The suffix *-lity* or *-rity* is expressed by disjoining a stroke:

.... possibility .... liability

... desirability .......... majority

.. minority .. similarity

In addition to the principles given here, there are many contractions (abbreviated words) in Pitman, the use of which enables the shorthand writer to gain a high degree of speed. A few examples follow:

... assignment ..... intelligent

.. democracy ..... manufacture

..... expensive .. universal

## Sample Letter

A business letter written in Pitman, together with a transcript of the shorthand, follows:

... ..
Dear-Sir:

As-we-have-not   heard   from-you

for-some-time,   we-are   wondering

whether   you   ever   received   our-letter

of   December   8   in-which   we-enclose

a   duplicate   of   a   bill   for   merchandise

shipped   to-you   in   July.

We-are   particularly   anxious;   with-the

end   of-the   year   approaching,   to-clear

up   as   many   of-our   outstanding

accounts   as   possible.

Please-let-us-hear   from-you   by-return-mail.

Very-truly-yours,

9

# THE GREGG SYSTEM

The Gregg System of shorthand, like Pitman, is written according to sound. The words *laugh, aim, cat, knee*, are therefore written as if spelled *laf, am, kat, ne*.

## Consonants

The consonants, represented by shorthand signs which are similar except in size, are arranged in pairs according to their similarity of sound (*k, g; t, d; p, b; f, v*)

The size, proportion, and s ant of all shorthand outlines, as used in the illustrations, should be followed.

Each consonant expressed by a shorthand sign has one or more word meanings. These are called Brief Forms, and represent high frequency words.

The *Consonants, Signs*, and *Brief Forms* are as follows:

| CONSONANTS | SIGNS | BRIEF FORMS |
|---|---|---|
| K | ⌒ | can |
| G | ⌒ | go, good |
| R | ⌣ | are, our, hour |
| L | ⌣ | will, well |
| N | — | in, not |
| M | — | am, more |
| T | ╱ | it, at |
| D | ╱ | would |
| H | • (a dot) | a, an |
| TH | ╱ | the |
| TH (second form) | ╱ | there, their |
| P | ( | put |

| CONSONANTS | SIGNS | BRIEF FORMS |
|---|---|---|
| B | ( | be, by, but |
| F | ) | for |
| V | ) | have |
| CH | / | which, change |
| J | / | (not a brief form) |
| SH | / | shall, ship |
| S | ) | is, his |

The signs for *k, g, r, l, n, m*, are written forward from left to right; those for *t, d*, and the two forms for the sound of *th* (as in *that* and *oath*) are written upward from the line of writing. The hard sound for *g*, as heard in *game* and *grow*, is represented by the sign for the letter *g*; the soft sound for *g*, as heard in *gem* and *margin*, is represented by the sign for the letter *j*.

The signs for *p, b, f, v, ch, j, sh*, and the two forms for *s* are all written downward. The sound of *ch* is that heard in *chair*, and the sound of *sh* is that heard in *fresh*. As *s* is one of the most frequent letters in the language, two signs are provided to facilitate joining with other letters, thus ) or (

The difference in size for the signs *sh, ch, j*, written as / , / , / , should be noted carefully.

## Vowels

There are two types of vowel signs: circle-vowels and hook-vowels. The circle-vowels, used for sounds of *a* and *e*, are written O and ● ; the hook-vowels, for sounds *o* and *oo*, are written ʊ and ∩

The four vowel signs are O , ● , ʊ , ∩ . Each one represents a group of three related sounds—a short sound, a medium sound, and a long sound. All of these together represent the twelve vowel sounds in the language.

The circle vowel for *a* is used to express the pronoun *I*, and the circle vowel for *e* is used for the pronoun *he*.

The exact shade of pronunciation for each vowel sound is indicated as follows: the short sound has no marking; the medium sound is indicated by a dot under the vowel; the long sound by a short dash. While these markings are sometimes useful, they are rarely needed to indicate exact shades of sound. For example, the outlines for

*calm*     and *came*

are alike except for the dot under *calm* and the dash under *came*. Yet, when either word appears in a sentence, the marking of the vowel is not necessary. In the sentence

The air is calm.

no special marking under *air* or *calm* is necessary because the exact sounds of the vowels are perfectly clear in reading the sentence. Again, in the sentence

He came for me.

the outline for *came*, without any vowel marking, can only be read as *came* if the sentence is to have meaning.

The related vowel sounds (*short, medium,* and *long*) for each vowel sign follow:

### THE *A* GROUP

| VOWEL SOUND | VOWEL SIGN | OUTLINE |
|---|---|---|
| short *a* as in *cat* | | |
| medium *a* as in *calm* | | |
| long *a* as in *came* | | |

### THE *E* GROUP

| | | |
|---|---|---|
| short *i* as in *din* | | |
| medium *e* as in *den* | | |
| long *e* as in *dean* | | |

### THE *O* GROUP

| | | |
|---|---|---|
| short *o* as in *rot* | | |
| medium *o* as in *raw* | | |
| long *o* as in *wrote* | | |

### THE *OO* GROUP

| | | |
|---|---|---|
| short *u* as in *cup* | | |
| medium *oo* as in *cook* | | |
| long *oo* as in *food* | | |

### Punctuation Marks

The punctuation marks which are used most frequently are: period   ; question mark   ; paragraph mark

### Phrasing

The shorthand signs for *I can go there* are

For greater speed in writing, however, some words are joined together in phrases. Thus the foregoing sentence may be written

Other sentences, written with separate signs for each word, follow:

1. He will not go there.

2. I will not go there.

3. Will he have it for me?

4. He will not put it there.

5. Will he ship it for me?

6. I am going to be there.

7. At the hour he will go.

A dot placed at the end of a word, as used after *going* in sentence No. 6, expresses the common ending *ing*.

By joining in phrases the simple Brief Forms given in the above six sentences, the shorthand outlines appear as follows:

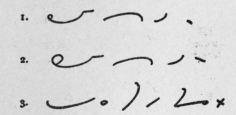

1.

2.

3.

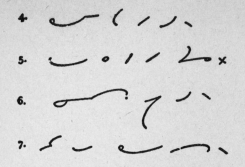

4. 
5. 
6. 
7. 

## Diphthongs

The four vowel sounds are used in forming the four diphthongs of the language. The diphthongs are expressed by joining into one symbol the exact sounds of the circles and hooks from which the diphthongs are composed.

| DIPH-THONG | VOWEL SOUNDS | DIPH-THONG SIGN | AS IN | WRITTEN |
|---|---|---|---|---|
| u | e + oo |  | unit |  |
| ow | a + oo |  | ounce |  |
| oi | aw + e |  | oil |  |
| i | a + e |  | sky |  |

The diphthong is a "broken circle," and the break is made in any part of the circle, usually just before another letter is added, thus:

tie ; pie ; sky ; sign ;
tried

## Joinings

Words and phrases are formed by joining the *signs* for consonants and vowels. The basic rules for correct joinings follow:

The circle-vowels and are written inside of all curves. For example:

egg ; gay ; air ;

Abe (the strokes under the outline indicate capitalization); pay ; if ;

happy (the h-dot is written first).

When joined to a single straight stroke, the circle is written toward the right as the hands of a clock move, thus:

aim ; may ; tea ;

day ; head

(the upper dot is for *h* and the lower dot represents

medium sound of *e*); each ; knee ;

me The circle is also written clockwise between straight lines in the same direction, thus:

deed ; main

Whenever the circle comes between two strokes which form an angle, the circle is placed outside the angle, thus:

cake rain

dream make

team met

chat chap

chief page

lane

The circle is also written inside of the curve when a curve and a straight line meet without forming an angle, thus:

read ; taken ; ticket .

Circle vowels coming between opposite curves (such as *r* , *g* , or *p* ,

*v* ), must be written on the back of the first curve, thus: rag ; pave ;

lake

## Consonant Combinations

There are a number of frequent consonant combinations that should be noted and practiced:

kr as in *cream*

or *creed*

gl as in *glee*

or *eagle*

gr as in *gray*

or *eager*

kl as in *clay*

or *clan*

rk as in *ark*

or *dark*

lk as in *milk*

or *silk*

Other consonant combinations which must be learned are:

pr as in *pray*

pl as in *pledge*

br as in *brave*

bl as in *blame*

fr as in *fresh*

fl as in *flash*

### Signs for S

There are two signs for the letter *s*, both written downward, ) or ( to increase facility in joining. Two simple rules govern joinings for the letter *s*.

1. When *s* is joined to curves, use the form which continues in the direction of the curve to which it is joined, thus:

series     sales

safe     saves

seeks     sag

busy     vast

2. When *s* is joined to straight lines or when an angle is formed, use the *s* which makes a sharp angle, thus:

seen     same

staff     seeds

days     dance

needs     chance

After downward straight lines the clockwise *s* is used as in:

ages

13

### The Writing Line

The first consonant of a word always rests on the line of writing, except *s*. When *s* begins a word and it is followed by another consonant, the consonant following *s* rests on the line. For example, when the first consonant is a horizontal or upward stroke, no special treatment is necessary, as in:

makes —∅3    dress ↗

but when the first consonant after *s* is a downward stroke, then *s* does not rest on the line of writing, thus:

safe ♀    sable Ɛ    sage ♀

### Blended Consonants

Frequently recurring syllables are often expressed by joining two consonants into one continuous stroke. Thus, *d* and *t* joined into one long stroke express the syllables *ted, ded, det,* as in the words:

treat ↗    tread ↗

treated ↗

net ↗    need ↗

needed ↗

ate ∂    add ∂

added ∂

Also, by blending *m* and *n* into one long stroke the syllables *men* or *mem,* and similar sounding syllables may be expressed thus:

mend ———    memory ———∂

minimum ———∂    emanate ∂———∂

Another simple blend, formed by joining letters,

is the syllable for *ses,* written ∫ or ∠ , as in:

senses ∂∠    cases ♀

analysis ∂∠

Other syllables, illustrating the blending principle and formed by joining consonants into one rapid symbol, follow.

| SIGN | | AS IN | |
|---|---|---|---|
| ten, den | ∫ | written | ∂ |
| | | sentence | ∂ |
| | | denote | ∫ |
| tem, dem | ∫ | temple | ∫ |
| | | freedom | 2∫ |
| ent, end | ∫ | sent | ∫ |
| | | bond | ∫ |
| emt, emd | ∫ | prompt | ∫ |
| | | trimmed | ∂ |
| def, dev, tive | ∩ | defend | ∩ |
| | | divide | 2∩ |
| | | positive | ∩ |

14

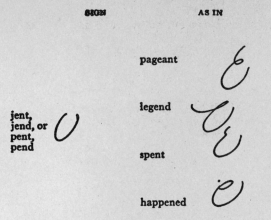

| SIGN | AS IN |
| --- | --- |
| jent, jend, or pent, pend | pageant / legend / spent / happened |

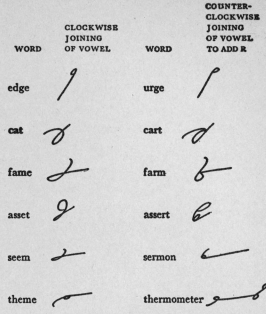

| WORD | CLOCKWISE JOINING OF VOWEL | WORD | COUNTER-CLOCKWISE JOINING OF VOWEL TO ADD R |
| --- | --- | --- | --- |
| edge | | urge | |
| cat | | cart | |
| fame | | farm | |
| asset | | assert | |
| seem | | sermon | |
| theme | | thermometer | |

It should be noted that the number of syllables expressed by these blended consonants are more numerous than shown above, since no attention is paid to minor spelling differences in the vowel sounds of such syllables.

Blended consonants are also used in phrasing, as follows:

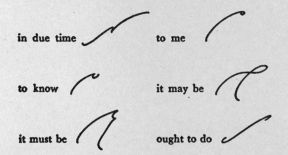

in due time     to me

to know     it may be

it must be     ought to do

### Expressing R by Reversing the Circle-Vowels

When the joining of circle-vowels to straight lines is not made in accordance with the rules given under "Joining," but reversed, then it is possible to express the letter r by omitting it. This is done when the circle, which must be written toward the left (or counter-clockwise), occurs before or after straight lines, between a horizontal and an upward stroke, between a downward stroke followed by a forward one, and in the syllables *ser* and *ther*. In each instance, the sound of r, though not written, is read into the word after the circle. For example:

| WORD | CLOCKWISE JOINING OF VOWEL | WORD | COUNTER-CLOCKWISE JOINING OF VOWEL TO ADD R |
| --- | --- | --- | --- |
| hat | | heart | |
| may | | mar | |
| day | | dared | |

### The Letters *W*, *Y*, and *X*

The letter *w* is expressed by the *oo*-hook. In the middle of words, however, *w* is expressed by a dash placed under the vowel which follows the *w* sound.

Examples of *w* expressed by the *oo*-hook:

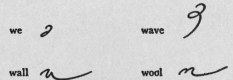

we     wave

wall     wool

Examples of *w* expressed by a dash placed under the vowel:

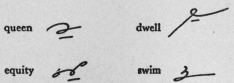

queen     dwell

equity     swim

The sound for *y*, when followed by a hook-vowel, is expressed by the sign for *e*; *ye* is expressed by a small loop; *ya* is expressed by a large loop:

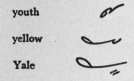

youth

yellow

Yale

The letter *x* is expressed by the sign for *s* slanted toward the right; *xes* is a blend of the two *s*'s:

mix     mixes

fix     fixes

### The Signs for NG and NK

The sign for the basic letter — is lengthened and slanted slightly downward for the sounds *ng* and *nk*, as follows:

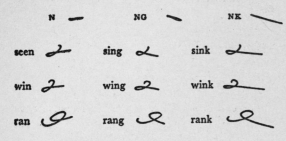

| N — | | NG ⁀ | | NK ⁀ |
|---|---|---|---|---|
| seen | | sing | | sink |
| win | | wing | | wink |
| ran | | rang | | rank |

### The Hook-Vowels

The hook-vowels for *o* and *oo* are written in their natural positions, except in certain cases.

Examples of words with the *o*-hook in its natural position follow:

John          Paul          Jones

Before *n*, *m*, *r*, and *l*, the *o*-hook is placed on its side, as follows:

| on | | home |
| or | | college |

Examples of words with the *oo*-hook in its natural position follow:

| who | | whom |
| us | | sugar |

The *oo*-hook is turned on its side after *n* and *m*, and after *k* and *g* if followed by *r* or *l*, thus:

| noon | | moon |
| cur | | cool |

### Common Prefixes and Suffixes

At the beginning of words the prefixes *con-*, *com-*, *coun-*, are usually expressed by *k*, thus:

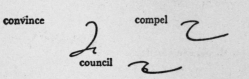

| convince | | compel |
| | council | |

The letter *s* expresses *sub-*, as in:

| submit | | subway |

*Ex-* is represented by *es*, thus:

| expense | | exceed |

The vowel is dropped in the prefixes *en-*, *in-*, *un-*, *em-*, thus:

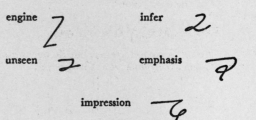

| engine | | infer |
| unseen | | emphasis |
| | impression | |

When the prefix is followed by a vowel, the **initial** vowel is retained:

emit

The vowel is dropped in the prefixes *be-*, *de-*, *re-*, *dis-*, and *mis-*. For example:

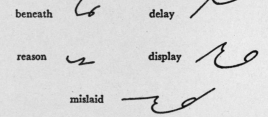

| beneath | | delay |
| reason | | display |
| | mislaid | |

The suffix *-ly* is expressed by the circle, thus:

| safely | | hardly |

The suffixes *-ily* and *-ally* are expressed by a loop.

| heartily | | socially |

The suffix *-tion* is expressed by *sh*, thus:

| nation | | emotion |

The suffix *-ings* is expressed by the left *s*, and *-ingly* by a small circle in place of the *-ing* dot, thus:

| meetings | | willingly |

The suffix *-ble* is expressed by *b*, as in:

sensible

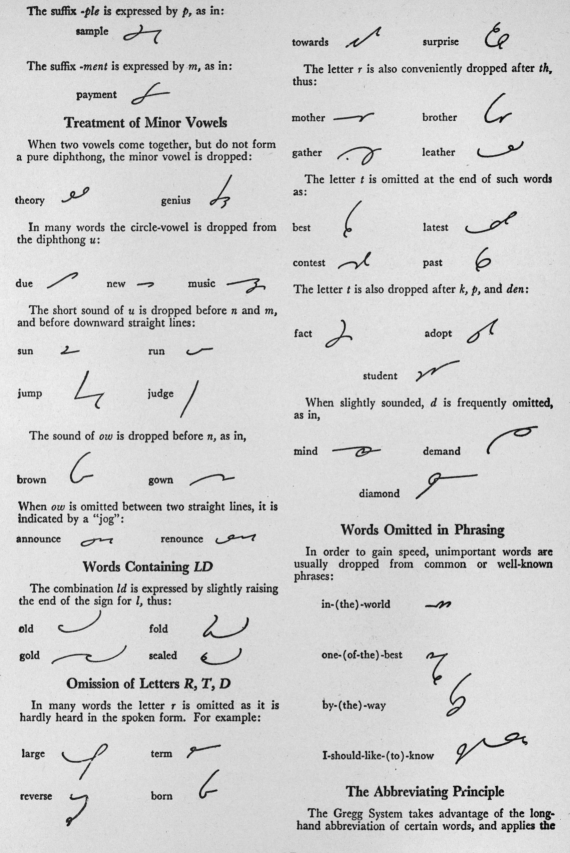

The suffix *-ple* is expressed by *p*, as in:

sample

The suffix *-ment* is expressed by *m*, as in:

payment

## Treatment of Minor Vowels

When two vowels come together, but do not form a pure diphthong, the minor vowel is dropped:

theory            genius

In many words the circle-vowel is dropped from the diphthong *u*:

due            new            music

The short sound of *u* is dropped before *n* and *m*, and before downward straight lines:

sun            run

jump            judge

The sound of *ow* is dropped before *n*, as in,

brown            gown

When *ow* is omitted between two straight lines, it is indicated by a "jog":

announce            renounce

## Words Containing LD

The combination *ld* is expressed by slightly raising the end of the sign for *l*, thus:

old            fold

gold            sealed

## Omission of Letters R, T, D

In many words the letter *r* is omitted as it is hardly heard in the spoken form. For example:

large            term

reverse            born

towards            surprise

The letter *r* is also conveniently dropped after *th,* thus:

mother            brother

gather            leather

The letter *t* is omitted at the end of such words as:

best            latest

contest            past

The letter *t* is also dropped after *k, p,* and *den*:

fact            adopt

student

When slightly sounded, *d* is frequently omitted, as in,

mind            demand

diamond

## Words Omitted in Phrasing

In order to gain speed, unimportant words are usually dropped from common or well-known phrases:

in-(the)-world

one-(of-the)-best

by-(the)-way

I-should-like-(to)-know

## The Abbreviating Principle

The Gregg System takes advantage of the long-hand abbreviation of certain words, and applies the same principle to the abbreviation of words in shorthand. All unnecessary endings are dropped from the shorthand forms. For example:

*amount* is written *amt.*

*Reverend, Rev.*

*answer, ans.*

*magazine, mag.*

*January, Jan.*

*association, assoc.*

*memorandum, memo.*

In many shorter words the abbreviated form stops with a diphthong or an accented vowel, thus:

arrive        strike

proud         repeat

cure          excuse

peculiar

In another group of words, the abbreviated shorthand outline ends with the accented syllable, thus:

authen(tic)

cap(able)

estab(lish)

## Similar Word-Beginnings and Word-Endings

Another method of cutting words short is achieved through the word-building principle based on similarity of many word-beginnings and word-endings. Some prefixes are disjoined to express a syllable plus *tr* and a vowel. For example, disjoined *k* (written a little above the line) expresses *con* plus *tr* and a vowel, giving the full prefix *contra*. By adding

another *k*, the word *contract* is formed. Similarly *ks* disjoined is *constru,* and when *k* is added, it forms the word *construct*
Disjoined *n* stands for *inter* or *intel,* making it possible to write easily words like *interest* and

*intelligent*

Other similar word-beginnings are disjoined to express similar prefixes, as follows:

| PREFIXES | | AS IN | |
|---|---|---|---|
| agr- | | agreeable | |
| | | agreement | |
| decl- | | declare | |
| | | declaration | |
| incl- | | include | |
| | | inclusive | |
| self- | | selfish | |
| | | self-control | |
| trans- | | transfer | |
| | | transact | |
| super- | | superintendent | |
| | | supervise | |

A few illustrations of similar word-endings (joined and disjoined) are given here:

To write Gregg Shorthand with any degree of speed, it is necessary to master all of the Brief Forms, the many frequently recurring phrases, abbreviating devices, and a short vocabulary.

| SUFFIXES | | AS IN | |
|---|---|---|---|
| -scribe | 2 | subscribe | 2 |
| | | subscription | 2 |
| -pose | 6 | compose | 2 |
| | | composition | 7 |
| -spect | 6 | inspect | . 7 |
| | | inspection | 7 |
| -ical, -icle | ⌒ | musical | ⌒ |
| | | article | ⌒ |
| -bility | ( | possibility | ( |
| | | sensibility | ( |
| -fication | ) | classification | ) |
| | | notification | ) |
| -gram | ⌒ | telegram | ⌒ |
| | | program | ⌒ |

### Sample Letter

An illustration of a business letter written in Gregg, together with a transcript of the shorthand, follows

Dear-Sir:

As we-have-not heard from-you

for-some-time, we-are wondering

whether you ever received our letter

of December 8 in-which we-enclosed

a duplicate of a bill for merchandise

shipped to-you in July.

We-are particularly anxious, with-the

end of-the year approaching, to-clear

up as-many of-our outstanding

accounts as possible.

Please-let-us hear-from-you

by-return-mail.

Very-truly-yours,

# SPEEDWRITING

Speedwriting is a system of shorthand in which the letters of the alphabet, alone and in various combinations, are used to represent words and phrases. A few ordinary punctuation marks, such as the comma and hyphen, are used along with the alphabet to denote certain syllables or sounds. It can be written with pen or pencil, or on any typewriter. Silent letters are omitted, and many other abbreviating principles are employed. Frequently recurring words and common phrases are stressed.

All unnecessary writing movement in the formation of letters is discarded as waste effort. A small, round writing style is recommended, for example:

ABCDEFGHIJKL
MNOPQRSTUVW
XYZ
abbcdeffgghhijjkk
llmnopqrrstuvwx
yyzz

When letters with beginning loops begin words, time is saved by eliminating these loops. For example, as shown in the above alphabet, the first *b* is better for beginning a word. The same preference applies when letters with loops are at the end of words.

The punctuation marks used in Speedwriting are the same as those used in longhand writing. To indicate a paragraph, the punctuation mark with which the paragraph should end is repeated, for example, `. , ?? , !!` .

Sometimes the same wordsign (code word) has more than one meaning, in which case the context of the material to be transcribed will show which meaning is intended.

The Speedwriting Manual contains fifty-nine lessons with a summary of principles at the end of each group of ten lessons. Each lesson contains a number of principles (rules) as well as a set of illustrative code words. The words selected for illustration and practice are presented in the order of their frequency of use in the English language. For example, the words in Lessons One through Five contain the hundred most frequently recurring words. In Lessons Six through Nine, the hundred words of next highest frequency are presented, and so on through the book.

## Principles of Speedwriting

The first five lessons in the Speedwriting Manual cover the following vocabulary lists and principles:

### VOCABULARY

| | | | | | |
|---|---|---|---|---|---|
| all | *l* | like | *lk* | this | *th* |
| as | *as* | little | *ll* | time | *ti* |
| can | *k* | more | *mo* | to | *to* |
| do | *do* | *other | *O* | we | *w* |
| for | *f* | some | *so* | well | *l* |
| in | *n* | than | *n* | **will(v.) | *l* |
| is | *s* | that | *ta* | work | *wk* |
| it | *t* | there | *tr* | you | *u* |
| know | *no* | | | | |

*To express the syllable *ther*, the *o* is capitalized.
**The noun *will* is written, *wl*.

### PRINCIPLES

All silent letters are omitted, as in:
know, *no*; dough, *do*; rough, *rf*; die, *di*.

When *c* has the sound of *k*, write *k*:
could, *kd*; cough, *kf*; college, *klj*.

Write *t* to express *to* in infinitives only:
to do, *tdo*; to have, *tv* (using the code for have); to be, *tb*; to see, *tse*; to know, *tno*.

Before a noun, pronoun, or adjective write *to*:
to bed, *tobd*; to me, *tome*; to the, *tot* (the code for the word "the" is expressed by *t*).

When *as* is repeated in a phrase, omit the vowel:
as well as, *sls*; as long as, *slgs*.

### VOCABULARY

| | | | | | |
|---|---|---|---|---|---|
| a | *a* | how | *hw* | only | *nl* |
| about | *ab* | me | *me* | our | *r* |
| after | *af* | much | *mc* | over | *V* |
| and | *a* | my | *mi* | place | *pl* |
| are | *r* | now | *nw* | take | *tk* |
| come | *k* | of | *v* | which | *wc* |
| day | *a* | on | *o* | with | *w* |
| go | *g* | one | *on* | your | *u* |
| had | *h* | | | | |

### PRINCIPLES

Write *w* to express the sound of medial and final *ow*:
cow, *kw*; mouse, *mws*.

Write *c* to express the sound of *ch*:
chap, *cp*; check, *ck*; touch, *tc*.

Disregard the spelling of such words as *try, my, few, new, weigh, sleigh,* and write only what you hear:
tri, mi, fu, nu, wa, sla.

Write *l* to express final *ly, ily, ley*:
nearly, *nel*; family, *fml*; valley, *vl*.

### VOCABULARY

| | | | | | |
|---|---|---|---|---|---|
| again | *ag* | him | *m* | the | *t* |
| any | *n,* | his | *s* | they | *ty* |
| be,-ing | *b* | long | *lg* | thing | *tg* |
| before | *bf* | not | *n* | way | *wa* |

20

| ever,-y | ev | or | or | what | wa |
|---|---|---|---|---|---|
| from | fm | out | ou | who | ho |
| good | g | see | se | would | d |
| he | e | such | sc | year | y |
| here | he | | | | |

### PRINCIPLES

Use a wordsign and another syllable, or two word-signs to form a word:

therefore, *trf;* today, *tod.*

Omit *and* in such phrases as:

more and more, *momo;* over and over, *VV.*

Write figures for all numbers, except "1" which, when standing alone, is written *on.*

Write *g* to express final *ing* and *thing*:

knowing, *nog;* nothing, *ng.*

Write a comma to express the medial or final sound of *ie*:

anything, *n,g;* money, *mn,.*

*n* may safely be omitted in such words as:

long, *lg;* thing, *tg;* ring, *rg;* sing, *sg.*

### VOCABULARY

| an | a | into | nt | their | tr |
|---|---|---|---|---|---|
| at | at | make | mk | them | tm |
| been | b | man | m- | then | tn |
| but | b | many | m | up | p |
| by | b | men | mn | was | z |
| great | gr | new | nu | were | w |
| have | v | no | no | when | wn |
| her | h | old | ol | where | wr |
| if | if | so | so | *will(n.) | wl |

*The verb *will* is written, *l.*

### PRINCIPLES

Write *s* to express initial *some*:

something, *sg;* somehow, *sw;* sometimes, *stis.*

The past tense and the present participle of many verbs may safely be omitted:

I have worked for you before, *ivwk fubf.*
I am doing well, *imdo l.*

Write *v* to express final *ever*:

whenever, *wnv;* whoever, *hov;* however, *hwv.*

In most cases *t* may safely be used to express the sound of *th*:

them, *tm;* then, *tn.*

When final *s* has the sound of *z*, write *z*:

raise, *rz;* tease, *tz;* wise, *wz.*

Lessons Six through Ten, in addition to new vocabulary lists, contain the following principles:

Write *y* to express the sound of *oi*:

toy, *ty;* joy, *jy;* boil, *byl;* oil, *yl.*

Write a comma to express final *st*:

just, *j,;* past, *p,;* missed, *m,;* cost, *k,.*

Capitalize the principle syllable of a word to add the sound of *er, der, ter,* and *ther*:

major, *Mj;* similar, *Sml;* hearer, *He;* larger, *Lj;* order, *Or;* other, *O;* another, *aO;* over, *V.*

For this rule, it should be noted that the principal syllable of a word is the first syllable of the root word, as in the illustration for *another.*

Write *p* to express medial and final *ple*:

deplete, *dpe;* triple, *trp;* sample, *smp.*

Use an oblique line (shilling mark) to express medial and final *rd* and *rt*:

artist, *a/,;* insert, *ns/;* card, *k/;* hard, *h/;* bird, *b/.*

To form the plural or to add *s* to words ending with a punctuation symbol, repeat the symbol:

cards, *k//;* rents, *r--;* masts, *m,,;* classes, *kl";* binds, *bi--;* blesses, *bl".*

Write *Z* to express the sound of initial, medial, or final *sh*:

shadow, *Zdo;* shoes, *Zz;* flashy, *flZ,;* dish, *dZ.*

Use a hyphen (-) to express the sound of medial or final *nd, nt,* and *ment*:

band, *b-;* paint, *pa-;* lend, *l-;* sent, *s-;* sentiment, *s--.*

Write *q* to express the sound of medial or final *nk*:

rink, *rq;* sinks, *sqs;* banquet, *bqt.*

The semicolon (;) may be used to indicate final *ity*:

nobility, *nb; ;* oddity, *od; ;* divinity, *dvn; ;* laxity, *lx; ;* city, *s; ;* pity, *p;.*

When writing with pen or pencil, the semicolon may be changed to a blend as for *city* which is written *s).*

Write only as much of a word as is necessary to suggest the word:

look, *lo;* name, *na;* together, *tog;* friend, *fr;* bring, *br.*

Use the apostrophe (') to indicate final *ss*:

lass, *l';* kiss, *k'.*

Write *k* to express the syllables *cog, col, com, con, cor, coun, cum*:

collect, *kk;* comfort, *kf/;* comment, *k-;* connect, *knk;* council, *ksl;* recognize, *rkz.*

The letters *d, m, n, nd, r, s, t,* and *v* may safely be omitted when preceded by a strongly accented vowel or diphthong, as in the following:

| LETTERS | | AS IN | |
|---|---|---|---|
| d | maid, ma | paid, pa | |
| m | home, ho | same, sa | |
| n | down, dw | clown, klw | |
| nd | found, fw | round, rw | |
| r | fear, fe | dear, de | |
| s | induce, ndu | reduce, rdu | |
| t | sight, si | right, ri | |
| v | leave, le | receive, rse | |

The principles given in Lessons Eleven through Fifty-nine can be summarized as follows:

| WRITE | TO EXPRESS | EXAMPLE |
|---|---|---|
| *a* | Initial *ar* | arm, *am*; argue, *agu* |
| *a* | *aw, au* | law, *la*; author, *A* |
| *o* | Initial *or* | orphan, *ofn*; orchard, *oc/* |
| *u* | Initial *ur* | urge, *uj* |
| *b* | *ble, bly* | tablet, *tbt*; forcibly, *fsb* |
| *c/* | *nce, ncy* | dance, *dc/*; fancy, *fc/* |

When the sound of "ance" or "ence" occurs in the middle of a word, the oblique line (/) is dropped: extensive, *xtcv*; pencil, *pcl*.

When the sound of "ance" is preceded by a vowel, the "c" is dropped: insurance, *nsu/*; compliance, *kpi/*.

| WRITE | TO EXPRESS | EXAMPLE |
|---|---|---|
| *e* | Initial *er* | earn, *en*; early, *el* |
| *f* | Medial and final *ful, fy* | useful, *usf*; verify, *vf* |
| *f* | Medial and final *fere, fore* | interfere, *Nf*; therefore, *trf* |
| *j* | Medial and final *tion* | reactionary, *rkjy*; nation, *nj* |
| *K* | Initial *contra* | contract, *Kk*; control, *Kl* |
| *L* | Initial *letter, liter* | letterhead, *Lhd*; literary, *Ly* |
| *n* | Initial *en, in* | enlarge, *nlj*; inform, *nfm* |
| *N* | Initial *enter, intel* | entertain, *Ntn*; intelligent, *Nj* |
| *p* | *pr, pur, pro* | pride, *pi*; purchase, *pcs*; product, *pdk* |
| *q* | *qu* | quiz, *qz* |
| *Q* | *quadr* | quadrant, *Q-* |
| *s* | Medial *st* | vastly, *vsl*; constant, *ks-* |
| *s/* | *self* | himself, *ms/*; herself, *hs/* |
| *s/* | *selves* | ourselves, *rs/* |
| *S* | *str* | strike, *Si*; industry, *ndS* |
| *S* | *star, ster, stir, stor, stur* | start, *St*; register, *rjS*; stirrup, *Sp*; restore, *rS*; disturb, *dSb* |
| *x* | Final *acial* | racial, *rx* |
| *x* | *us, acious* | bonus, *bnx*; gracious, *gx* |
| *y* | *ary, ury, ery, iry, ory* | momentary, *mo-y*; treasury, *tsy*; finery, *fiy*; wiry, *wy*; sorry, *sy* |

| WRITE | TO EXPRESS | EXAMPLE |
|---|---|---|
| *A* | *asm* | spasm, *spA* |
| *Ag* | *aggra, agre, agri* | aggravate, *Agva*; agree, *Ag*; agriculture, *Agkl* |
| *Al* | *alter* | alternative, *Alnv* |
| *dc* | *decla, decli* | declare, *dc*; decline, *dcn* |
| *D* | *deter* | determine, *Dm* |
| *Dg* | *degre* | degree, *Dg* |
| *f* | *fer, for* | conference, *kfc/*; forgive, *fgi* |
| *G* | *gram* | program, *pG* |
| *i* | *im* | impart, *ip/* |
| *I* | *ism* | journalism, *jnlI*; optimism, *opmI* |
| *n* | *inclu, enclo* | include, *ncd*; enclosure, *ncz/* |
| *Pa* | *patri* | patriotism, *PatI* |
| *rc* | *recla* | reclamation, *rcmj* |
| *s* | *ser* | service, *svs*; survey, *sva* |
| */* | *ward* | forward, *f/*; upward, *p/* |
| *T* | *atic, itic* | emphatic, *mfT*; critic, *krT* |
| *z/* | *zure* | leisure, *lz/*; measure, *mz/* |
| *'* | *ness* | lateness, *la'*; fearfulness, *fef'* |
| *El* | *electri, electro* | electric, *Elk*; electron, *Eln* |
| *Ig* | *igno* | ignore, *Ig* |
| *j/* | *cient, ciency* | sufficient, *sfj/*; proficiency, *pfj/* |
| *Mg* | *magne* | magnet, *Mgt*; magnificent, *Mgf* |
| *s* | *sub* | subway, *swa*; subtract, *strk* |
| *Sg* | *signa, signi* | signal, *Sgl*; signify, *Sgf* |
| *;* | *ate* | adequate, *aq*; ; nominate, *nm*; ; operate, *op*; ; discriminate, *dskm*; |
| *T* | *trans* | transform, *Tfm*; transfer, *Tf*; transportation, *Tp/j* |
| *x* | *aks* | accept, *xep*; accident, *xd-* |
| | *ex* | exact, *xk*; excel, *xl* |
| | *ox* | oxygen, *xjn* |
| *a-* | *anta, anti* | antagonize, *a-gnz*; anticipate, *a-spa* |

| WRITE | TO EXPRESS | EXAMPLE |
|---|---|---|
| " | lessness | carelessness, *ka"* |
| C | circ, circum | circle, *Cl;* circumstance, *C,* |
| f/ | fication | classification, *klsf/* |
| K | ical, icle | radical, *rdK;* bicycle, *bsK* |
| la | elate, ulate | relate, *rla;* formulate, *fmla* |
| P | para, peri | paramount, *Pmw* period, *Pd* |
| R | retre, retro | retreat, *Rt;* retrograde, *Rga* |
| S | astic, estic | drastic, *dS;* domestic, *dmS* |
| v | ive, utive | responsive, *rspcv;* executive, *xkv* |
| X | exter, extre | exterior, *Xr;* extreme, *Xm* |
| A | attra, atro | attractive, *Akv;* atrocious, *Ax* |
| H | hydra | hydrant, *H-* |
| i; | itis | appendicitis, *ap-si;* |
| Me | meter | kilometer, *klMe* |
| Ml | multi | multigraph, *MlG* |
| N | entic | authentic, *atN* |
| ol | ology | psychology, *skol;* zoology, *zol* |

Omit *n* before *ch*, *j* or *nce*.
   branch, *brc;* lunch, *lc;* range, *rj;* ordinance, *odc/*

Omit *d* before *j, m, v*:
   adjudge, *ajj;* admit, *amt;* advertise, *avz;*

Omit *r* in words of more than one syllable after the letters *b, f, k, v*:
   breakfast, *bkf,;* freedom, *fdm;* credit, *kdt;* converse, *kvs.*

### PHRASING

Shorthand phrasing is the writing of two or more words without lifting the pencil. Care should be taken to combine only such words as can be written together naturally. The beginner will find it best to write short phrases at first as that will make for ease in reading as well as in writing.

In certain commonly used phrases, the outlines may be shortened, either by omitting unnecessary letters or by omitting obvious words. For example: of course, *vks;* point of view, *pyvu;* more and more, *momo.*

## Sample Letter

ds:
Dear Sir:

as wvn h fm u

As   we have not   heard   from   you

f sli wr W—

for   some time,   we are   wondering

W u ev rse r L

whether   you   ever   received   our   letter

v dc 8 n wc w nc

of   December   8   in   which   we   enclosed

a dpka v a bl f mc-z

a   duplicate   of   a   bill   for   merchandise

z lou n jl..

shipped   to you   in   July.

wr P ax wl

We are   particularly   anxious,   with the

e- vl y apc lkle

end   of the   year   approaching,   to clear

p as m v r ous—

up   as   many   of   our   outstanding

akls as psb..

accounts   as   possible.

pl llus he fm u

Please   let us   hear   from   you

brlnml..

by return mail.

vlu,

Very truly yours,

# Typewriting Lessons for Home Study

## THE TYPEWRITER

The first typewriter was patented in 1868 by Christopher Latham Sholes, a resident of Milwaukee, Wisconsin. Through more than seventy-five years of service its usefulness and speed have been established.

The typewriting exercises in this section are designed to help develop right typewriting habits, ease of operation, smoothness of control, accuracy, and speed.

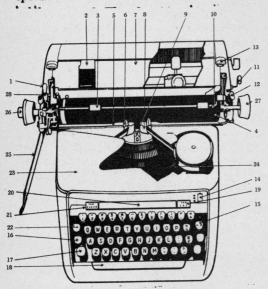

Fig. 1—Typewriter.

9. PRINTING-POINT INDICATOR — indicates the writing position on the line scale.
10. PAPER HOLDER BAIL RELEASE LEVER—when pulled forward, releases paper holder bail so that paper can be placed under it.
11. PAPER RELEASE LEVER—loosens or holds the paper firmly in place.
12. CARRIAGE RELEASE LEVERS (right and left)—permit free movement of carriage to any desired point on the line scale.
13. MARGINAL STOPS (right and left)—set the beginning and end of the typing line.
14. RIBBON INDICATOR—adjusts ribbon for writing on upper or lower half. When the indicator is in the central position, the typewriter can be used to cut stencils.
15. MARGINAL RELEASE KEY—allows the carriage to move beyond the marginal setting.
16. SHIFT LOCK (right and left)—used for locking carriage when all capital letters are to be typed.
17. SHIFT KEYS (right and left)—held down when capital letters are to be typed.
18. SPACE BAR—for spacing between words.
19. TABULATOR SET KEY—sets the tabulator stops at fixed positions.
20. TABULATOR BAR—moves the carriage to any position where a tabulating stop has been set.
21. TABULATOR CLEARANCE KEY—for removing all unneeded tabulator settings.
22. BACK SPACER—when pressed down, the carriage moves back one space at a time. Useful when inserting omitted letters, making corrections, tabulating, and centering.
23. FRONT PLATE—can be removed by pressing hand in back of plate and then pushing forward; is put back by setting lower portion in position and snapping into place.
24. TOUCH TUNING—permits tension adjustment to individual touch.
25. LINE SPACE LEVER—used to return carriage to the beginning of a new line of writing.
26. VARIABLE LINE SPACER—used for changing line spacings, and for typing on ruled lines.
27. CYLINDER KNOBS (right and left)—for turning the cylinder to insert the paper.
28. AUTOMATIC LINE FINDER—when lever is raised a word may be written between two lines, but closer to one than the other. The cylinder is returned to original spacing by lowering lever and turning cylinder knob to line of writing.

## Operative Parts of the Typewriter

Before starting to typewrite, it is very important that the location and function of the following typewriter parts (Fig. 1) be memorized:

1. LINE SPACE REGULATOR—permits adjustment for single, double, or triple line spacing.
2. PAPER GUIDE—makes it possible to insert the paper accurately and evenly in the typewriter.
3. PAPER HOLDER BAIL—holds the paper firmly in place against the cylinder.
4. CYLINDER OR PLATEN—the rubber roll around which the paper is held in position.
5. CYLINDER SCALE—a guide for the exact writing line; also indicates the exact positions of the letters.
6. CARD HOLDERS—used when writing cards and addressing envelopes.
7. PAPER REST—used as a rest for the paper placed in the machine in readiness for typewriting.
8. PAPER CENTERING SCALES—for centering paper on cylinder.

The typist should also know the location and use of these additional typewriter parts, not indicated in Figure 1:

CARRIAGE—the upper part of the typewriter frame which holds the cylinder. When desired, the carriage can be moved freely from side to side. However, when a key or the space bar is struck, the carriage moves one space at a time.

RIBBON SPOOLS (right and left)—receive the ribbon which moves continually from one spool to the other as the typewriter keys are struck.

TABULATOR STOPS—used for setting fixed positions for paragraphs and columns.

TABULATOR RACK—the bar on which the tabulator stops are fastened.

Except for slight differences, typewriter parts and their uses are substantially the same on nearly all standard makes of typewriters.

For efficiency, each part of the typewriter must be operated correctly. The fingers of the left hand should be used for handling parts on the left side of the machine; the fingers of the right hand should take care of the parts on the right side of the machine. Making long reaches across the machine should be avoided.

### Correct Posture

The correct position for sitting at the typewriter is shown in Figure 2. One should sit comfortably far

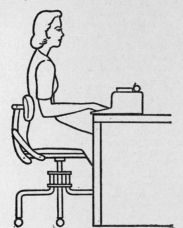

Fig. 2—Correct typing posture.

back in the chair, keeping the body erect, slightly forward, and directly in front of the typewriter. Feet should be kept flat on the floor. The elbows should rest easily at the sides. The fingers should be curved and poised over the second row of keys above the space bar. A correct writing position is essential as it develops alertness and ease of operation.

hold of the longer end. The paper release should be reset at once in readiness for another paper.

**The Paper Guide and the Marginal Stops.** The marginal stops control the length of the typewritten line. The placement of the paper guide along the scale on the paper table determines whether the typed line will appear closer to the left edge of the paper, the right edge of the paper, or be centered in the middle of the paper with the same margins on either side of the typed line.

In order to arrange all typing work neatly with similar margins on both sides, we must decide on a centering point. For convenience, let us choose *40* on the typewriter scale as the centering point. To find the correct place to set the paper guide, with *40* as the center, first make a small crease in the middle of the sheet of paper. Set the carriage so that the center point of *40* appears in back of the printing-point indicator. Insert the paper with the crease exactly behind the printing point. If the crease, on inserting the paper, is not directly behind the printing point, press down the paper release lever to allow the paper to be moved freely until the crease is in back of the printing point. Close the paper release lever and check the alignment to see that (a) the indicator registers at *40* on the scale, and that (b) the crease is behind the printing point. Next move the paper guide so that the left edge of the paper rests against it. This will be the correct position for the guide when the middle of the paper is at *40*.

Lines of any length can be centered. For example, to center a line of *60* spaces, set the marginal stops at *10* and *70*; for a line of *50* spaces, set the stops at *15* and *65*; for a line of *40* spaces, set the stops at *20* and *60*; for a line of *70* spaces set the stops at *5* and *75*. To illustrate the correct centering of lines, the following diagram (Fig. 3) will prove helpful:

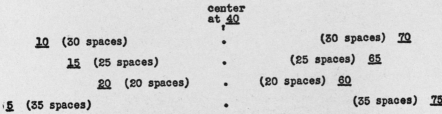

Fig. 3—Centering diagram.

### Handling the Paper, Marginal Stops, and Carriage

**Handling the Paper.** To insert the paper, place it between the paper rest and cylinder. While holding it up with the left hand against the paper guide, turn the right cylinder knob and roll the paper into position. If it needs straightening, press down the paper release lever with the right hand (always use the hand nearer to the part to be operated), line up the top edge of the paper with the line scale on the cylinder, and close the paper release lever. To remove the typed sheet, the paper is loosened by pressing down the paper release, and is pulled out by taking

Whatever the length of line, the same number of spaces are on the left of the center point (40) as are on the right of it. In the line of 60 spaces, half (or 30) is subtracted from 40 to find the setting of the left marginal stop; and 30 spaces are added to 40 to set the right marginal stop. In all typing work, the length of line to be used must first be decided upon, and the line then centered by placing the marginal stops at the correct points on the scale. This method of centering a line works for either pica or elite type. A sample of each type is shown:

Pica type. 10 spaces to 1 inch.

Elite type. 12 spaces to 1 inch.

**The Carriage Return.** At the end of a line of typewriting, the carriage must be returned to the starting point. This is done by operating the line space lever which does two things at one time: (1) it moves the paper up for a new line of writing, and (2) it returns the carriage to the beginning of the new line of writing. By setting the line space regu-

bon is attached to the empty spool and wound around it until the eyelet (B) in the ribbon reaches the hub of the spool. The ribbon spools are placed in the ribbon cups, making sure that the new ribbon is attached to the ribbon guide in exactly the same way as the old ribbon. When putting on a two-color ribbon, the least used color should be the lower one.

FIG. 4—Typewriter ribbon mechanism.

lator, it is possible to have the typewritten lines one, two, or three spaces apart. To operate the line space lever, the first finger, firmly supported by the other fingers, is placed in the curve of the lever and the carriage is thrown back quickly with a fast movement of the hand.

## Care of the Typewriter
## and Changing Ribbons

**Care of the Typewriter.** The typewriter should be cleaned every day. Parts that are not easily accessible should be cleaned with a long-handled brush. The type should be cleaned regularly with a stiff-bristled brush, and wiped every so often with type cleaning fluid. The rod on which the carriage moves should be oiled whenever the carriage does not move back and forth easily. This oiling is done by moving the carriage to the extreme right and then to the extreme left, placing a drop of oil on the rod between the carriage bearings. To make the marginal stop rods move freely, they should be wiped occasionally with a cloth moistened with oil. Oil should always be used sparingly and any excess wiped off with a soft cloth. The type bars should never be oiled. When the typewriter is not being used, it should be kept covered.

**Changing Ribbons.** Most typewritten work should be done with a black ribbon. If a two-color ribbon is used, the change from one color to the other is done by adjusting the ribbon indicator.

The ribbon should be changed as often as necessary so that the work will appear clear and attractive. Before putting on a new ribbon the position of the old ribbon on the machine should be studied carefully. The old ribbon is wound onto one of the ribbon spools by means of a handle located at the right side of the machine. The typewriter carriage should be moved to the center, the shift lock key pushed down, the ribbon spools lifted out of the ribbon cups (A), and the ribbon taken out of the ribbon guide (E) (Fig. 4). The end of the new rib-

The levers (C) should be pulled forward; the ribbon passed through openings in the cups in front of small rollers or guides, and then through slots in reversing levers (D). It is next placed in back of ribbon guide (E), and threaded down through slots (F) in the ribbon guide. To lower the ribbon guide in readiness for typewriting, one of the shift keys should be pressed down, thereby releasing the shift lock.

The procedure for changing ribbons on standard typewriters other than the Underwood is essentially the same.

## Key Stroking

**Learning the Position of the Keys.** Before the keys can be struck correctly, their position and the fingers used for striking each key must be memorized. Starting with Lesson I, Exercise 1, and throughout the section, all typing is done according to the "touch system."

**Striking the Keys Correctly.** The keys of a typewriter should be hit directly in the center with a sharp, quick stroke. Each stroke should be firm, equal in force, and rhythmically even. The keys should never be pushed or held.

## TYPEWRITING

### Lesson I—The Touch System

The touch method of typing eliminates having to look at the typewriter keyboard (Fig. 5). The fingers are trained to find and strike the keys accurately.

The diagonal line through the center cuts the keyboard into a left side and a right side. The fingers of the left hand strike the keys on the left side of the line; the fingers of the right hand strike the keys on the right side. There is a definite pattern for training the fingers to strike the keys so that the same finger always hits the same key.

26

The keys are arranged in four rows and eleven columns. The keys in the columns run up and down from upper left to lower right, just as the diagonal

EXERCISE I

Insert a sheet of paper in the typewriter, **center it** at *40*, set the marginal stops at *15* and *65* for **a type-**

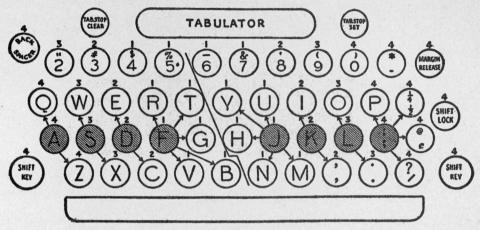

FIG. 5—Keyboard chart.

line through the center of the keyboard does. You learn to control and strike all the keys from a position called the *home* or *guide keys*. The *home keys* for the left hand, beginning with the little finger to the first finger, are a s d f. The *home keys* for the right hand, from the little finger to the first finger, are ; l k j.

With the fingers on these guide keys, it is important to get the feeling of just where the *home keys*

writing line of 50 spaces, and type five full-length lines of the following, repeating the combinations of characters in the order given until each line is filled:

asdf ;lkj asdf ;lkj asdf ;lkj

Practice this exercise until you learn the correct action for striking the guide keys from the home position. At first, type slowly and carefully to ac-

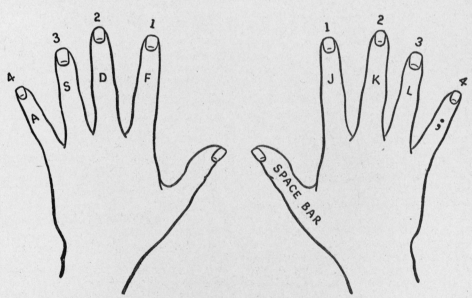

FIG. 6—Guide key fingers.

are in relationship to the rest of the keys. The next step is to practice using these keys. The fingers should be kept curved over the home keys and each key hit with a firm, quick stroke.

The space bar should be tapped lightly with the thumb of the right hand.

quire an even, accurate stroke. As soon as you gain confidence in controlling the guide keys and in striking them properly, begin to work for both speed and accuracy.

Now that you know the correct stroking and the proper finger position for the home keys, type the words listed below. The marginal stops should be set at *10* and *70* for a typing line of 60 spaces. Type two full-length lines of each word, and strike each letter with the correct guide key finger.

```
ask    lad    fad    all
dad    jad    sad    salad
fall   falls  asks   lads
```

A great deal of careful practice is essential if any degree of typewriting proficiency is to be attained.

## Lesson II—R and E; U and I

It is usually helpful to name and number the fingers that are kept over the guide keys (Fig. 6). For the left hand, the first finger is called the F finger, the second is the D finger, the third is the S finger, and the fourth is the A finger. For the right hand, the first finger is called the J finger, the second is the K finger, the third is the L finger, and the fourth is the ; finger.

When a key is located in its proper diagonal column above or below the guide key, it must be "reached" and struck by the correct guide key finger. As soon as you are familiar with the location of the various typewriter keys and know which fingers to use, you should learn the "reach" for the letters R and E on the left side and for U and I on the right side. You will notice that R is in the F column, and that E is in the D column; therefore, the F finger also controls the letter R, and the D finger controls the letter E. Similarly, you will notice on the chart that U is in the J column and that I is in the K column; therefore the J finger controls the letter U, and the K finger controls the letter I.

### EXERCISE 2

Set the marginal stops at *15* and *65* and type five full-length lines of the following, repeating the combinations of characters in the order given until each line is filled:

**frf ded juj kik frf ded juj kik**

Do not look at the keys when typing; rely on your sense of touch; avoid errors by typing slowly and smoothly.

### EXERCISE 3

With the marginal stops set at *15* and *65*, type two lines of each of the words listed below. Concentrate on the correct fingering. Strike the space bar once with the right thumb after writing each word. In typing the first word, fur, f is struck with the first finger of the left hand, u with the first finger of the right hand, and r with the first finger of the left hand.

```
fur    due    red    kid
fir    irk    fed    refer
ire    fire   fired  is
if     fee    jeer   defer
```

### EXERCISE 4

Use a line of 60 spaces, and type two **full-length** lines of each pair of words:

```
fill   fills
sail   sails
aid    aids
led    sleds
sea    seals
```

### EXERCISE 5

Type two lines, 60 spaces long, of each of the following phrases:

```
is as      is as if
will ask   a fair deal
```

## Lesson III—G and T; H and Y

The new keys in this lesson are G, T and H, Y. The Keyboard Chart shows that the letter G is nearest to the guide key F, and is therefore struck with the F finger. G is also in the second row of keys, and serves as the pivot for the diagonal column running through it. Thus T, which is above G, is also controlled by the F finger.

On the right side of the keyboard you see that the letter H is nearest the guide key J, and is therefore struck with the J finger. As H is in the second row of keys, it serves as the pivot for the diagonal column running through it. Y, which is above H, will also be controlled by the J finger.

### EXERCISE 6

Set the marginal stops at *10* and *70*, and without looking at the keyboard, type two full-length lines of fgf with the F finger and jhj with the J finger as follows:

**fgf jhj fgf jhj fgf jhj fgf jhj**

### EXERCISE 7

With the marginal stops at *10* and *70*, type full-length lines of the following until it can be done easily and accurately:

**ftf jyj ftf jyj ftf jyj ftf jyj**

### EXERCISE 8

Set marginal stops at *15* and *65*, and type one full-length line of each of the following words which contain the new letters G, T, Y, H:

```
it     hit    get     yet    let
hat    the    try     fry    sigh
glad   that   hall    lady   flag
dash   has    had     hash   flags
task   says   fast    rugs   flash
rush   hard   days    day    glass
three  third  thirty  harsh  shall
```

28

## EXERCISE 9

Use a line of 60 spaces and type one full-length line of each of the following phrases:

```
if the          if it
if it has       the lad has
the silk flag   a tall glass
```

## EXERCISE 10

Set marginal stops at *15* and *65*. Type each of the following phrases twice in the order given, double spacing between every two phrases:

```
if the if the    if it if it
if it has if it has
a fur rug a fur rug
a tall glass a tall glass
the lad has the lad has
the silk flag the silk flag
```

Repeat this exercise several times until you can type each phrase easily and accurately.

## Lesson IV—Capital Letters and Sentences

Capital letters are typed by using the shift keys. Every key on the keyboard is provided with two characters, a *lower case* character (small letter) and an *upper case* character (capital letter). To type a capital of any letter on the left side of the keyboard, use the right shift key; and to type a capital of any letter on the right side of the keyboard, use the left shift key.

The left shift key is controlled by the A finger; the right shift key by the ; finger. Notice that *only* the little fingers operate the shift keys. The shift key, instead of being hit like the other keys, is held down firmly during the striking of the capital letters, and then released for typing the small letters. When holding down the shift key with the little finger, try as far as possible to keep the other fingers over their respective Guide Keys.

## EXERCISE 11

Set marginal stops at *10* and *70*. Hold the shift key down firmly when typing the capital letters. Note that the *upper case* character on the ; key is the :. Type one full-length line of each of the following, repeating the combination of characters in the order given until the line is filled:

```
fff FFF jjj JJJ fff FFF jjj JJJ
ggg GGG hhh HHH ggg GGG hhh HHH
rrr RRR uuu UUU rrr RRR uuu UUU
eee EEE iii III eee EEE iii III
aaa AAA ;;; ::: aaa AAA ;;; :::
```

## EXERCISE 12

With the marginal stops at *10* and *70*, type one full-length line of each of the following names:

```
Fred  Harry  Kate  Larry  Jerry
Jake  Hal    Saul  Duke   Adele
```

## EXERCISE 13

In Lesson IV the *period* is used. It is on the lower bank of keys under the guide key L, and is therefore struck with the L finger. A period at the end of a sentence is followed by two typewriter spaces (two taps of the space bar).

Set the marginal stops for a line of 50 spaces, and type two full-length lines of the following:

```
l.l l.l l.l l.l l.l l.l l.l l.l
```

## EXERCISE 14

Set the marginal stops at *10* and *70*, and type two full-length lines of each of the following sentences. Retype any that seem difficult.

```
Fred will get it.
I see Kate.
I see Adele.
He sees Saul.
He is glad the tie suited Harry.
This is easy.
```

## Lesson V—W and O; V and M

In this lesson you learn the correct fingering for the letters W, O and V, M. On looking at the Keyboard Chart you will see that W is in the column over S and is struck with the S finger; O is in the column over L and is struck with the L finger; V is in the column under F, and is struck with the F finger; M is in the column under J, and is struck with the J finger.

## EXERCISE 15

Set the marginal stops at *15* and *75* and type one full-length line of each of the following, repeating the combinations of characters in the order given until the line is filled. Retype any lines that give trouble.

```
sws lol sws lol sws lol sws lol
sss www lll ooo sss www lll ooo
fvf jmj fvf jmj fvf jmj fvf jmj
fff vvv jjj mmm fff vvv jjj mmm
```

## EXERCISE 16

Use a line of 60 spaces and type two lines of each word:

```
we        or        for       of
go        to        two       too
so        got       four      you
who       work      your      well
low       me        my        word
will      over      gave      time
five      whose     seem      made
eve       every     them      might
have      more      Lewis     mighty
William   Morris    Marty     Timothy
```

## EXERCISE 17

Set marginal stops at 15 and 65. Type each sentence three times, using single spacing within the same sentence and double spacing between each group of three sentences.

We were glad to get your order.

We wish to get the goods for you.

Our fall styles will sell well.

Fred must have more time for it.

He will go over every item of this order.

Tim said he will meet me at my home today.

## Lesson VI—Q and P; B and N

The new letters in this lesson are Q, P, B, N. The Keyboard Chart shows that Q is on the left side of the keyboard in the A column and is therefore struck with the A finger. P is on the right side of the keyboard in the ; column and is therefore struck with the ; finger.

## EXERCISE 18

Set margins at 10 and 70 and the Line Space Regulator for single spacing. Use the Marginal Release Key when extra space is needed at the end of a line. Type three full-length lines of each of the following, repeating the combinations of characters in the order given until the lines are filled:

```
aaa qqq aaa ;;; ppp ;;;
asdfaqa ;lkj ;p; asdfqa ;lkj ;p;
fqf jpj fqf jpj fqf jpj fqf jpj
```

The letter B is at the left center of the keyboard in the diagonal column under G which is struck with the F finger. Therefore B is also struck with the F finger. On the right side of the keyboard the letter N is in the diagonal column under H which is struck with the J finger. Thus the J finger controls N.

It is important to find each key by the sense of touch.

Place your fingers on the Guide Keys. Stretch the F finger to the letter B, and without striking the key reach back and forth from F to B until you get the feel of what is actually the longest letter-reach on the keyboard. Then stretch the J finger to the letter N. This reach, which is short, should also be practiced until it feels easy.

## EXERCISE 19

With the marginal stops set at 10 and 70, type three full-length lines of each of the following combinations of characters:

```
fff bbb fff jjj nnn jjj
asdfbf ;lkjnj asdfbf ;lkjnj
fbf jnj fbf jnj fbf jnj fbf jnj
```

## EXERCISE 20

Many new words can now be written with the letters contained in Lesson VI. An even touch and the use of the correct fingers on the typewriter keys is more important at the beginning than speed, which is bound to come as the result of good typewriting habits.

Type two lines, single space, of each of the following words, using a line of 60 spaces. Double space after every two lines.

| quit | quite | quiet | quote |
| quake | queer | queerly | quire |
| require | quart | quarts | quarter |
| quarry | quail | quaint | quay |
| paid | pass | passed | paper |
| repay | report | reports | repeat |
| appeal | reprove | repel | dispel |
| depot | be | by | but |
| been | better | begin | believe |
| before | build | building | in |
| not | note | nine | noon |
| men | month | knowing | known |

## EXERCISE 21

Use a line of 60 spaces and type each of the following sentences three times. Single space between lines of the same sentence; double space between each group of three sentences.

The quarry was not far away.

We ordered a few quarts of milk.

I will pay for the report.

He was ready to pay the debt for the papers.

The lad took a few quart jugs home.

We are pleased to repay the bill for postage.

Many people will find work this month.

He paid the note before the tenth of the month.

I believe the job will be done soon.

They will be in the country in June.

You had to pay a quarter to get in before.

30

## Lesson VII—C, X, and ,

Three new keys—C, X, and ,—are taken up in this lesson.

When your fingers are over the Guide Keys, you will notice that C is diagonally under D, and that the D finger strikes C. Practice reaching from D to C, keeping the other fingers as close as possible to the Guide Keys.

As X is under S, it is struck with the S finger. Practice the reach from S to X until it can be made easily.

The *comma* is diagonally under K and is thus struck with the K finger. Reach back and forth from K to , until you get the knack of it.

The *period* (Lesson IV, Exercise 13) is on the right side of the keyboard and under L. The reach with the L finger from the letter L to . should be practiced again.

### EXERCISE 22

Punctuation marks should always be struck lightly. Set margins at *15* and *65*, use single spacing, keep fingers over the Guide Keys, and type two full-length lines of each of the following, repeating the combinations of characters in the order given until the lines are filled:

```
ddd ccc kkk ,,, ddd ccc kkk ,,,
sss xxx lll ... sss xxx lll ...
dcd k,k dcd k,k dcd k,k dcd k,k
sxs l.l sxs l.l sxs l.l sxs l.l
```

### EXERCISE 23

Set margins at *10* and *70*, and set the line regulator for single spacing. Type accurately one or two lines of each word. Keep the fingers curved and hit the keys with a sharp, quick stroke.

| | | | |
|---|---|---|---|
| can | came | clear | care |
| nice | come | cash | lack |
| back | carry | claim | could |
| cool | course | chance | check |
| cent | call | stock | once |
| close | ducks | pick | piece |
| peace | fix | fixes | fixed |
| six | tax | taxes | taxed |
| vex | vexed | exact | exceed |
| excuse | expect | extra | excel |
| expert | wax | extract | express |
| axis | lax | expense | examine |

### EXERCISE 24

Set margins for a line of 50 spaces; set line regulator for single spacing. The middle of the paper should be in back of the type guide when the indicator points to *40* on the scale. Strike the comma and period keys lightly. Tap the space bar once after a comma, and twice after a period at the end of a sentence.

Always keep your eyes on the sentences to be copied; never watch your fingers or the typewriter keys.

The colors are red, white, and blue.

If you come early, we will cash the check.

If you pay now, you can get the discount.

The pioneer was brave, young, and cheerful.

He can speak, write, sing and play.

They bought shirts, ties, and handkerchiefs.

## Lesson VIII—Z and /

The correct fingering for Z and / is given in this lesson. Since Z is in the A column, it is struck with the A finger. The oblique or fraction line / is on the right side of the keyboard in the ; column, and is therefore struck with the ; finger. (See Ex. 26.)

However, before starting to practice using these keys, it is suggested that you adopt a daily warming-up exercise known as the Experts' Rhythm Drill (Ex. 25). Always sit erect; keep your fingers curved over the guide keys; don't look at the keyboard; use the correct fingering; hit the keys firmly; and return the carriage quickly.

### EXERCISE 25

Set the marginal stops at *10* and *70*. Use single spacing, and type five full-length lines of the following Experts' Rhythm Drill:

```
a;sldkfjghfjdksla;sldkfjghfjdksl
```

### EXERCISE 26

Set the marginal stops for a line of 50 spaces, use single spacing, and type three full-length lines of each of the following, repeating the combinations of characters in the order given until the lines are filled:

```
faza j;/; faza j;/; faza j;/;
aaa zzz ;;; /// aaa zzz ;;; ///
aza ;/; aza ;/; aza ;/; aza ;/;
```

### EXERCISE 27

Use a line of 60 spaces, and type one full-length line of each of the following words. Type two or more lines of any word that seems difficult.

| | | | |
|---|---|---|---|
| size | dozen | zeal | zero |
| gaze | zest | lazy | prize |
| azure | zone | blaze | blazed |
| hazel | hazard | puzzles | puzzled |
| wizard | organize | dazzle | realize |
| ozone | zipper | zigzag | zebra |
| zinc | analyze | zenith | zinnia |

31

## EXERCISE 28

With the marginal stops at *10* and *70*, write each sentence three times. Single space between each group of three sentences, and double space between the new sentences.

        The lad was puzzled with the puzzle.

        Look at the star in the zenith of the azure sky.

        They analyzed the data of the zinc products.

        They supported the cause with great zeal.

        This organization favors the zoning law.

        A blazing fire was seen on the horizon.

        The initials on the letter are RS/TM.

## Lesson IX—Keyboard Check-up

In order to make certain that each letter is being struck with the correct finger, a hand diagram is given (Fig. 7). Each finger is marked with the let-

## EXERCISE 29

Set marginal stops at *10* and *70*, use single spacing, allow 5 spaces between the two alphabet groups on each line, and type five full-length lines of the following:

        abcdefghijklmnopqrstuvwxyz

## Lesson X—Figures 4, 5, 6, and 7

When you know how to type all the letters on the keyboard, you are ready to learn the position and typing of the numbers.

If you will turn to the Keyboard Chart (Figure 5) you will notice that numbers make up the top row of keys and that each key is at the head of one of the diagonal columns containing a guide key. The first numbered keys to be considered are 4, 5, 6, and 7. Figure 4 is at the top of the column over F, and 5 is at the top of the column over G. Therefore 4 and 5 are struck with the F finger since the letters F and G are also struck with the F finger. Figure 6 is at the top of the column over H, and 7 is at the top of the column over J. Thus both 6 and 7 are struck by the J finger which is also used to strike the letters H and J. In reaching for these numbered keys, the other fingers should be kept as close as possible to the guide keys.

## EXERCISE 30

Set marginal stops for a line of 60 spaces. Use single spacing and type two full-length lines of each

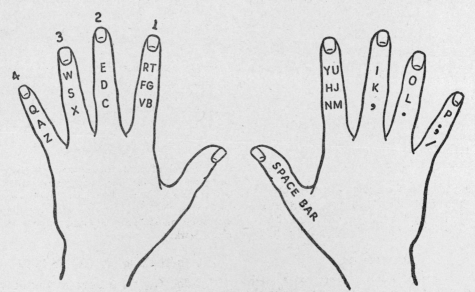

FIG. 7—Hand diagram for typewriter keys.

ters that it controls, thus enabling you easily and quickly to review and memorize the letters and the correct fingering.

A good exercise for daily practice is to type the alphabet several times, being sure to strike each letter with the correct finger.

of the following, repeating the combinations of characters in the order given until the lines are filled:

        fr4f ju7j fr4f ju7j
        f444f j777j f444f j777j
        f4f j7j f4f j7j f4f j7j

```
fgt5f jhy6j fgt5g jhy6j
f555f j666j f555f j666j
f5f j7j f5f j7j f5f j7j
```

### EXERCISE 31

With a line of 60 spaces and single spacing, type each of the following sentences three times. Double space after each set of three sentences. Strike the space bar once after a comma.

The numbers are 44, 55, 66, 77, and 455.

The style numbers are 456, 567, 564, and 754.

Set them up in groups of 444, 555, 666, and 777.

Ship the orders marked 54, 76, 575, and 676.

The tickets are numbered 45, 67, 474, and 656.

## Lesson XI—Figures 3, 8, and 1; and ?

Three new numbered keys—3, 8, 1—and the interrogation mark—?—are introduced in this lesson. On looking at the Keyboard Chart, you will note that 3, in the diagonal column over D, is struck with the D finger; and 8, in the diagonal column over K, is struck with the K finger. The figure *one* is obtained by striking the small letter l with the L finger. The ?, in the ; column, is controlled by the ; finger. The left Shift Key should be held down firmly for the striking of the ?. However, on some typewriter keyboards the ? is the shift of the comma key. It is then struck with the K finger.

### EXERCISE 32

With the marginal stops set for a line of 50 spaces, use single spacing and type three full-length lines of each of the following, repeating the combinations of characters in the order given until the lines are filled:

```
de3d ki8k de3d ki8k de3d ki8k
d3d k8k d3d k8k d3d k8k d3d k8k
l3l l8l l3l l8l l3l l8l l3l l8l
;?; ;?; ;?; ;?; ;?; ;?; ;?; ;?;
```

### EXERCISE 33

Type each group of two sentences on a single line, and type each line three times. Strike the space bar twice after a ? at the end of a sentence.

How many books did he buy?
He bought 144 books.

What is the size of his shirt?
It is size 15.

Did they order many bonds?
They ordered 38.

Can he do it?
He said that he can.

When will he come?
He will come in 8 hours.

Is the picture on page 31?
Or is it on page 81?

## Lesson XII—Figures 2, 9, and 0; " and ( )

The numbered keys 2, 9, 0; the special shift key characters " (quotation mark) and ( ) (opening and closing parentheses) are taken up in this lesson.

The figure 2, in the S column, is struck with the S finger; the figure 9, in the L column, is struck with the L finger; and the figure 0, in the ; column, is struck with the ; finger. The Shift Key is used for the special characters. The quotation mark is made by holding down the Shift Key and striking 2 with the S finger. The opening parenthesis is the shift of figure 9, struck with the L finger; the closing parenthesis is the shift of the figure 0, struck with the ; finger. Always use the little fingers for the Shift Keys. To get a capital or upper case letter, hold the Shift Key down firmly, strike the letter, and then release the Shift Key.

### EXERCISE 34

Using single spacing and a line of 50 spaces, type three full-length lines of each of the following, repeating the combinations of characters in the order given until the lines are filled:

```
sw2s lo9l sw2s lo9l sw2s lo9l
;p0; ;p0; ;p0; ;p0; ;p0; ;p0;
s2s l9l ;0; s2s l9l ;0; s2s l9l
s"s l(l s"s l(l s"s l(l s"s l(l
;); ;); ;); ;); ;); ;); ;); ;);
```

### EXERCISE 35

Type each of the following sentences three times, using single spacing. No extra space is allowed between the opening quotation mark and the word that follows, or the last letter of a word and the closing quotation mark. The same rule applies to parenthesis marks.

Is the number 290 or 209?

The rug is 9 feet wide and 12 feet long.

Read the poems on page 129 to 138.

Solve 4 examples on page 28, and 6 on page 57.

He cried, "They shall not pass."

His motto is "Talk less and listen more."

The date (set for next week) is May tenth.

### EXERCISE 36

Strike the small letter 1 for the figure *one*. Be sure to strike the numbers with the correct fingers. Use a line of 60 spaces and type five full-length lines of the numbers in the order given.

12345 67890 12345 67890

## Lesson XIII—$, %, —, &, #, and '

Six new signs, introduced in this lesson, are the upper case, shift key characters $, %, _ (underscore), &, #, and ' (apostrophe). When striking any of these characters, the shift key at the opposite side of the typewriter should be held down. The $ sign, which is the shift of 4, and the % mark, which is the shift of 5, are struck with the F finger while the little finger of the right hand holds down the right shift key. The _ (underscore), the shift of 6, and the & sign, the shift of 7, are struck with the J finger while the little finger of the left hand holds down the left shift key. The # (number sign) is the shift of 3 and is struck with the D finger. The ' (apostrophe) is the shift of 8 and is struck with the K finger.

### EXERCISE 37

Using single spacing and a line of 50 spaces, type two full-length lines of the following combinations of characters in the order given. Double space after each two-line group.

```
fr4$f ju7&j  fr4$f ju7&j
f$f  j&j  f$f  j&j  f$f  j&j
f5%f  j6_j  f5%f  j6_j
f%f  j_j  f%f  j_j  f%f  j_j
de3#d ki8'j  de3#d ki8'j
d#d  k'k  d#d  k'k  d#d  k'k
#$%  _&'  #$%  _&'  #$%  _&'
```

Now you are ready to type sentences in which the new special signs are used. The opposite shift key should be held down firmly, and the special character keys struck with the correct fingers. To underscore a word, move the carriage back to the beginning of the word and strike the _ (underscore) for each letter in the word. The underscoring of a sentence or group of words may be continuous, including the spaces between the words, or may be only under each letter.

### EXERCISE 38

With a 50-space line and single spacing, type each sentence three times. Double space after each three-line group.

The bill for $44.00 was paid last month.

The note bears interest at 6% per annum.

An underscored word is printed in italics.

Johnson & Bigelow is the name of this company.

We ordered style #33 and style #37.

We found Harry's hat and Dan's coat.

## Lesson XIX—¢, ½, —, @, ¼, *, and :

There are three end keys on the right side of the keyboard that are controlled by the ; finger. Six special characters are on these keys. The lower-case characters are the ¢, ½, and — (hyphen); the upper-case characters are the @, ¼, and * (asterisk). Be sure to reach for these end keys with the ; finger. The : (colon) is the upper case character on the ; key. The space bar should be tapped twice after the :.

### EXERCISE 39

Set the marginal stops at 15 and 65 and type one full-length line of the following reaches with the little finger of the right hand:

```
;¢;  ;¢;  ;¢;  ;¢;  ;¢;  ;¢;  ;¢;  ;¢;
;½;  ;½;  ;½;  ;½;  ;½;  ;½;  ;½;  ;½;
;—;  ;—;  ;—;  ;—;  ;—;  ;—;  ;—;  ;—;
;@;  ;@;  ;@;  ;@;  ;@;  ;@;  ;@;  ;@;
;¼;  ;¼;  ;¼;  ;¼;  ;¼;  ;¼;  ;¼;  ;¼;
;*;  ;*;  ;*;  ;*;  ;*;  ;*;  ;*;  ;*;
;;;  ;;;  ;;;  ;;;  ;;;  ;;;  ;;;  ;;;
```

### EXERCISE 40

Use a line of 60 spaces and type two lines of each of the following sentences. The / (oblique or fraction line) is used to make fractions that are not on the keyboard. Between a whole number and its accompanying fraction, tap the space bar once.

The price is usually 7¢ a pound.

The fraction ½ may also be typed as 1/2.

Seven-eighths may be written as 7/8.

He bought 2 dozen oranges @ 84¢ a dozen.

The sum of 1½ and 1¼ is 2 3/4.

An * (asterisk) is used to indicate a footnote.

34

The seasons are: spring, summer, fall, and winter.

## Lesson XV—Special Characters

In this lesson the making of special characters not on the typewriter keyboard is discussed. Some of these special characters are made by using one key; others require the use of two keys; and still others make it necessary to operate the Variable Line Spacer.

If the special characters mentioned here are not part of your typewriter keyboard, they may be made as follows:

*Division Sign* ÷. Strike the colon, then backspace and strike the hyphen. A space may be left before and after the sign.

*Multiplication Sign* x. The small letter x is used, preferably with a space before and after it. When x is used in giving dimensions, it means "by".

*Equals Sign* =. Strike the hyphen, then backspace, turn the cylinder very slightly by using the Variable Line Spacer, and type another hyphen.

*Minus Sign* --. Two hyphens may be used for a minus sign. The underscore mark may also be used by turning the cylinder back to the point where the minus sign should go. The Variable Line Spacer is used in turning the cylinder. Space may or may not be left before and after the hyphen.

*Plus Sign* -/-. Type two hyphens, backspace, and hold the back spacer so that the fraction line will come between the hyphens.

*Degree Sign* o. Use the Variable Line Spacer to turn the cylinder forward a half space and type the letter o; for example; 75°.

*Exclamation Mark* !. Type the apostrophe, then backspace and strike the period. Strike the space bar twice when an exclamation mark comes at the end of a sentence.

*Dash* --. Two hyphens typed closed together make the dash. Space is not usually left before and after this sign.

*Underscore* _. Use the shift of figure 6 for the underscore mark. Type it as many times as there are letters or words to be underscored. Do not underscore punctuation marks or the space between words.

*Care of* c/o. When the abbreviation of "Care of" is preferred, type small c, the fraction line /, and small o.

*Chemical Symbols.* In the formula $H_2SO_4$, type the letters first, leaving spaces for the numbers. Move the carriage back to the free spaces, turn the cylinder back a half space, and type the numbers.

*Exponents.* To type the expression $(a \times b)^3$, turn the cylinder forward a half space for the exponent 3.

### EXERCISE 41

Use a line of 60 spaces and type each of the special characters several times, or until you can type them neatly and accurately. For additional practice typewrite each of the following three times:

$80 \times 5 = 400$, and $80 \div 5 = 16$.

The readings were 98° and 99°.

The term $3x^2$ means 3xx.

Laugh with folks -- not at them.

$50 + 25 = 75$, and $50 - 25 = 25$.

$C + H_2SO_4 = 2SO_2 + CO_2 + 2H_2O$.

"Man the lifeboats!"

Mail it to Peter Brown, c/o John Rogers.

## Lesson XVI—Paragraph Indention and Simple Tabulation

The Tabulator Set Key and the Tabulator Bar or Key are taken up in this lesson. The Tabulator Set Key is used for setting paragraph indentions and the starting points for columns in tabulation work. The Tabulator Bar is used to make the carriage jump quickly to the point on the scale where new paragraphs are to begin, or where columns are desired.

**Paragraph Indentions.** Paragraphs are usually indented five spaces. If you use a line of 60 spaces, with margins set at *10* and *70*, the paragraph should begin at *15* for a five-space indention. Before setting the typewriter for indentions, clear all previous tabulator settings in the machine by operating the Tabulator Clearance Key and moving the carriage back and forth several times. When the machine is free of all stops, move the carriage to *15* and set a stop at that point with the Tabulator Set Key. By pressing the Tabulator Bar, the carriage moves from the left margin to *15* at one stroke. An extra line should always be allowed between paragraphs.

### EXERCISE 42

Set marginal stops at *10* and *70*, and a tabulator stop at *15* for paragraph indention. Use single spacing and type lines 60 spaces in length of the following paragraphs from a speech made by Franklin Delano Roosevelt, leaving a double space between paragraphs.

In expressing our faith of the Western World, let us affirm:

That we maintain and defend the democratic form of constitutional representative government.

That through such government we can more greatly provide a wider distribution of culture, of education, of thought and of free expression.

That through it we can obtain a greater security of life for our citizens and a more equal opportunity for them to prosper.

That through it we can best foster commerce and the exchange of art and science between nations; that through it we can avoid the rivalry of armament, avert hatred and encourage good will and true justice.

And that through it we offer hope for peace and a more abundant life to the peoples of the whole world.

**Simple Tabulation.** Typewritten material can be arranged in columns by using the Tabulator Set Key and the Tabulator Bar.

### EXERCISE 43

Set marginal stops at *20* and *60*; set tabulator stops at *31*, *42*, and *53*. Insert paper so that its center is in back of the center point of *40* on the scale. Type the tabulation below; first single spaced, and then double spaced.

| | | |
|---|---|---|
| results | instead | through |
| ability | against | because |
| further | regards | package |
| between | charged | letters |
| approve | farmers | company |

## Lesson XVII—Developing Speed and Accuracy

When you know how to operate the parts of the typewriter, and have mastered the keyboard, your next step is to develop speed and accuracy. From a speed of 20 to 30 words a minute, you can easily increase your typewriting speed to 30, 40, 50, and more words a minute simply by conscientious and regular practice.

In this lesson three exercises are given. The sentence exercises will help increase your speed, the alphabetic sentences will help develop greater accuracy, and the straight copy material will serve as a test of typewriting speed and accuracy. After typing the material in this lesson, begin to choose material of your own. Typewrite selections from your favorite columnist, or passages from a good story. With daily practice, it is possible to become an expert typist.

### EXERCISE 44

Set the marginal stops for a line of 70 spaces and type a full page of each sentence.

Initiative is doing the right thing without being told.

The object of teaching a child is to enable him to get along without his teacher.

Better mend one fault in yourself than a hundred in your neighbor.

Learn to think with sincerity, for it is the first attribute of greatness.

The three great angels of life are thought, conduct, and toil.

There is no freedom on earth for those who deny freedom to others.

Let no act be done without its purpose, nor otherwise than in accordance with the perfect principles of art.

Irony and pity are both of good counsel; the first with her smiles makes life agreeable, the other sanctifies it with her tears.

Strong men can always afford to be gentle.

Government of the people, by the people, for the people, shall not perish from the earth.

### EXERCISE 45

Set the marginal stops for a line of 70 spaces, and type each sentence twenty times.

The quick brown fox jumps over the lazy dog.

Please pack this box with my five dozen jugs of quality veneer.

The quick movement of our enemy would jeopardize sixty gunboats.

The sixty-five quickly jumping dogs and foxes were just shot by the crazy maniac.

After our breezy excursion along the mountain and river slope we took refreshments and gathered jonquils.

We quickly chased the zebras to a quiet drinking place just near my five bundles of flax.

The jolly boys were exceptionally kind to several dozen children who quickly escaped from danger.

The zeal of the brave boys quickly won praise from the exact old judge who wanted to give them an award.

Sixty young school chums jeopardized their lives by fighting zealously in a quaint market warehouse.

Please give him just five requisitions for sixty dozen new black pencils the same quality as we had before.

### EXERCISE 46

Set the marginal stops at *15* and *70* and type Lincoln's Gettysburg Address for accuracy and speed:

### LINCOLN'S GETTYSBURG ADDRESS

| | Strokes |
|---|---|
| Fourscore and seven years ago our fathers brought forth | 55 |
| on this continent a new nation, conceived in liberty and | 111 |
| dedicated to the proposition that all men are created equal. | 171 |
| Now we are engaged in a great civil war, testing whether that | 232 |
| nation, or any nation so conceived and so dedicated, can long | 293 |
| endure.  We are met on a great battlefield of that war.  We | 352 |
| have come to dedicate a portion of that field as a final | 408 |
| resting place for those who here gave their lives that that | 467 |
| nation might live.  It is altogether fitting and proper that | 527 |
| we should do this.  But, in a larger sense, we cannot dedicate | 589 |
| --we cannot consecrate--we cannot hallow--this ground.  The | 648 |
| brave men, living and dead, who struggled here have consecrated | 711 |
| it far above our poor power to add or to detract.  The world | 771 |
| will little note nor long remember what we say here, but it | 830 |
| can never forget what they did here.  It is for us, the living, | 893 |
| rather to be dedicated here to the unfinished work which they | 954 |
| who fought here have thus far so nobly advanced.  It is rather | 1016 |
| for us to be here dedicated to the great task remaining before | 1078 |
| us--that from these honored dead we take increased devotion | 1137 |
| to that cause for which they gave the last full measure of | 1195 |
| devotion; that we here highly resolve that these dead shall | 1254 |
| not have died in vain; that this nation, under God, shall have | 1316 |
| a new birth of freedom; and that government of the people, by | 1377 |
| the people, for the people, shall not perish from the earth. | 1437 |

**How to Test Your Typewriting Ability.** It is important to know how fast you can typewrite and how accurate you are, because if you plan to work in an office, your prospective employer will ask about your typewriting ability, and may wish to give you a test before employing you. To determine a typist's accuracy and speed, a timed test is given and the words per minute are estimated as follows:

| | |
|---|---:|
| Total number of strokes typed.......... | 1437 |
| Divide by 5 for approximate number of words ............................ | 287 |
| Number of errors in typing and spacing is multiplied by 10 and deducted, as follows: 5 errors x 10 = .............. | −50 |
| Net number of accurate words.......... | 237 |
| Divide by number of minutes of typing (5) to get the number of words per minute ........................... | 47 |

It is a good plan to keep a record of all speed and accuracy tests. In this way you have a definite idea of the progress you are making.

The article in Exercise 46 should be typed several times until you have reached a speed of at least 40 words a minute. When you can type at that rate, take other timed tests on articles of your own choice, always striving for greater accuracy and speed.

## Lesson XVIII—How to Typewrite a Business Letter and Address Envelopes

**Business Letters.** In this lesson the correct and attractive setup and arrangement of business letters is taken up. Such letters usually contain the following formal parts:

| | |
|---|---|
| Date Line | Complimentary Close |
| Inside Address | Signature and Title |
| Salutation | Identification Initials |
| Body of the Letter | Enclosure (if any) |

The firm name and address is usually displayed at the top of the *letterhead*. The *date line* gives the month, date, and year the letter is written. The *inside address* is that of the person or company to whom the letter is written. The *salutation* is the formal opening or greeting line. The *body of the letter* contains the full message. The *complimentary close* is the formal closing line. The *signature and title* is the longhand signature of the dictator of the letter and his official title in the firm. The *identification initials* are those of the dictator and the transcriber and should be typed at the lower left corner of the letter. An *enclosure* is indicated under the identification initials, either by the abbreviation "Enc." or the word spelled out.

Standard business stationery measures 8½ x 11 inches.

When typewriting the model letter forms in this lesson, notice particularly the placement, spacing, and arrangement of each part of the business letter. There are many acceptable business letter styles, but only the most commonly used are given here. Many firms have their own particular style for letters, and

these can be followed easily by modifying slightly the Indented, Block, and Semi-Block styles illustrated in Exercise 47.

For convenience, letters are classified as short, medium, and long. *Short letters* do not exceed 75 words in length; *medium letters* contain about 75 to 150 words; and *long letters* have about 150 to 200 words. Any one of these letters may be arranged neatly on a single sheet of paper. Letters containing more than 200 words usually require a second page.

Letters of more than one page should carry an identifying line, typed 4 line spaces from the top of all pages which follow the first page. This line should give, properly spaced out between margins, the name of the person to whom the letter is addressed, the page number, and the date, as follows:

**Mr. G. L. Gray  -2-  May 8, 19--**

One or two double spaces should be left between this identifying line and the rest of the letter.

### EXERCISE 47

Instructions for eight different styles of one-page business letters are given here and on the two following pages, designated as Sample Letter A, Sample Letter B, etc., through Sample Letter H. First, type each letter at least three times, following instructions exactly. When finished, check with the copy in the text for any errors in spelling or punctuation. Then compare the appearance and arrangement of your finished letters with the illustrations (Figures 8 through 15) following Sample Letter H, which show typewritten models of these eight letters. If upon comparison you find that your placement, spacing, or other details of presentation are not accurate, retype each letter (without the model) until you can make a perfect copy. (Note that the number of words in the body of each letter is given in parentheses at the beginning of the instructions for each.)

#### Sample Letter A

*Indented Style, Open Punctuation, Double Spacing, Enclosure* (46 words). As this is a short letter, double spacing is used. Set marginal stops at 20 and 65. Start the date line about 15 single spaces from the top of the paper and at 45 on the scale. Come down 6 single line spaces to the inside address. Indent 5 spaces for each new paragraph. Start the complimentary closing at 40 on the scale. After the closing, leave a double space for the firm name which should be written in capitals. Allow 4 single spaces between the firm name and the title of the person writing the letter. The initials of the dictator and of the stenographer are typed near the lower left corner.

July 16, 19—

Don Harris & Company
75 Adams Street
   Dayton, Ohio
Gentlemen:

   We enclose a statement of your account for $475.68 which was figured on your usual discount of 5%.

   You will notice that the statement includes an overdue item of $64.51 for purchases during April. We shall appreciate your sending a check for $475.68 by return mail.

Very truly yours,

FRM/PE            ACE SPORTING SHOP
Enclosure              Credit Manager

# Shorthand, Typewriting, and Clerical Skills

## Sample Letter B

*Indented Style, Close Punctuation, Single-Spaced Inside Address, Double-Spaced Message, Enclosure (54 words).* The marginal stops and arrangement of this letter are the same as for Sample Letter A. Close punctuation refers to the placing of commas at the end of the first two lines, and a period at the end of the last line of the address. The dictator's and transcriber's initials are in small letters, and an enclosure which has an account number is typed under the initials.

January 3, 19—

Mrs. George Anderson,
820 Marcy Avenue,
Dallas, Texas.

Dear Mrs. Anderson:

We greatly appreciate your patronage and wish to continue to serve you through your Charge Account.

However, we should like to call your attention to an unpaid balance of $127.54 concerning which we sent you a statement some time ago.

Will you please send us your check for this amount as soon as possible.

Sincerely yours,
MAYNARD & COLLINS
Elizabeth Sloan
Accounting Dept.

es/hw
Enc. 23847

## Sample Letter C

*Block Style, Open Punctuation, Single Spacing (162 words).* Set marginal stops at 15 and 70. Start the date line 12 single spaces from the top of the paper and at 55 on the scale. Allow 4 single line spaces before typing the inside address. Start the closing at 40 on the scale.

March 24, 19—

The Bradford Bonding Company
114 John Street
New York 4, N. Y.

Gentlemen:

During the past five years our company has bonded all employees who are responsible for the handling of any company funds. Our contract has been held by the Royal Company in Detroit.

As this company plans to withdraw from this particular field, it will be necessary for us to place this business with another company. Will you request one of your representatives to visit us? Please ask him to come prepared to give full details about your plan and the cost of your service.

In order that your representative may have some advance information about our requirements, we are sending you a copy of our latest payroll summary sheet. This form contains the names of all employees who are to be bonded and describes the nature of their duties.

Our present contract with the Royal Company will expire on April 15. Therefore, we must act immediately in placing this business with another company. Please have your representative call at an early date.

Very truly yours,
RHODES JEWELRY COMPANY
General Manager

GSL/WJ

## Sample Letter D

*Block Style, Close Punctuation, Single Spacing (96 words).* Marginal stops are set at 15 and 70. Start the date line 14 single spaces from the top of the paper and at 55 on the scale. Allow 4 single line spaces before typing the inside address. Start the closing at 40 on the scale.

January 2, 19—

Mr. James Maxwell,
1247 Bedford Avenue,
Lincoln, Nebraska.

Dear Mr. Maxwell:

You are doubtless aware of the growing interest of many of our young men in the Saturday night meetings sponsored by the various clubs of the Lincoln YMCA.

As the program staff is eager to expand the athletic and cultural activities of the Y, we are writing to ask you, as a former member, to come to a meeting on Friday, January 11, at 7:30 p.m., in Room 318, so that we may discuss future plans for the organization of a new activities program.

We should appreciate your letting us know whether we may expect you.

Sincerely yours,
Charles R. Alden
Program Director

CRA/GB

## Sample Letter E

*Semi-block Style, Open Punctuation, Single Spacing (73 words).* The arrangement for this letter follows that of Sample Letter D. The line "Attention of Mr. Lewis" is centered and underscored, and written 2 line spaces below the inside address.

June 15, 19—

The Midway Mart, Inc.
1001 Market Street
Los Angeles, California
Attention of Mr. Lewis

Gentlemen:

We are informed by the railroad company that they will assume full responsibility for the case of two dozen damaged lampshades delivered to your company on June 12.

Please mail us the agent's receipt for the merchandise; and return the lampshades, for which we shall issue a credit memorandum for the full amount plus freight charges.

We regret that this shipment was damaged, and hope you have not been inconvenienced because of it.

Very truly yours,
Robert J. Holmes
Credit Manager

RJH/VN

## Sample Letter F

*Semi-block Style, Close Punctuation, Single Spacing (108 words).* The arrangement for this letter follows that of Sample Letters D and E.

June 18, 19—

Acme Publishing Company,
555 Lexington Avenue,
Chicago, Illinois.
Subject: Business Education

Gentlemen:

We are planning to reorganize the work of our business education department for the school term beginning next February.

At the present time we offer our pupils a limited

range of miscellaneous business electives. It is our plan to increase these electives to provide a complete major in each of the three fields: stenography, bookkeeping, office practice.

We are interested in examining the most recently published books in business education with a view to their adoption as classroom textbooks. We should be glad to have you send us copies of all new business books suitable for high school pupils, published by your company between now and November 1.

> Very truly yours,
> BARTON BUSINESS SCHOOL
> Harold Wilson, Chairman
> HW/E      Education Department

### Sample Letter G

*Semi-block Style, Open Punctuation, Single Spacing, Enclosure* (98 words). Set margins at *10* and *75* for the letter as a whole, and at *20* and *65* for the two numbered paragraphs. This further indenting within the regular margins is a good way to set off material of special interest. Start the date line about 14 single line spaces from the top of the paper and at *60* on the scale.

> March 5, 19—

Mrs. E. J. Thomas
654 Main Street
Albany 3, New York

My dear Mrs. Thomas:

Wise spending, economy, and balanced budgets are topics which are not new to housewives who find it necessary to watch expenditures and conserve.

Since food takes a large part of the family's income, it is important to economize intelligently, for health depends to a large extent upon the right food.

To help reduce grocery bills:

(1) choose foods that are inexpensive and yet meet health needs;
(2) study the markets and apply business principles to food buying.

Our bulletin No. 456 deals primarily with the latter method of cutting food costs. Mail the enclosed card, asking for your copy.

> Very truly yours,
> MGB/KS      Mary G. Byron, Chairman
> Enc.

### Sample Letter H

*Block Style, Close Punctuation, Single Spacing* (146 words). Margins are set at *15* and *70*. Start the date line about *12* single spaces from the top of the paper and at *55* on the scale. This letter has a four-line inside address. The special line within the letter is set off for emphasis by centering and underscoring. If preferred, this line could be capitalized.

> July 17, 19—

Mr. G. L. Graham, Manager,
The Anchor Bookstore,
20–31 Main Street,
Schenectady, New York.

Dear Sir:

We have on hand a quantity of paper of the grade that we formerly sold through you to the Central High School Bookroom. We should like to dispose of our surplus of this stock before we take inventory, and if you can use it, we shall be glad to quote you a very special price. We have enough paper to make

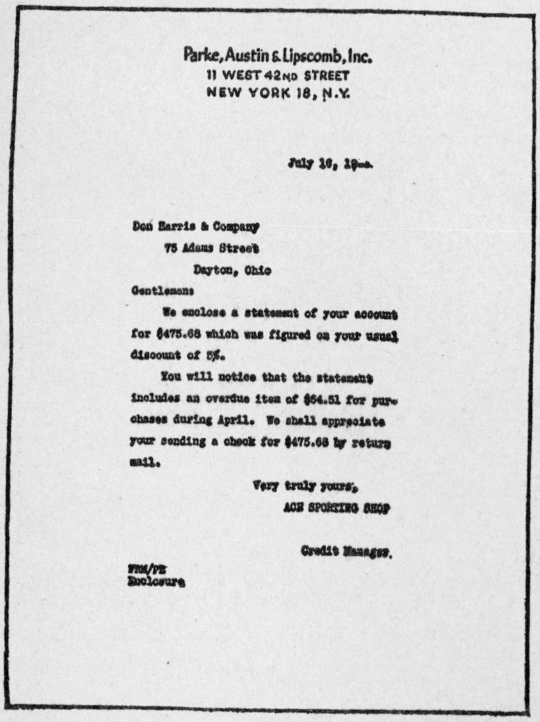

<u>980 dozen fillers, banded 50 sheets to the filler.</u>

You have been paying 96¢ a dozen and from this price we will allow you a discount of 25%, making our present price 72¢ a dozen fillers, F.O.B. Schenectady. I think you will agree with me that this is a very good offer for this quality of paper.

If you can use this paper, we shall be glad to bill half of the order as of October 1, and the other half as of December 1.

> Yours very truly,
> M. C. JEWETT COMPANY
> L. M. Jewett,
> LMJ/VRP      Secretary.

Fig. 8—Model for Sample Letter A

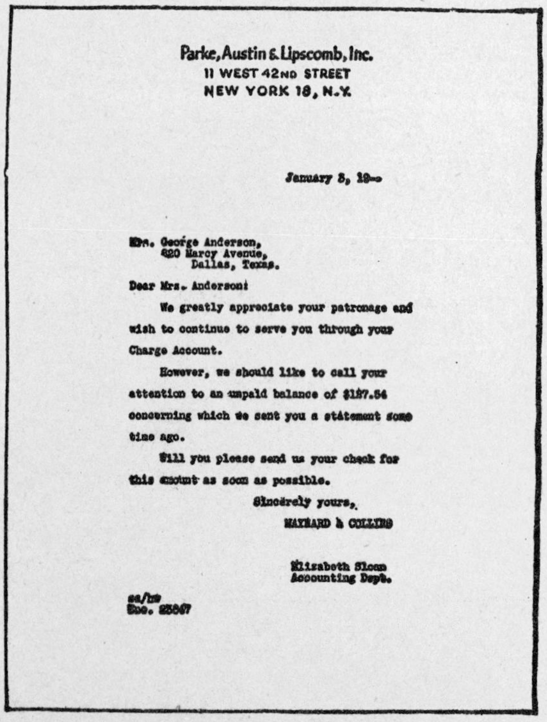

Fig. 9—Model for Sample Letter B

Parke, Austin & Lipscomb, Inc.
11 WEST 42ND STREET
NEW YORK 18, N.Y.

March 24, 19—

The Bradford Bonding Company
114 John Street
New York 4, N. Y.

Gentlemen:

During the past five years our company has bonded all
employees who are responsible for the handling of any
company funds.  Our contract has been held by the
Royal Company in Detroit.

As this company plans to withdraw from this particular
field, it will be necessary for us to place this business with another company.  Will you request one of
your representatives to visit us?  Please ask him to
come prepared to give full details about your plan, and
the cost of your service.

In order that your representative may have some advance
information about our requirements, we are sending you
a copy of our latest payroll summary sheet.  This form
contains the names of all employees who are to be bonded
and describes the nature of their duties.

Our present contract with the Royal Company will expire
on April 15.  Therefore, we must act immediately in
placing this business with another company.  Please
have your representative call at an early date.

Very truly yours,

RHODES JEWELRY COMPANY

General Manager

GBL/EB

FIG. 10—Model for Sample Letter C

Parke, Austin & Lipscomb, Inc.
11 WEST 42ND STREET
NEW YORK 18, N.Y.

January 2, 19—

Mr. James Maxwell,
1847 Bedford Avenue,
Lincoln, Nebraska.

Dear Mr. Maxwell:

You are doubtless aware of the growing interest of many
of our young men in the Saturday night meetings sponsored by the various clubs of the Lincoln YMCA.

As the program staff is eager to expand the athletic
and cultural activities of the Y, we are writing to ask
you, as a former member, to come to a meeting on Friday,
January 11, at 7:30 p.m., in Room 318, so that we may
discuss future plans for the organization of a new
activities program.

We should appreciate your letting us know whether we
may expect you.

Sincerely yours,

Charles R. Alden
Program Director

CRA/GB

FIG. 11—Model for Sample Letter D

Parke, Austin & Lipscomb, Inc
11 WEST 42ND STREET
NEW YORK 18  N Y.

June 15, 19—

The Midway Mart, Inc.
1001 Market Street
Los Angeles, California

Attention of Mr. Lewis

Gentlemen:

We are informed by the railroad company that they
will assume full responsibility for the case of two
dozen damaged lampshades delivered to your company on
June 12.

Please mail us the agent's receipt for the merchandise; and return the lampshades, for which we shall
issue a credit memorandum for the full amount plus
freight charges.

We regret that this shipment was damaged, and hope
you have not been inconvenienced because of it.

Very truly yours,

Robert J. Holmes
Credit Manager

RJH/UB

FIG. 12—Model for Sample Letter E

Parke, Austin & Lipscomb, Inc
11 WEST 42ND STREET
NEW YORK 18  N Y.

June 18, 19—

Acme Publishing Company
555 Lexington Avenue,
Chicago, Illinois.

Subject:  Business Education

Gentlemen:

We are planning to reorganize the work of our business education department for the school term beginning
next February.

At the present time we offer our pupils a limited
range of miscellaneous business electives.  It is our
plan to increase these electives to provide a complete
major in each of the three fields: stenography, bookkeeping, office practice.

We are interested in examining the most recently
published books in business education with a view to
their adoption as classroom textbooks.  We should be
glad to have you send us copies of all new business
books suitable for high school pupils, published by
your company between now and November 1.

Very truly yours,

ELRTON BUSINESS SCHOOL

Harold Wilson, Chairman
Education Department

GBZ/B

FIG. 13—Model for Sample Letter F

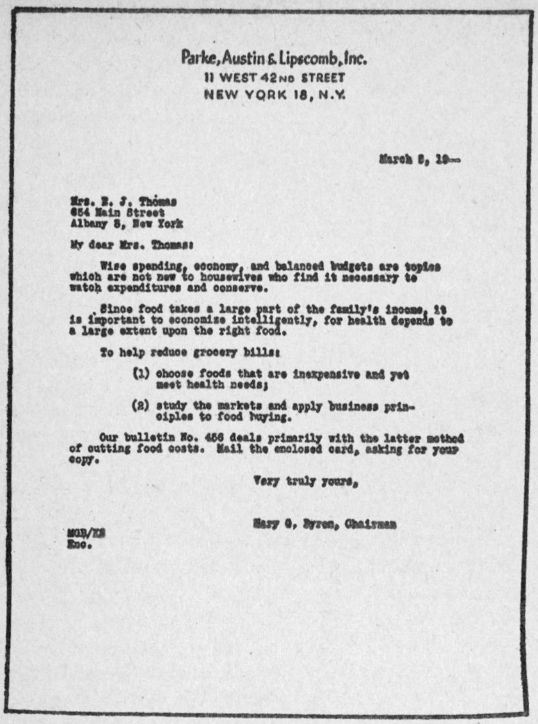

FIG. 14—Model for Sample Letter G

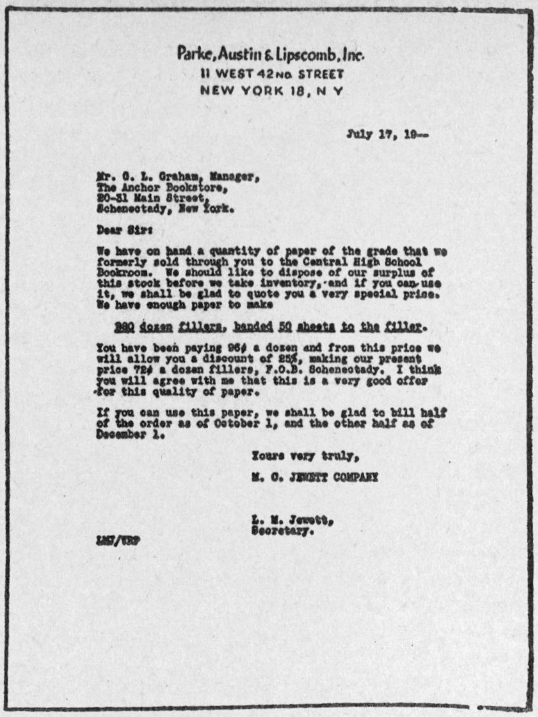

FIG. 15—Model for Sample Letter H

**Envelopes.** Sizes of envelopes generally used by business offices are No. 6½ (3½ x 6½ inches), No. 9 (3⅞ x 8⅝ inches), and No. 10 (4⅛ x 9½ inches). The two latter envelope sizes are used with the 8½ x 11-inch letterhead paper.

The address on an envelope is usually typed toward the lower right-hand half of the envelope. On a No. 6½ envelope, the first line of an address should be placed 10 or 12 line spaces from the top and 1 or 2 spaces to the left of center (Fig. 16).

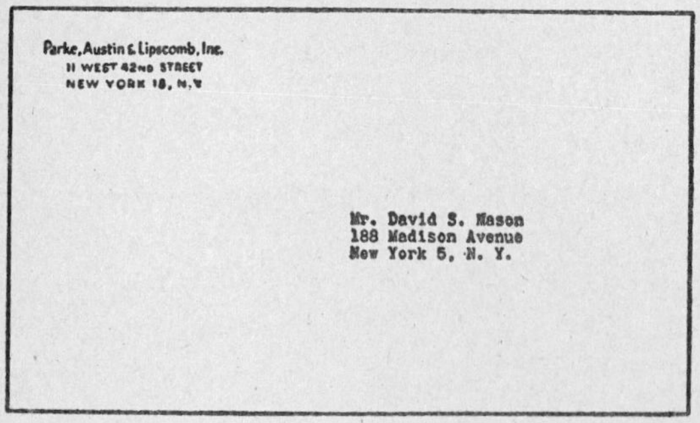

FIG. 16—Model of address on envelope

On No. 9 and No. 10 envelopes, the first line of an address should be placed about 13 line spaces from the top and about 5 spaces to the left of center. A company may, however, prefer some other placement of address, which should be followed.

The style of address on the envelope should follow that of the inside address of the letter. If the indented style and open punctuation are used in the letter, the indented style and open punctuation should be used on the envelope:

**Mr. Robert B. Wells**
**432 Broad Street**
**Dayton, Ohio**

The most commonly used types of addresses are: (1) indented, single spaced, with open punctuation; (2) indented, single spaced, with close punctuation; (3) block style, single spaced, with open punctuation; (4) block style, double spaced, with close punctuation. Practice typing these different styles of addresses on Nos. 6½, 9, and 10 envelopes, paying particular attention to arrangement and correct placement.

It is frequently necessary to write directly to a company but to have the letter brought to the *attention of* a particular individual who may handle or be concerned with the contents of the letter. The *attention of* line, which in the letter itself is usually centered after the address, as in Figure 12, should be typed toward the lower left-hand corner on the envelope. The form may be either:

**Attention of Mr. Lewis**

or

**Attention: Mr. Lewis**

When an envelope is addressed in this way, it may be opened, in the absence of the person to whose attention it is addressed, by anyone connected with the company. Thus an order or some matter requiring immediate attention is taken care of without delay.

## Lesson XIX—Tabulating and Centering

Much of the factual information which business organizations use must be tabulated so that it can be referred to easily. In general, tabulations contain main headings, subheadings, and column headings. Since all parts of a tabulation must be centered, the rule for centering should be reviewed (see Fig. 3, and its text, at beginning of Typewriting Lessons).

To center the heading, THE UNION SUPPLY COMPANY, count all the spaces, including those between words. Divide these 24 spaces by 2 which gives 12. Subtract 12 from the center-point of 40 to get 28. Move the typewriter carriage until the indicator points to 28 on the scale. The heading will be accurately centered when the typing starts at this point.

Correct placement of tabulations is obtained by *vertical placement* and *horizontal centering.*

*Vertical Placement.* There are six typewriting lines to an inch. Therefore, on a sheet of 8½ x 11 paper there are 66 writing lines. From this number subtract the number of lines needed for the tabulation. Divide by 2 for the number of lines to leave at the top of the paper before beginning the tabulation.

If a tabulation requires 26 spaces, subtract 26 from 66, which leaves 40. Half of 40 is 20, the number of spaces to leave above the tabulation.

In vertical placement, the number of free lines that should be left at the top of standard lettersize paper for tabulations containing 20, 33, 41, or 30 lines are 23, 16, 12, and 18.

*Horizontal Centering.* Count the total number of spaces required in all columns, adding the spaces between columns. The total number of spaces in the entire line is then divided by 2. Subtract this amount from 40 to get the starting point of the line, and add the same number to 40 to get the end of the line. Set the marginal stops at these two points, and then plan the setting of the tabulator stops for each column.

Let us assume a tabulation of three columns, containing 14, 10, and 12 spaces respectively, with 7 spaces between each of the columns, as shown in Figure 17.

Add these spaces ($14 + 7 + 10 + 7 + 12$) to get the total number of spaces required in the writing line. The sum of the spaces is 50. To center these spaces on the line, divide by 2 which gives 25, and place one marginal stop at 15 which is 25 spaces to the left of 40 (the center) and another marginal stop at 65, the same number of spaces to the right of 40, as shown in Figure 18.

To set the tabulator stops for the second and third columns, start by adding to 15, the point at which the left marginal stop is set, the 14 spaces in the first column, and the 7 spaces between the first and second columns, thus: $15 + 14 + 7 = 36$. Therefore, the point at which to set the tabulator stop for the second column is at 36. The position of the third tabulator stop is found by adding $36 + 10 + 7 = 53$, the point at which to set the third tabulator stop (see Fig. 19).

If a line is made up of an odd number of spaces, the fraction which results after dividing the spaces by 2 is dropped when subtracting to get the left marginal stop (LMS), and is kept when adding to get the right marginal stop (RMS). For example, if a line has 55 spaces, the marginal stops are obtained as follows: $55 \div 2 = 27\frac{1}{2}$. The LMS is $40 - 27$, or 13; and the RMS is $40 + 28$, or 68.

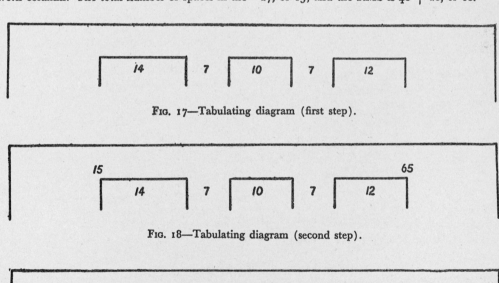

FIG. 17—Tabulating diagram (first step).

FIG. 18—Tabulating diagram (second step).

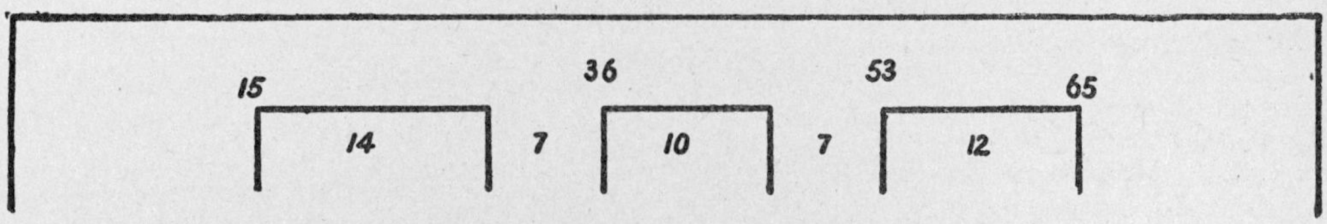

FIG. 19—Tabulating diagram (third step).

Using 40 as the center-point, find the number on the scale to which the indicator should be moved in order to center each of the following lines:

Thomas Jefferson

Lawrence High School

UNITED STATES OF AMERICA

UNION TRUCKING CORPORATION

The above names should begin at points 32, 30, 28, and 27. For lines containing 40, 45, 50, 60, and 75 spaces, the left and right marginal stops should be set at 20 and 60, 18 and 63, 15 and 65, and 3 and 78.

**Tabulation Plan Sheet.** Before making a tabulation, a plan sheet containing all the necessary data should be prepared.

First examine the following model tabulation:

### Tabulation No. 1

#### WORDS FREQUENTLY MISSPELLED

| | | |
|---|---|---|
| accurate | definite | medicine |
| adequate | eligible | molasses |
| adjacent | exercise | mortgage |
| airplane | familiar | mucilage |
| allotted | forcibly | nauseous |
| argument | forehead | optimist |
| assassin | fourteen | parallel |
| athletic | grievous | paralyze |
| attacked | guardian | pavilion |
| audience | humorous | pinnacle |
| bachelor | identity | poignant |
| believed | inveigle | reveille |
| boundary | judgment | scissors |
| business | lavender | strategy |
| calendar | lethargy | syllable |
| colander | maneuver | tortoise |
| courtesy | marriage | valuable |

Now prepare a Plan Sheet such as is shown in Figure 20, to serve as a guide for typing Tabulation No. 1, so that once you start typing, you can continue the tabulation without hesitation to the end.

Now examine the following model tabulation:

### Tabulation No. 2

PERRY MANUFACTURING COMPANY
BUFFALO, NEW YORK
Men's Outfitters

| MODEL | STYLE | PRICE |
|---|---|---|
| T-528 | Fitted Topcoat | $25.50 |
| T-531 | Reversible Topcoat | 28.25 |
| T-533 | Chesterfield | 32.75 |
| T-425 | Polo Overcoat | 39.00 |
| T-427 | Ulster | 40.60 |
| T-430 | Guard Overcoat | 42.50 |

In preparing a Plan Sheet for Tabulation No. 2, the number of spaces in each of the first three lines of the heading are counted, and each line is then centered. The first line contains 27 spaces; half of 27 is 14, which when subtracted from 40 (the center-point) leaves 26, the point at which the typing of the line should start to be centered properly. The next two lines, which contain 17 and 16 spaces, respectively, are centered in the same way.

To set the LMS and RMS, count the number of spaces across to be occupied by the complete tabulation, including the spaces between the columns. There is a total of 41 spaces, half of which is 21, and 21 from the center-point 40 leaves 19, the point at which the LMS should be set. For the RMS, add the LMS 19 and the total number of 41 spaces across to get 60, the point at which the RMS should be set.

As columns 1 and 3 each occupy 5 spaces (except for the addition of the dollar sign in column 3), the proper placement of these two columns within the 41 spaces is a simple matter—column 1 starts at 19, column 3 at 55.

To center column 2, the word STYLE is first centered by counting the number of spaces, 5, dividing by 2 which equals 3, and subtracting 3 from center-point 40 which equals 37, the point at which to start typing. The items in this column are centered by counting the number of spaces in the longest line, which, in this tabulation, has 18 spaces. Here again, 18 is divided by 2, which gives 9, and 9 sub-

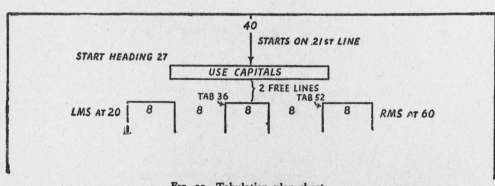

Fig. 20—Tabulation plan sheet

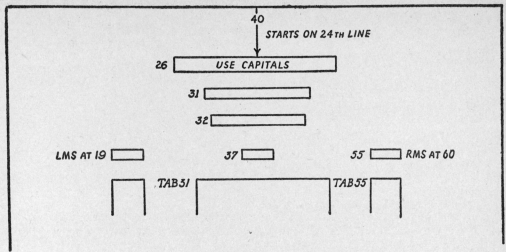

FIG. 21—Tabulation plan sheet.

tracted from the center-point 40 gives 31, the point at which to start typing the items in column 2.

The Plan Sheet for this tabulation is shown in Figure 21.

Now examine these two additional model tabulations:

### Tabulation No. 3
#### FIFTEEN LARGEST CITIES IN THE UNITED STATES

| Rank | City | Approximate Population |
|------|------|------------------------|
| 1 | New York | 7,500,000 |
| 2 | Chicago | 3,400,000 |
| 3 | Philadelphia | 1,930,000 |
| 4 | Detroit | 1,620,000 |
| 5 | Los Angeles | 1,500,000 |
| 6 | Cleveland | 878,000 |
| 7 | Baltimore | 859,000 |
| 8 | St. Louis | 816,000 |
| 9 | Boston | 771,000 |
| 10 | Pittsburgh | 672,000 |
| 11 | Washington | 663,000 |
| 12 | San Francisco | 635,000 |
| 13 | Milwaukee | 587,000 |
| 14 | Buffalo | 576,000 |
| 15 | New Orleans | 495,000 |

### Tabulation No. 4
#### BASKETBALL SCHEDULE
#### Cole High School
#### Cole, Wisconsin
#### CURRENT SEASON

| Date | School | Played at |
|------|--------|-----------|
| Feb. 3 | Miller | Home |
| 5 | Open | -- |
| 10 | Hackamore | Hackamore |
| 12 | Winkel | Home |
| 17 | Roundelay | Home |
| 19 | Pringle | Pringle |
| 26 | Open | -- |
| Mar. 3 | Gotham | Gotham |

You are now ready to prepare Plan Sheets for Tabulation Nos. 3 and 4. Bearing in mind the previous examples, you can then set up the material attractively on 8½ x 11 paper.

# Helpful Hints for Secretaries

The duties of a secretary, explained in this section, consist in knowing about and in being able to carry out the various customs and procedures with which the average business office is concerned. There are also numerous special aids and devices with which the efficient secretary should be familiar.

The successful secretary must have superior stenographic skill, a clear and intelligent understanding of the rules and principles of sound business practice, and a dependable and agreeable personality.

## DICTATION AND TRANSCRIBING

**Taking Dictation.** When your employer wishes to dictate, be prompt, cooperative, and courteous in the way in which you perform this very important duty.

Each morning check to see that your pen is filled and in good writing order. Also, have some well-sharpened pencils ready in case of necessity. Your notebook, pen, and pencils must always be ready for immediate use, and your notebook should be dated each day.

During pauses or interruptions in the dictation, read your notes back and insert notations for proper punctuation, capitalization, and paragraphing.

Write names and addresses in shorthand; correct

spelling can be checked later by referring to the letterhead of the correspondence being answered.

Draw a line through each page of shorthand notes after they have been transcribed.

Keep a rubber band around the finished notes in your notebook so that your place is always ready for starting the next dictation.

If dictation is sometimes too fast or not clear, read the doubtful part to the dictator at the end of the dictation. It is wiser to ask about it than to be inaccurate.

When there is an enclosure, it should be mentioned at the end of the notes so that the word "enclosure" will be typed at the end of the letter directly under the dictator's initials.

**Steps in Transcribing Shorthand Notes.** Transcribing is a threefold job. You must read your shorthand notes correctly, typewrite accurately and neatly, and consider the best English usage. If an outline may be read in more than one way, read through the entire sentence before writing it to be sure of the correct meaning. And whenever something does not sound quite right, always ask about it.

Proofread your letter before removing it from the machine, as any necessary corrections can be made more easily while the paper is still in the typewriter.

The correct size of envelope should accompany each transcribed letter. In handing the correspondence to the dictator for his signature the finished letter and the envelope should be face-up, with the flap of the envelope tucked under the top edge of the letter.

When the letters are signed, take them to your desk for proper folding, insertion, stamping, and mailing. In large concerns these duties are performed by a special mailing department.

# PLANNING POSITION OF LETTER ON LETTERHEAD

A chart for the neat arrangement of letters is shown for paper measuring 8½ x 11 inches. Use the table only as a temporary guide, for with increased practice you will learn to make necessary changes in spacing between the parts of a letter.

The letterhead is generally printed or typed one inch from the top of the paper. When it is necessary to type the letterhead, leave 6 free line spaces (there are 6 single line spaces to the inch on the typewriter) and write the first line of the letterhead on the seventh typewriting space. A three-line letterhead will therefore occupy lines seven, eight, and nine. The date usually starts 6 single line spaces below the letterhead, or on the fifteenth line from the top of the paper. Six single line spaces should be allowed between the date and the inside address. However, this spacing will sometimes vary, depending on the length of the letter.

For good placement of a business letter you must be able to estimate the number of words in the letter. To do this, count the number of lines that are to be typed and multiply by the average number of words to a line. For example, if your shorthand notes take up 20 lines and you write about 10 words to a line, the letter would contain about 200 words. If this represents a full page in your shorthand notebook, a half page of notes would contain about 100

words, three-quarters of a page about 150 words, and so on.

After the number of words in a letter have been estimated, set the letter up on the typewriter according to the following letter-placement table.

| KIND OF LETTER | NUMBER OF WORDS | SPACING | MARGINAL STOPS | DATE LINE FROM TOP OF PAGE |
|---|---|---|---|---|
| Short | up to 75 | Double | 20—60 | 15 spaces |
| Medium | 75—150 | Single | 15—65 | 15 spaces |
| Long | 150—200 | Single | 10—70 | 14 spaces |

This is a very simple table, and uses what is called the 6—6—6 arrangement; that is, there are 6 single spaces down to the letterhead, 6 down to the date line, and 6 down to the inside address. Slight changes in the table are left to the practical experience and judgment of the person doing the typewriting.

# AIDS IN TYPEWRITING

It is important that a secretary know how to use the typewriter's many mechanical devices, especially the Variable Line Spacer for typing on ruled lines, the Tabulator Stops for paragraphs and tabulations, the Right Marginal Stop for indicating the end of a line, and the Marginal Release Key.

**When and How to Divide Words.** With the Right Marginal Stop set correctly, a bell rings when the typewriter carriage is within a few spaces of the end of a line. This warning helps in the arranging of a nearly even right margin. If the bell sounds when you are in the midst of typing a long word, be sure to divide the word into its correct syllables. Consult the dictionary whenever you are in doubt about the correct division of a word. One-syllable words— *though, rough, scheme, through, fought, height, thought, strength*—cannot be divided. Never divide a word after a single letter in such words as *ahead, away,* and do not separate two-letter endings, such as *ly, ed, er, an,* from the rest of the word. It is better to complete the word by using the Marginal Release Key to get the extra letter or two on the line.

Try to avoid dividing the name of a person or place. If possible the complete name should always be on one line.

The last word in a paragraph and the last word on a page should not be divided. Also, more than two consecutive lines should not end in word divisions, as it is difficult to read such lines, and the over-all effect is poor.

**Preparing Carbon Copies.** Carbon paper is made in a number of weights, but two grades are most frequently used: (1) heavy carbon paper and (2) light carbon paper. Heavy carbon paper is used in making from 1 to 4 copies at a time; light carbon paper for from 5 to 10 copies at one time. If it is usually necessary to make more than 10 copies at a time, it is best to use light carbon paper and a hard-surface platen.

When working with carbons, always arrange the sheets of typewriting paper and the carbon paper in proper order, and insert the papers evenly in the machine. For example, six copies of a letter require six sheets of paper (an original, and five carbons) and five carbon papers. Place the first sheet of typing paper flat on the desk, and then a carbon paper with its carbon surface face down on top of it. Do the same for the second, third, fourth, and fifth sheets, placing a carbon paper on top of each successive sheet. When these are arranged in this order, place the letterhead (original copy) on top of all the papers. The top edge of the papers should be away from you, and the bottom edge near you. Pick up the papers so that the bottom edge is raised upward and the top edge is downward. Straighten the papers on a flat surface so that the top and left edges of all papers are absolutely even, and insert carefully in typewriter. If further straightening is necessary, use the paper release lever. The procedure for making carbon copies is the same whether one or many carbon copies are to be made.

Before typing, check to see that each sheet of carbon paper is placed so that the carbon side faces the paper intended for the copy. It is very important to check the arrangement of the sheets of paper and the carbons, because if everything is not in order, the letter or material to be copied must be typed again, thus resulting in a waste of time and paper.

Many secretaries allow about a half inch of the carbon paper to stick out from between the bottom edges of the typing paper. This permits the quick separation of the carbon papers from the typing sheets simply by holding the typed sheets with the fingers of one hand and the carbon papers with the fingers of the other and pulling them apart smoothly and carefully.

## ERASURES

When a mistake is made it should be erased very neatly, leaving no evidence of the erasure. Before you do any erasing, *always* move the typewriter carriage over to one side away from the typing point so that the eraser dust will not drop down and clog the mechanism of the machine.

To erase on a carbon copy or copies, place an eraser shield (of celluloid or heavy paper) between each sheet of carbon paper and the carbon copy or copies being made, and erase carefully. The firmness of the shield protects the copies in back of it from becoming smudged. If there are several carbon copies to be corrected, continue with the rest of the erasing in the same way. After the necessary erasing has been done, return the carriage to the exact point on the line and make the correction.

**Correcting Words by Crowding and Spreading.** Sometimes a correction must be made by replacing a six-letter word with one of seven letters, or with one of five letters. Such corrections require the clean erasure of the original word and the typing in its place of the new word. This is known as correcting by crowding or spreading.

In crowding letters, move the carriage to the point where the beginning of the word should be typed and depress the back-spacer before striking each letter in the new word. In spreading letters, move the carriage to the point where the word should begin and with the carriage release lever control the carriage so as to allow more space between each letter in the new word. After a few attempts, this method of making corrections will become very easy.

## FORM LETTERS

Many large organizations use form letters in replying to certain types of letters of which they receive several in the course of the day's business. By making up form letters, which may be copied word for word or changed slightly to fit the particular inquiry, much time is saved that would otherwise be taken up in the dictation of answers to each letter.

The secretary should know just which of her employer's letters should be brought to his personal attention, and which can be answered by her, either with a form letter or with a variation of one.

If the employer prefers to sign all form letters, they should be written promptly and placed in a neat pile on his desk, separate from the letters he has dictated and which he will want to read carefully. When the secretary signs such letters, she should write her employer's name in the usual place and put her own initials immediately underneath.

## HANDLING OFFICE MAIL

Office mail falls into two general classifications—outgoing and incoming. Outgoing mail must be signed, folded, sealed, stamped, and mailed. Incoming mail must be opened, sorted, distributed, and then filed.

### Incoming Mail

In large offices, incoming mail is usually handled by a special department. However, in the small office, the secretary must be familiar with all routine practices for handling the incoming mail. Mail must be opened, sorted, classified, and distributed to the proper person as quickly as possible. Before opening letters, those marked "Personal" should be delivered sealed to the designated person or officer. All other mail should be opened carefully so as not to cut any of the contents. When there are enclosures, they should be checked to see that nothing has been omitted. The enclosures should be carefully clipped or stapled to their respective letters before delivering them to the person or persons to whom addressed. When incoming letters contain money or checks, such letters should be sent immediately to the cashier's office so that the necessary bookkeeping record may be made. Letters containing money enclosures usually are answered by a member of the accounting department.

**Dating and Distributing the Mail.** Many concerns stamp the date and time of receipt of all incoming mail in a clear space on the upper part of the letter. This stamp frequently bears a notation which the secretary fills out when a letter is to be sent to more than one member of the firm.

**Arranging Incoming Mail.** All incoming mail requiring the attention of the person addressed should be systematically arranged and placed on his desk so that matters requiring immediate attention will receive first consideration. For example, the mail for the desk of a busy executive would be arranged as follows:

(1) Telegrams
(2) Letters referring to special appointments for the day
(3) Regular mail
(4) Personal mail
(5) Advertisements
(6) Newspapers and magazines

## Outgoing Mail

In handling outgoing mail the secretary must be sure that the letter is complete in every respect and ready for her employer's signature. If the letter is to be sent by "Special Delivery" or "Air Mail," such notations must appear on the envelope, preferably immediately under the postage. When mail is addressed for the special attention of someone, the words "Attention of . . ." should be typed in the lower left-hand corner of the envelope.

It is also the secretary's duty to make certain that any enclosures mentioned in the letter are carefully checked and securely placed in the envelope.

After the envelopes are sealed, the correct amount in postage stamps should be placed evenly in the upper right-hand corner.

**Folding Letters.** All letters must be properly folded for insertion in their envelopes.

For the standard business size envelope (No. 6½), letters are folded as follows:

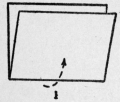

*First*—Fold the lower edge of the letter to within ¼ inch of the top edge. Crease the fold neatly.

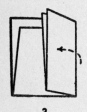

*Second*—Fold the right side of the paper toward the left so that the folded portion will be about ⅓ of the width of the paper. Crease the fold neatly.

*Third*—Fold the left side of the paper toward the right to within ¼ inch of the right edge. Crease and fold neatly.

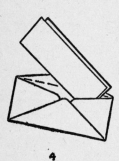

*Fourth*—Hold the folded letter in the right hand, and the open envelope, face downward, in the left hand. Place the letter in the envelope so that the last fold is inserted first.

*Note:* Always allow for a slight overlay at each fold, as this makes it easier to unfold the letter.

Fig. 22—Folding letter for No. 6½ envelope.

For the standard legal size envelope (No. 10), letters are folded as follows:

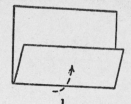

*First*—Fold the lower edge of the letter to a point about ⅓ from the top edge of the letter. Crease the fold neatly.

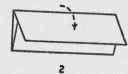

*Second*—Fold the top edge of the letter down to a point about ¼ inch from the lower edge. Crease the fold neatly.

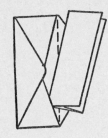

*Third*—Hold the folded letter in the right hand, and the open envelope, face downward, in the left hand. Place the letter in the envelope so that the last fold is inserted first.

Fig. 23—Folding letter for No. 10 envelope.

**Sealing Envelopes by Hand.** In small offices envelopes are seldom sealed by machine. A batch of 8 or 10 envelopes can be quickly sealed by hand by overlapping the opened gummed flaps of the envelopes so that all may be moistened with one stroke of a wet sponge. Each envelope is then picked up with one hand, passed on to the other, and the flap sealed by closing the fingers over the envelope. This is repeated until all the envelopes are sealed.

## Postal Information

Every secretary should be familiar with the general rules and regulations of the Post Office Department. She will find it helpful to know about rates and fees for Air Mail, Special Delivery, Registered Mail, Money Orders, and Insured and C.O.D. mail. She should also become familiar with the regulations governing parcel post and printed matter.

## OFFICE REFERENCE BOOKS

The busy secretary is constantly in need of exact facts and detailed information. There are many sources of such information, but only a few of the more important reference books are mentioned here:

Unabridged dictionary
Complete world atlas
World Almanac for the current year
Local telephone directories
City directory
State directory

Congressional Directory
Style manual
Handbook of business English
Book of synonyms and antonyms

When tracing data and information on special problems, it is often necessary to consult reference volumes at the library. Some of those most frequently used are:

Rand McNally Bankers Directory
Dun & Bradstreet Ratings and Reports
United States Customs Information
The Custom House Guide
Moody's Manuals (financial data for investors)
Poor's Manuals (financial data for investors)
The Official Hotel Red Book and Directory
Bullinger's Postal and Shipper's Guide
American Medical Directory
The New York Times Index (news items and reports indexed under name or subject)
Reader's Guide to Periodical Literature (items indexed by author and subject)
Lloyd's Register of World Shipping
The United States Official Postal Guide
Who's Who in America

Some specialized problem may make it necessary to consult a number of other source books, made available in the reference rooms of most public libraries. Only through constant use of these can the secretary appreciate their usefulness as sources of information.

## THE SECRETARY'S DUTIES AS RECEPTIONIST

In every office the secretary's daily contacts with callers build or destroy good will. When the secretary acts as an office receptionist, it is necessary, as the firm's representative, to treat all callers with courtesy. The caller may be a prospective customer, a salesman, employee, creditor, applicant for a position, a friend, or a member of the family. In every case the secretary must act with agreeable tact and good judgment. She should make the caller's contact with the firm pleasant and satisfactory.

Knowing her employer's needs and desires, the secretary should get from the caller his name, business, and the nature of his errand. The secretary must be quick to judge what callers are welcome, and prevent any unwanted callers from taking up the valuable time of a busy executive.

When a caller has an appointment, but arrives ahead of time, the secretary should see that there is some interesting reading matter available for him to look at while waiting.

When special papers and reports will be required during a consultation or interview with certain individuals, such material should be taken from the files and placed on the executive's desk in readiness.

## HANDLING TELEPHONE CALLS

Since the telephone is one of the important business instruments used by the secretary, it is essential that it be used skillfully and effectively to win the confidence and good will of the person at the other end of the line. A pleasing voice, resonant, low, well-controlled, and firm, is a decided asset and should be developed.

The following are good telephone rules to remember:

(1) Be prompt in answering the telephone.
(2) Avoid being misunderstood; speak directly into the mouthpiece; pronounce words clearly; enunciate numerals distinctly.
(3) When answering the telephone give the firm's name immediately, and then your own name if it will expedite matters.
(4) If the person wanted is not in, offer to take a message for him.
(5) Write down every message completely and put it in a conspicuous place on the desk of the person for whom it is intended.
(6) Check the accuracy of names and numbers received over the telephone by repeating them very clearly.
(7) Be brief, courteous, and businesslike.
(8) When another is telephoning, stop typing if it seems to interfere with his hearing the message.
(9) Keep an index of frequently called numbers beside the telephone.
(10) Consult the telephone directory for information about long-distance calls, regular charges, reduced rates, and other special services.

# Filing Equipment and Systems

Filing is an important activity in most business offices, and every secretary should have a knowledge of the best and correct filing methods.

The systematic and orderly arranging and keeping of correspondence and other business papers and documents so that they can be found easily and quickly constitute the filing process. A dictionary and a telephone directory are good illustrations of excellent filing schemes because words and names have their particular places in which they can always be found.

In order to find the right place for all business records, it is first necessary to classify the records properly. All records of a similar nature should be kept together for easy reference. This classifying of papers according to a systematic scheme is known as *indexing*. Before taking up the subject of indexing, we shall consider several types of filing equipment and systems of filing.

## FILING EQUIPMENT

The most commonly used filing equipment is the *vertical file cabinet*. Correspondence is filed by placing the correspondence on edge, in folders, behind lettered guides. All correspondence relating to a certain matter is thus brought together in one folder for convenience in handling.

The *Spindle File* is a very simple filing device. It

is a long metal pointer resting on a base. Papers are filed by piercing them over the sharpened pointer and allowing them to rest safely near the base. It keeps papers together until they can be filed more permanently.

The *Clipboard File* and the *Shannon File* are essentially lightweight baseboard files. The first keeps papers together by a strong clip at the top of the board; the second holds them together with two pegs over which the papers are placed and held securely by arch-shaped metal snaps.

The *Letter-Box File* is large enough to hold a number of standard-size letters, and is often provided with an alphabetic index so that letters are put away in proper order.

*Visible Files* are available in flat or vertical styles. They are particularly good for filing names because one can see at an instant several names at one time. The vertical visible file has from 10 to 20 panels hinged on a central upright brace. Each panel has places for as many as 40, 50, or 75 visible labels containing names and other information. Since the panels swing freely around the brace, it is possible to locate a name very quickly.

The *Card Index File Box* is a vertical type of filing equipment, designed for the easy handling of cards in an upright position. It can be obtained in standard card sizes. Libraries use this type of file.

## SYSTEMS OF FILING

**Basic Systems.** There are four basic systems of filing: Alphabetic, Geographic, Subject, and Numeric.

The *alphabetic system,* in which filing is according to personal names, is the most widely used. In this system all correspondence or other filing material is placed in alphabetical order according to the spelling of the last name of the person or firm to whom the correspondence is addressed or with whom the material is identified.

The *geographic system* is also an alphabetic arrangement, but consists in filing according to place names instead of personal names. This geographic system is especially useful for firms who carry on a nationwide business and who consult their correspondence and other records according to towns and cities, rather than individuals. However, within the geographic unit filing would be alphabetical according to the name of the person or firm.

The *subject system* of filing keeps together all correspondence and other matters relating to a single subject, arranging these subjects alphabetically. The subject system is especially useful for firms that consult their records in terms of topics, articles, or activities, rather than individuals or localities.

The *numeric system* is used by firms that prefer to have a code number for every correspondent. First of all, it is necessary to keep an alphabetically arranged card index file which shows the correspondent's code number; and these cards must be consulted before the correspondent's letters can be found in the files. The folders in the files are arranged in strict numerical order, so that it is a very easy matter to find material. However, the disadvantage of this system lies in the need for a second set of records giving the code numbers. Many large concerns, with separate filing departments, prefer the numeric system.

**Arrangement Within Folders.** In any of the four basic systems there is also the question of arranging the correspondence within a folder devoted to a single person, firm, place, or subject. Within such a folder, the correspondence should be kept according to date, always placing the correspondence with the most recent date at the top (or front) of the folder. Carbon copies of replies should take their place according to date in the same file, or they may be attached to the letter which they answer.

## INDEXING

In order to file papers correctly, it is essential to adopt a set of guiding rules for proper indexing. Indexing is the process of deciding under which name, place, or subject certain correspondence or other material shall be filed, and then how it shall be filed in relation to other names in the files. Some correspondence can be indexed in more than one way. Where doubt exists as to the correct way of indexing a name or subject, it is a good plan to use *cross-reference*.

For cross-reference purposes in a correspondence file, it is desirable to use letter-size sheets of paper since these will fit into the folders and files just as the correspondence itself does and will not fall out or be misplaced as small slips or cards would be. Such cross-reference sheets should be marked with a notation "See .................." which will be a cross-reference to the name or heading under which the correspondence will be found.

In the indexing and filing of correspondence according to the alphabet, it is customary to paste a label on each folder used for filing, giving the name of the person whose correspondence is contained in the folder. If the folder contains correspondence with more than one person, the range within the alphabet covered by the names should be indicated on the label. These labels should be prepared according to the accepted rules for alphabetical arrangement of names as used in business offices, which we shall outline here. In general, all names are arranged in order from *A* to *Z*; and "nothing comes before something," or if a name "ends first, it is filed first"; for example, *Green* comes before *Greene*. The more specific rules follow:

### Rules for Indexing

1. Names of individuals should be arranged so that the surname is first, the given name or initial next, and the middle name or initial last.

| NAME | INDEXED |
| --- | --- |
| George W. Adams | Adams, George W. |
| Martin Roy Jones | Jones, Martin Roy |
| T. Harold Snyder | Snyder, T. Harold |

2. Surnames containing prefixes, such as De, La, Mac, Mc, O', Van, etc., are considered as though they were not separated, but written as one word.

| NAME | INDEXED |
| --- | --- |
| John De Forest | DeForest, John |
| Richard La Follette | LaFollette, Richard |
| Jean Mac Bride | MacBride, Jean |
| Donald Mc Ann | McAnn, Donald |
| Hugh O'Neil | O'Neil, Hugh |
| George B. Van Gogh | VanGogh, George B. |

3. Titles such as Dr., Prof., Rev., Mr., Mrs., Miss, Jr., Sr., etc., are disregarded, and are placed at the end of the name in parentheses.

| NAME | INDEXED |
|---|---|
| Prof. William Blain | Blain, William (Prof.) |
| Dr. Martin Clark | Clark, Martin (Dr.) |
| Frank Hall, Jr. | Hall, Frank (Jr.) |
| Mrs. J. R. Marshall | Marshall, J. R. (Mrs.) |
| Rev. John Slater | Slater, John (Rev.) |

4. Treat abbreviations, such as Chas., Geo., Wm., Co., Inc., etc., as if they were spelled out in full.

| NAME | INDEXED |
|---|---|
| Chas. Adams | Adams, Charles |
| Wm. Baker | Baker, William |
| Geo. Donahue | Donahue, George |
| St. John's Hospital | Saint John's Hospital |
| Y. M. C. A. | Young Men's Christian Association |

5. Hyphenated surnames of individuals are treated as one word; hyphenated firm names, though treated as separate words, are not inverted for indexing.

| NAME | INDEXED |
|---|---|
| James Duff-Gordon | Duff-Gordon, James |
| Frank Harrison-Forbes | Harrison-Forbes, Frank |
| Scripps-Howard Co. | Scripps-Howard Co. |

6. Names of companies should be indexed as written if they do not contain the *full name* of an individual; if they contain the full name of an individual, the order for indexing is the surname, given name or names, and remainder of name or title.

| NAME | INDEXED |
|---|---|
| Corn Exchange Mart | Corn Exchange Mart |
| Hodges Tailoring Co. | Hodges Tailoring Co. |
| William Martin Co., Inc. | Martin, William, Co., Inc. |
| Robert Morris Hat Shop | Morris, Robert, Hat Shop |

7. Disregard such words as *a, an, and, &, the, for, of*, etc., in filing.

| NAME | INDEXED |
|---|---|
| The Marvel Bake Shop | Marvel Bake Shop (The) |
| Jones & Davis Co. | Jones (&) Davis Co. |
| School of Music | School (of) Music |

8. Names containing an apostrophe for the singular possessive case are indexed as though the *s* were not included. Disregard the apostrophe in names containing plural possessives.

| NAME | INDEXED |
|---|---|
| Bond's Bread Co. | Bond('s) Bread Co. |
| Bonds' Atlas Shop | Bonds (') Atlas Shop |

9. Names of hotels, schools, libraries, and other institutions should be indexed under their distinctive titles.

| NAME | INDEXED |
|---|---|
| Harvard University | Harvard University |
| Kings County Hospital | Kings County Hospital |
| Hotel Pennsylvania | Pennsylvania, Hotel |

10. Names that begin with numerals are indexed as though the numerals were spelled in full.

| NAME | INDEXED |
|---|---|
| 5th Avenue Library | Fifth Avenue Library |
| 1 Park Avenue Building | One Park Avenue Building |

# Business Machines and their Use

Where there is much repetitive work, office machines are a great saver of effort and time. The more common types of equipment the secretary is likely to encounter are discussed below.

## COPYING MACHINES

An enormous convenience for making a few exact, instant copies of all sorts of documents, copying machines range from large floor models, which can copy almost anything onto ordinary bond paper, to small desk-top models, which only copy black-and-white single sheets onto special coated paper. The electrostatic (Xerox and other brands) process will pick up most colors (except, usually, blue) and reproduce them in black and white. Thermal and light/heat processes usually only pick up black and white really well.

On the large flat-bed machines the original is placed face-down over a window on the top of the machine. Not only single sheets, but bound books and other thick items can be duplicated. Before pressing the copy button, make sure that the copy counter is set for the number of copies you want, and that the proper length of paper (letter- or legal-size) is in the machine.

On rotary-fed machines the material to be copied must be thin, flat, and of standard size, as it is fed right through the machine. Be sure to insert the original straight, so it won't get jammed in the works. Carriers made of plastic sheeting help preserve the originals and also make it possible to insert smaller-then-standard pieces such as cards and newspaper clippings.

## DUPLICATING MACHINES

Copies made in copying machines are relatively expensive. For more than a few copies it is more economical to make a master and run the copies off on a duplicator such as a stencil, spirit, or offset machine.

**Stencil Duplicators.** Also called mimeographing, the stencil process is an easy, inexpensive way of turning out 25–2500 copies where a legible but not top-quality appearance is needed. The master is made by cutting a stencil. Mimeograph stencils are made of plastic film with a backing of tissue, either letter- or legal-size. The typewriter cuts through the plastic, but not the porous backing, leaving holes in the shape of letters for the mimeograph ink to come through onto the copy.

Before cutting a stencil on your typewriter, type out the material on ordinary paper as you wish it to look. Insure clear, sharp duplicates by cleaning your machine's type bars. Inserting the carbon cushion sheet supplied with each box of stencils between the tissue backing and the plastic sheet, with the glossy side of the carbon toward the plastic, will make the letters appear darker on the duplicates. Set the ribbon indicator for "stencil" so that the ribbon stays out of the way and the type bars strike the stencil directly. Type with a firm, uniform touch so that the finished job will look smooth and regular. Such characters as *E, M,* and *W* require slightly greater typing pressure; *e, o, c, i, l,* and *f* require lighter pressure. Strike all punctuation marks very lightly. An electric typewriter can be made to cut the best-looking stencils, particularly when the pressure on the above letters is adjusted by a repairman.

Errors can be corrected by rubbing them with the rounded end of a paper clip and then applying a thin coating of stencil correction fluid. Wait a few seconds till the fluid dries, then type your correction with a rather light touch.

Drawings and written material can be cut into the stencil by hand, using a pointed stylus. An illuminated drawing board called a mimeoscope or light table is useful for this type of work.

Stencils can be made in thermal copiers from originals done on plain paper. Not only does this save cutting stencils by hand; longer runs are feasible, as duplicate stencils are easily made when the first one wears out. "Electronic" stencils made with special equipment can be used to reproduce half-tones and will last for runs of 5,000–10,000 copies.

To print a stencil, attach it face down to the top of the drum of the mimeograph machine and smooth it around the drum so that it is neat and straight. Remove the backing sheet at the perforated line and lock the bottom of the stencil into position. Use special mimeograph paper that will absorb the ink instantly. A trial run of 10–20 copies will probably be needed before the machine begins printing clearly.

**Spirit Duplicators.** Spirit (or "ditto") duplicating is one of the simplest ways of making a few hundred inexpensive copies. Carbons for making spirit masters come in five colors, purple being the most popular. Multicolored copies can be made by changing carbon colors when preparing the master. Masters can be typed, handwritten, drawn, or prepared in a thermal copying machine.

To type a master, place the master sheet in your typewriter with the spirit carbon behind it, so that the spirit carbon will deposit a reverse image on the back of the master sheet. If you are using a master set with the carbon attached to the master sheet, first pull out the protective tissue between the carbon and the master, and insert the set open end first so that corrections can be made if necessary. Leave at least ½ inch blank at top and bottom for attaching the master to the duplicator. Type with an even touch as with a mimeo stencil. The use of a backing sheet will produce sharper, darker copies.

Corrections need only be made on the reverse side of the master. There are correction pencils, fluids, and tapes for this purpose. A mistake can also be scraped off with a dull razor blade and then cleaned with a soft eraser. Type the correction with a strip of fresh spirit carbon cut from the margin or from an extra sheet of carbon. Remove this strip before resuming typing.

To make the duplicates, the master is inserted in the duplicating machine so that the side inked by the carbon will strike the blank paper. Wood alcohol—the "spirit"—dissolves a bit of the ink on the master onto each copy. Since a little ink is used up each time, after a few hundred copies the image will fade. A duplicate master made in a thermal copier can be used to extend the run.

**Offset Duplicators.** Offset (or multilith) duplicates are both cheaper and of higher quality than those made in copying machines, and, though it takes special skill to run the printers, the masters are easy to prepare. For short runs, paper "mats" can be made in electrostatic or thermal copiers or directly in the typewriter, and duplicate mats can be made in the offset printer itself to extend the run. Plastic and metal plates are also made for longer runs. Typing, printing, drawings, and photographs can be pasted up on the master, and the image reduced or enlarged. Corrections and updating are easy to do.

# DICTATING MACHINES

Dictating machines usually come in two parts: (1) the dictating, or input, unit used by the dictator and (2) the transcribing, or output, unit used by the typist. The input unit can be a small battery-operated unit usable anywhere, a desk-top machine, or a remote microphone or telephone hookup connected to a centralized bank of recording machines. Modern recorders have features such as provision for playback and corrections, indexing or timing systems, warning signals when the end of the recording capacity is neared, and voice-operated relays that stop the recorder during long pauses and restart it when the dictator begins speaking again.

Transcribing units can be equipped with a variety of earpieces to suit the typist, and have easily operated controls, such as foot pedals, by which the machine can be stopped, started, backed up, or moved forward. There are also speed controls so that the typist can select a comfortable pace, and volume and sometimes tone controls to ensure maximum audibility. So that material can be located quickly, there are provisions for indexing or rapid scanning.

There are two types of recording media: (1) embossing and (2) magnetic. The embossing type employs belts or discs which are not reusable. They are very inexpensive and are either discarded after use or filed as a record. Because they are not erasable the dictator must alert the typist to corrections by means of indexing slips and then re-dictate the material as it should be.

Magnetic recording media comes in belts, tape cassettes, tape reels, or endless tape loops. To make a correction, the dictator backs up the tape, erases it, and dictates the new material. Though more expensive than embossing media, magnetic media can be reused hundreds of times.

# ADDRESSING MACHINES

For frequent mailings to a long list of addresses, addressing machines save much typing. The two most commonly found machines are the Addressograph, which uses metal plates on which the addresses are embossed by a Graphotype machine, and the Elliott addressing machine, which uses stencils prepared on a typewriter. The plates or stencils are loaded on trays, ready for addressing thousands of pieces of mail per hour. After use, each plate slips back into a receiving tray or filing drawer in the same order in which it was placed in the machine. This makes it easy to change plates quickly and keep mailing lists up to date. The Addressograph can be adjusted to make two or more impressions of the same plate, as well as to print only parts of the plate. It is also possible to select certain plates and reject others.

## ADDING AND CALCULATING MACHINES

The familiar *ten-key adding machine* has a key for each digit, as well as buttons for plus, minus, repeat, subtotal, and total. With a little practice it can be run rapidly by the touch system. These machines are also called listing machines, because they print each number entered, as well as subtotals and totals, on a paper tape.

The *full-keyboard adding machine* has a separate vertical row numbered 1 to 9 for each column of units, tens, hundreds, thousands, etc. Zeroes register automatically if no key in a column is pressed. More than one key can be pressed at once. Though the touch system is not used, an operator skilled in correct finger combinations and techniques can work speedily.

Multiplication and division can be done on adding machines by repeat addition and subtraction, but it is much easier to do them on a calculator.

With the *key-driven calculator* (Comptometer and other brands) an operator can do high-speed addition and multiplication. Subtraction and division take special skill. This machine has a full-bank keyboard. Answers appear in a window on the machine rather than on a printed tape.

The *printing calculator* takes less practice to use, as all four operations can be done at the touch of a button. The machine looks much like a ten-key adding-listing machine except for the additional multiplication and division buttons. Some models have memory storage features, dual registers, and provisions for handling constant quantities.

Pocket and desk-top *electronic calculators* are rapidly gaining popularity. Having no moving parts, they are noiseless and extremely fast. Not only do they add, subtract, multiply, and divide; various models are preprogrammed to do complex operations (like square roots) instantly. Many machines have one or more "memories" for storing the result of a computation for use in future computations; and some can be programmed by means of magnetic cards or tape to do a whole series of operations automatically. These machines are of the ten-key type, with extra buttons for various operations, and come in both window and printing models.

## OTHER OFFICE EQUIPMENT

There are bookkeeping and billing machines from simple adding machines with wide carriages to whole punched-card and electronic data processing systems. Typewriters exist that can write in changeable type styles; do repetitive typing automatically, stopping where individual material is to be inserted; handle corrections and additions without hand retyping; or serve as input devices for computers. There are multi-button phones connected to many inside and outside lines; phones connected to loudspeakers; automatic dialers; phones connected to dictating equipment; dataphones which carry information from one business machine to another far away; and facsimile machines that transmit visual images over phone lines. The many other office devices include staplers, hole punchers, postal scales, postage meters, line-a-time typing aids, and check writers and protectors.

# Getting Your First Office Job

As soon as you are equipped with the necessary knowledge and skill acquired as the result of conscientious study and practice in shorthand, typewriting, and the various other procedures involved in the work of a business office, you are ready to go out and sell your services.

There are several ways to get a position, the most common of which are:
Answering "Help Wanted" advertisements
Advertising in "Situations Wanted" columns
Filling out applications
Registering at employment agencies
Personal inquiries
Personal recommendations of friends
It is well to remember that every employer who has a vacancy in his office is looking for a competent and attractive person.

If the first step for you to take in getting a position is to write a letter, then make certain that the appearance of your letter and its content convey the impression you wish them to make on someone who knows nothing about you, but who is interested in learning of your qualifications.

Your letter should be neat, accurately typed, and checked carefully to see that you have given clearly and concisely all the necessary information about yourself. The prospective employer is more apt to reply to a well-written letter and to ask you to come in for an interview.

If it is necessary for you to telephone instead of write for an appointment, your voice should be distinct and pleasant to whoever may answer the telephone. Ask for the proper person immediately, tell him briefly who you are, why you are calling, and that you would like to apply for the position.

When getting ready for an interview, be sure of your appearance and of what you are going to say before you start out. The conversation with a prospective employer will never follow exactly the pattern you may have outlined, but if you know what you want to say, you are bound to make a more favorable impression because you will be prepared.

You should always be on time for an interview; let your voice express a modest yet confident personality; and avoid extremes in clothes and hairdos. As soon as the interview is over, you should leave promptly.

# Business English and Effective Speaking

In this section we take up the fundamentals of Good English in writing and speaking. We begin with a consideration of ways of avoiding errors that arise through a lack of understanding of the parts of speech, and then take up such common sentence errors as run-on sentences, dangling expressions, and misplaced modifiers. How to acquire good habits in the generally troublesome fields of spelling, capitalization, and punctuation is next considered. Then we give useful reference lists of words often confused and preferred words and expressions.

The discussion of Effective Speaking takes up proper pronunciation, including several lists of words frequently mispronounced, with their correct pronunciation indicated, and presents information on how to prepare a speech and develop a style in speaking.

## Practical Guide to Good English

Business English, the English that is used in the day-to-day activities of the business world, conforms to the same rules and principles of grammar as apply to good English wherever used. In Business English we are concerned especially with these rules and principles of good English as used in particular business situations.

Business English must be clear and concise, and must convey an idea to the listener or reader in the most forceful way possible. At the same time the English that is used in business must be correct; the words chosen must mean what you intend them to mean, and the sentences you use must conform to the standards of grammatical correctness.

### PARTS OF SPEECH

In the same way that members of the crew of an airplane are labeled according to their *function*—pilot, navigator, radio operator—we find it helpful to label words according to their function in sentences.

*Nouns* are words that are used to name people, places, things, ideas, conditions, qualities, and emotions.

> Edward Jones, Delaware, typewriter, success, pleasure

*Pronouns* are words that are used as substitutes for nouns.

> we, it, you, them, our

*Verbs* are words that express an action, a condition, or a state about a person, place, or thing.

> We *are writing.*
> We *have manufactured.*
> He *will distribute.*
> She *is* rich.
> They *run* home.
> The guests *left* early.
> If you *deliver* the order by the tenth, we *can begin* the sale on schedule.

*Adjectives* are words that modify the meaning of nouns and pronouns.

> *happy* land, *loud* noise, *sweet* cake, *bright* light

The words *the, a, an* are adjectives, but are usually referred to as "articles."

*Adverbs* are words that modify the meaning of verbs, adjectives, and other adverbs.

> open *quickly, extremely* bright, walk *very cautiously*

*Prepositions* are words that connect nouns and pronouns to the rest of the sentence.

> *to* the door, *by* me, *from* California, *with* great joy

*Conjunctions* are words that join two or more words, phrases, and clauses, and show certain relationships, such as cause, result, condition.

> Ted *and* Flora, the same *as* mine, *if* he comes, *although* it is raining, *since* he is not yet here, *because* he slid into the base, tune the radio down *or* turn it off, let us pay our check *and* take a taxi to the station.

*Interjections* are exclamations that express sudden emotion.

> oh, ah, pshaw, alas

Of these eight parts of speech nouns, pronouns, verbs, adjectives, and adverbs present problems that often lead to errors in speaking and writing. We shall take up the problems of these parts of speech in order.

## Problems in Using Nouns

Among the most common errors that arise in the use of nouns are those that involve the following: forming the plural, indicating possession, and finding the correct verb form to go with collective nouns.

### FORMING THE PLURAL OF NOUNS

Most nouns add *s* to signify the plural, that is, more than one.

    cigarette, cigarettes
    sir, sirs

If the singular form already ends in the sound of *s, sh,* or *ch,* the plural is formed by adding *es.*

    mass, masses
    dish, dishes
    tax, taxes
    pouch, pouches

If the singular form of the noun ends in a *y* which is preceded by a vowel, we merely add *s.*

    key, keys
    tray, trays

If the singular form of the noun ends in a *y* which is preceded by a consonant, the *y* is changed to an *i* and *es* is added.

    baby, babies
    party, parties
    diary, diaries

Many nouns ending in *f* or *fe* form the plural by changing the *f* to a *v* and adding *es.*

    wife, wives
    loaf, loaves
    life, lives
    beef, beeves (*beefs* is also acceptable)

If the singular form of the noun ends in an *o* which is preceded by a consonant, we usually add *es* to form the plural.

    cargo, cargoes
    motto, mottoes
    tomato, tomatoes
    potato, potatoes

Some nouns ending in an *o* preceded by a consonant form the plural by adding *s* to the singular:

    solo, solos
    piano, pianos
    studio, studios

Symbols and numbers usually have their plurals represented by the addition of *'s*; the same is true of words which are spoken of as such.

    1, 1's
    three 4's
    Your letter has too many *and's.*

Certain words have special plural forms.

    crisis, crises              adieu, adieus or adieux
    focus, foci                 index, indexes or in-
    genus, genera                 dices
    alumnus, alumni             appendix, appendixes
      (men)                       or appendices
    alumna, alumnae             axis, axes
      (women)                   bureau, bureaus or
    bacillus, bacilli             bureaux
    basis, bases                agendum, agenda
    datum, data                 erratum, errata
    ellipsis, ellipses          thesis, theses
    stratum, strata             hypothesis, hypotheses
    parenthesis, paren-         phenomenon, phenom-
      theses                      ena
    radius, radii               oasis, oases
    addendum, addenda           synopsis, synopses
    cactus, cacti or            membrandum, memo-
      cactuses                    randa

Certain words form their plurals irregularly.

    ox, oxen                    man, men
    louse, lice                 mouse, mice
    sheep, sheep                moose, moose
    woman, women                tooth, teeth
    die, dies or dice           deer, deer
    child, children             goose, geese
    fish, fish or fishes

The plurals of compound words are often sources of error.

    chairman, chairmen          mother-in-law, moth-
    blow-out, blow-outs           ers-in-law
    stand-by, stand-bys         man-o'-war, men-o'-
    teaspoonful, teaspoon-        war
      fuls

### INDICATING POSSESSION IN NOUNS

When we wish to show ownership or possession with nouns in the singular we use the apostrophe with an *s* (*'s*).

    the businessman's guide, the soldier's uniform

When the word showing possession already ends in *s,* we may add either *'s* or simply the apostrophe without the *s* (*'*).

    Charles' handbook, Mr. Harris's home

Possessives of plural words are formed by adding the apostrophe alone.

    boys' coats, lawyers' briefs

When the plural of a word does *not* end in *s,* we add *'s.*

    men's clothing, children's toys, women's wear

In compound words we show possession by adding *'s* to the end of the word.

    brother-in-law's office, brothers-in-law's offices
    chairman's address, chairmen's addresses

### PROPER VERB FORMS WITH COLLECTIVE NOUNS

Nouns that refer to a group have both a singular and plural meaning and are called *collective nouns.* The word *jury,* for example, is plural when it means twelve *individuals*; it is singular when it means a *unit.*

    The jury is excused. (The judge considers the
      jury a *unit.*)
    The jury disagree. (Some of the jury take one
      side, some another. The emphasis is on the
      *individuals.*)

Some frequently used collective nouns which may be thought of as singular or plural according to the shade of meaning in the sentence are: *council, jury, majority, minority, number.*

Some words ending in *ics* may be considered to be collective nouns. These include words that mean a science or study, which are usually singular in meaning: *mathematics, physics, mechanics, economics, acoustics, ballistics, eugenics, phonetics, esthetics.*

    *Physics* takes up problems of light and heat.
    *Economics* is a social science.
    *Aesthetics* deals with beauty.

## Problems in Using Pronouns

Pronouns, which, we have seen, are words used in place of nouns, present problems in the following cases: in choosing the proper form of the verb with certain pronouns; in distinguishing between *who* and *whom*; in the use of pronouns ending in *self*; in forming the possessive properly; in distinguishing among who, that, and which; in finding the correct form of personal pronouns.

## PROPER VERB FORMS WITH CERTAIN PRONOUNS

The following pronouns always refer to *one* person or thing, and therefore are used with the singular form of the verb:

> any, anybody, anyone, each, either, every, everybody, everyone, neither, nobody, none.
> Everybody *is* welcome. (Not *are*.)
> None of the customers *is* dissatisfied. (Not *are*.)

When another pronoun refers to one of the above, it must be in the singular form.

> Everyone will please take *his* seat. (Not *their*.)

## DISTINGUISHING BETWEEN WHO AND WHOM

*Who* is usually the subject of a verb. *Whom* is usually the object of a verb or preposition.

> I am uncertain *who* you think should be invited. (*Who* is the subject of the verb *should be invited*.)
> I am uncertain *whom* we should invite. (*Whom* is the object of the verb *should invite*.)
> For *whom* is this order? (*Whom* is the object of the preposition *for*.)

## THE USE OF PRONOUNS ENDING IN SELF

The correct use of pronouns ending in *self* is to show emphasis or reflexive conduct, that is, conduct that refers back to the subject.

> I, *myself*, have seen the display. (Emphasis.)
> The driver injured *himself*. (Reflexive.)

It is incorrect to use such pronouns as substitutes for ordinary subjects and objects.

> The company wrote to Mr. Jones and *me*. (Not *myself*.)
> *He* and Mr. Brown accepted the terms. (Not *himself*.)

### FORMING POSSESSIVE PRONOUNS

The following pronouns *never* contain the apostrophe ('):

> hers, its, ours, theirs, and yours.
> The sales department passed *its* quota. (Not *it's*, which means "it is.")
> This invention is *yours*.
> *Yours* truly. (Not *your's*.)
> This machine is *hers*.

## DISTINGUISHING AMONG WHO, THAT, WHICH, AND WHAT

*Who, that, which, what* are called relative pronouns. They refer to antecedents and also introduce dependent clauses. Note these distinctions in their use:

*Who* refers to persons.
> We had a caller *who* was very interesting.

*Which* refers to things.
> This is the ledger *which* you lost.

*Which* always refers to a single word and not to an entire preceding statement. An incorrect use of *which* would be: "The salesman sold twenty cars, *which* pleased his employer." This should be changed to read: "It was the salesman's record of selling twenty cars *which* pleased his employer." This sentence is correct because *which* refers to a single word, *record*. In the incorrect sentence, *which*

did not refer to any single word but to the statement that he had sold twenty cars.

*That* refers to persons or things. However, it is preferable to write *who* when referring to persons.

> He told a story *that* was instructive. (Thing.)
> I have a friend *that* (or *who*) really knows the market. (Person.)

*What* applies to things, and approximates *that which*.

> Give me *what* you don't want.

## USING THE CORRECT FORM OF PERSONAL PRONOUNS

Personal pronouns are those pronouns which stand directly for names of persons, places, or things.

The following personal pronouns are used as subjects of verbs or their equivalents: *I, you, he, she, it, we, they*.

The following personal pronouns are used as objects of verbs, prepositions, or participles: *me, you, him, her, it, us, them*.

The following examples show the personal pronouns as the equivalents of the subject *it*:

> It is *I*. (Not *me*.)
> It is *he*. (Not *him*.)
> It is *she*. (Not *her*.)
> It is *we*. (Not *us*.)
> It is *they*. (Not *them*.)

The following examples show the personal pronouns used as objects.

> Between *you* and *me*. (Not *I*.)
> Between *him* and *her*. (Not *he* and *she*.)
> Every customer except *him* has answered. (Not *he*.)
> The distributor sent a circular to *us* dealers. (Not *we*.)

# Problems in Using Verbs

Verbs show action or a state of being. They change their spelling and assume various forms under different circumstances. They change in accordance with the number of the subject, singular or plural, which relationship we call *agreement*. They also change according to the time expressed, changes which we call changes of *tense*.

## MAKING VERBS AGREE WITH SUBJECTS

A singular subject takes the singular form of the verb.

> I *am*. He *is*. It *was*.
> She *takes* a trip.

Expressions that come between subject and verb sometimes confuse a writer. In the following examples, the subjects are singular and take the singular form of the verb despite the words which come between subject and verb. The subjects are shown in capital letters, the verbs in italics.

> Your CONFIDENCE in placing this unusual order with us *is* appreciated.
> The FIRE, set by incorrectly wired machines, *has resulted* in a loss of ten thousand dollars.
> The DRIVER, with his horse, *was* visible a block away.
> CARNEGIE, as well as Bessemer, *was* a founder of the steel industry.

A simple test in sentences like these is to omit the intervening words and say the subject and verb together: "confidence is," "fire has resulted in," "driver was," etc.

A plural subject takes the plural form of the verb.

> WE *are*. THEY *are*.
> THEY *take* a trip.

As with singular subjects and verbs, the words between a plural subject and its verb should be disregarded in choosing a verb that agrees with its subjects.

> The SHELVES of the oak-panelled bookcase with the broken glass *have been removed*.
> His REASONS for not signing *were* excellent.
> His SUGGESTIONS, together with the memorandum he wrote, *were* very helpful.

The form of the verb is not affected by the predicate noun, that is, by the noun following any form of the verb *to be*. In the sentence "The topic of his address was fashions," *fashions* is the predicate noun and is plural in meaning, but the verb still agrees with the subject, which is *topic*.

> His business *is* woolens and cottons.

The words *each, every, neither* are singular in meaning.

> Each guest *is* served.
> Every purchaser of textiles *is* not a good judge of quality.
> Neither buyer *was* at fault.

The word *number* has two uses. When it means a numerical quantity, it is singular in meaning.

> The number of dozens *is* ten.

When it means a collection of individual things, it has a plural meaning.

> At the auction, a number of items *were* sold.

## CHOOSING THE PROPER TENSE OF VERBS

As already stated, a verb properly used expresses not only an act but places that act in time. That aspect of a verb which indicates time we call *tense*. Errors are often made in forming certain tenses of verbs and also in choosing the proper tense to place an act in a certain time.

**The Principal Parts of Verbs.** In order to form tenses properly we must know the principal parts of verbs. They are called principal parts because they are the foundation on which all forms of the verb are constructed.

There are three principal parts of verbs. They are the *present tense*, the *past tense*, and the *past participle*.

The present tense indicates that an action occurs in the present; the past tense, that it occurred in the past.

> I *write* shorthand. (Present tense.)
> I *wrote* shorthand. (Past tense.)

The past participle, on the other hand, is not a tense at all. It may not be used alone as a verb. It can be part of a verb, used with an auxiliary verb, or as the first word of a participial phrase. The two most commonly used auxiliaries are *to have* and *to be*. Let us consider the past participle of the verb *take, taken*.

> She *has taken* a business course. (The verb *has taken* contains the auxiliary verb *has*, and the past participle *taken*.)
> The diamond watch *was taken*. (Was + taken.)
> I *have* often *been taken* for him. (Have been + taken.)

The past tense and past participle of many verbs regularly end in *d*, or *ed*, which is added to the present tense. Such verbs are known as *regular verbs*.

| PRESENT TENSE | PAST TENSE | PAST PARTICIPLE |
|---|---|---|
| (I) love | (I) loved | loved |
| grant | granted | granted |
| awaken | awakened | awakened |

Since the regular verbs all follow virtually the same pattern, they present no difficulty.

There are other verbs, however, which form the past tense by changing the vowel of the verb or by using a completely different word; furthermore, the past participle is often different from the past tense. These verbs are known as the *irregular verbs*.

The irregular verbs are important for two reasons. The first is that their misuse is a sign of illiteracy. The second is that there is a danger of confusing the past participle with the past tense. This confusion is based on an analogy with the regular verbs among which the past participle and past tense are always identical in spelling.

> He *rang* the bell. (Not *rung*.)
> She *swam* the channel. (Not *swum*.)
> The cat *sprang*. (Not *sprung*.)
> They *came* yesterday. (Not *come*.)
> Who *did* it? (Not *done*.)
> He *began* the project. (Not *begun*.)
> The patient *drank* the milk. (Not *drunk*.)
> I *saw* the exhibition. (Not *seen*.)

Here is a list of frequently used irregular verbs and their principal parts:

| PRESENT TENSE | PAST TENSE | PAST PARTICIPLE |
|---|---|---|
| awake | awaked, awoke | awoke, awaked |
| bear | bore | borne |
| beat | beat | beaten |
| begin | began | begun |
| bend | bent | bent |
| blow | blew | blown |
| break | broke | broken |
| bring | brought | brought |
| burst | burst | burst |
| buy | bought | bought |
| cast | cast | cast |
| choose | chose | chosen |
| come | came | come |
| do | did | done |
| draw | drew | drawn |
| drink | drank | drunk |
| drive | drove | driven |
| eat | ate | eaten |
| fall | fell | fallen |
| fly | flew | flown |
| go | went | gone |
| hang | hung (an object) | hung (an object) |
| | hanged (a person) | hanged (a person) |
| know | knew | known |
| give | gave | given |
| grow | grew | grown |
| lay | laid | laid |
| lie | lay | lain |
| leave | left | left |
| let | let | let |
| lose | lost | lost |
| pay | paid | paid |
| put | put | put |
| ride | rode | ridden |
| ring | rang | rung |
| rise | rose | risen |
| run | ran | run |
| see | saw | seen |
| seek | sought | sought |

| PRESENT TENSE | PAST TENSE | PAST PARTICIPLE |
|---|---|---|
| send | sent | sent |
| set | set | set |
| shake | shook | shaken |
| sing | sang | sung |
| shrink | shrank | shrunk |
| speak | spoke | spoken |
| steal | stole | stolen |
| swim | swam | swum |
| swing | swung | swung |
| take | took | taken |
| tear | tore | torn |
| teach | taught | taught |
| tell | told | told |
| throw | threw | thrown |
| wear | wore | worn |
| wring | wrung | wrung |
| write | wrote | written |

**The Present Perfect Tense.** Whenever a verb contains a past participle, it is said to be in a *perfect tense*, that is, in perfected or completed time. It is not used to express action at one definite time.

If the auxiliary verb *to have* is used in the present tense with the past participle, then we say that the entire verb is in the *present perfect tense*.

> I *have gone,* she *has written,* we *have managed.*

The uses of the present perfect tense are:

(1) To describe a period of time beginning in the past and extending to the present.

> He *has worked* since noon.
> Mr. Jones *has been* vice-president for ten years.

A common mistake is to use the present tense in such cases.

> He *is* working since noon. (Incorrect.)
> Mr. Jones *is* vice-president for ten years. (Incorrect.)

(2) To describe a past action when no specific time is mentioned.

> How many times *have* you *seen* the customer?
> We *have* already *been* to the factory.
> I *have seen* the President.
> *Has* the five o'clock bell *rung* yet?
> Many improvements *have been made* in our product.

If we wish to be definite about the past time, we must use the past tense and *not* the present perfect.

> I *saw* the customer last week. (Not *have seen.*)
> We *went* to the factory last year. (Not *have been.*)
> I *saw* the President last May. (Not *have seen.*)
> *Did* the bell *ring* five minutes ago? (Not *has rung.*)
> Many improvements *were made* in our product in January. (Not *have been.*)

(3) To describe an action just concluded.

> They *have* just *arrived.*
> My brother *has returned.*

Each of the following sentences is correct, but observe the differences in meaning that are expressed by the use of a particular tense.

> We *lived* in Chicago for five years. (Obviously not now.)
> We *have lived* in Chicago for five years. (Still living there.)
> You *did* not *do* a single thing today. (The day is done.)

You *haven't done* a single thing today. (Still a chance; the day is not over.)

**The Past Perfect Tense.** If the auxiliary verb *to have* is used in the past tense with the past participle, the entire verb is in the *past perfect tense.*

> I *had gone,* she *had written,* we *had managed,* they *had arranged.*

The past perfect tense has the following use: when we wish to distinguish between two or more past events, the earlier event is placed in the past perfect, the later event in the past tense.

> The car *had driven* up when I arrived.
> When I called, I was told that Mr. Smith *had gone.*
> An investigation revealed greater damage than *had been supposed.*
> A better offer was made after he *had signed.*

Note that two or more events occurring simultaneously in the past are both placed in the past tense.

> The car *drove up* as I *arrived.*
> When I *called,* I *was told* Mr. Smith *was going.*
> An investigation *revealed* greater damage than *was supposed.*
> A better offer *was made* while he *was signing.*

**The Future Tense.** To express action in future time the present tense is joined with *shall* or *will* to form the future tense. I *shall leave;* the car *will wait.* The distinction in use of *shall* and *will* is vanishing in modern usage, but the traditional differences in the two words are worth noting.

*Shall* and *will* are words used to express ordinary expectation, determination, intention, defiance, threat, and prohibition.

> ORDINARY EXPECTATION:
> I *shall* write him tomorrow.
> He *will* visit us some day.
> You *will* be delighted.
> We *shall* invite your friends.
> They *will* discuss the problem.

Note that *I* and *we* use *shall* for ordinary expectation, while the other persons use *will.* The uses are reversed for determination, defiance, and threat or prohibition.

> DETERMINATION:
> We *will* defend our rights in this matter to the end.
> DEFIANCE:
> I *will* do as I please.
> We *will* not be intimidated.
> THREAT OR PROHIBITION:
> He *shall* pay for this!
> You *shall* not go.
> They *shall* not pass!

As far as the first person is concerned, people now say both "I *shall* go" and "I *will* go" when they mean ordinary intention or expectation.

In clauses beginning with *if* and *when,* in which the verb has a future significance, we use the present tense and *not* the future.

> If it *rains,* don't expect me. (NOT: if it *will rain.*)
> Give him my regards when you *see* him. (NOT: when you *will see.*)
> I *shall* retire when I *have* enough. (NOT: when I *shall have* enough.)

**Using Certain Auxiliary Verbs.** Auxiliary verbs are verbs that help to construct tenses and other forms of verbs. We have already seen how parts of the verb *to have* and *shall* and *will* are used as

58

auxiliaries. Here we shall take up several other auxiliary verbs.

SHOULD AND WOULD. Most people interchange *I should* with *I would*; actually, the first is correct, but, as in the case of *shall* and *will*, the distinction is losing its importance.

*Should* and *would* appear in indirect discourse, that is, in reporting a statement without using the identical language of the statement. We use *should* if the word *shall* was used in the original statement, and we use *would* if the word *will* was used.

He promised me he *should* be on time. (I *shall* be on time.)
The stock clerk asked whether he *should* check the invoice. (*Shall* I check?)
He *said* it would rain. (It *will* rain.)
The man declared he *would* not apologize. (I *will* not apologize.)

WILL AND WOULD. After the present tense of such verbs as *say, tell, promise, assert, report,* we use *will.* After the past tense of these verbs, we use *would.*

He says he *will* attend.
He said he *would* attend.
She tells me she *will* be early.
She told me she *would* be early.
I promise that I *will* obey the rules.
I promised that I *would* obey the rules.

**The Past Tense after "If."** A frequent situation in writing is one in which the writer declares that a certain course of action *would* take place on the condition that certain other circumstances hold good. These other circumstances are placed in the clause beginning with *if.* The correct tense of the verb, in these cases, is the *past tense.*

If you *accepted* our terms, work would begin at once. (NOT: if you *would accept.*)
If he *worked* harder, he would get a raise. (NOT: if he *would work.*)
If I *decided* to go, would you come along? (NOT: if I *would decide.*)

**The Past Perfect after "If."** When we wish to say that a certain course of action *would have been followed* depending on other circumstances, the condition is expressed by a verb in the past perfect tense after the word *if.*

If you *had accepted* our terms, work would have begun at once. (NOT: if you *would have. accepted.*)
If he *had worked* harder, he would have got a raise. (NOT: if he *would have worked.*)
If I *had decided* to go, would you have come along? (NOT: if I *would have decided.*)

## Adjectives and Adverbs

How often we hear statements like "We sure did have a good time last night" and "Carl is a real bright fellow." In these sentences the adjectives *sure* and *real* have been used in place of the adverbs *surely* and *really.* This confusion arises from a confusion of the functions of adverbs and adjectives. Adverbs modify verbs, adjectives, and other adverbs; adjectives modify nouns and pronouns. Adverbs answer such questions as how, when, where, and why. Note the use of adjectives and adverbs in the following pairs of sentences:

ADJECTIVE: This is a *real* treat.
ADVERB: He is a *really* good singer.
ADJECTIVE: Edward writes with *sure* strokes.
ADVERB: This *surely* tastes good.

ADJECTIVE: You should drive especially *carefully* at night.
ADVERB: *Careful* work produces the best results.
ADJECTIVE: The wall was *badly* scorched.
ADVERB: The axle is in *bad* shape.

We have said that adverbs modify verbs; these verbs, however, must be verbs of action such as *run, open, question, point.* There is another class of verbs which we call copulative verbs and which do not take adverbs. Copulative verbs include *to be* and substitutes for *to be* such as *look, seem, appear, taste, feel, smell.* Notice the following sentences:

The house is *quaint.*
The soup tastes *good.*

In each of these sentences the adjectives modify the subjects, *house* and *soup,* and not the verbs, *is* and *taste.* Consequently, since nouns may be modified only by adjectives, the adjectives *quaint* and *good* are used.

Consider the sentence "The rose smells sweet." Here we really mean that *the rose is sweet to smell,* and not that the rose has a nose with which it performs the act of smelling. That is what we would be actually saying if we said a person "smelled *sweetly.*"

In the following examples, note the differences between the copulative verbs and the verbs of action:

| COPULATIVE VERBS WITH ADJECTIVES | VERBS OF ACTION WITH ADVERBS |
| --- | --- |
| The wine *tastes sour.* | The man *tastes* the wine *carefully.* |
| The picture *looks beautiful.* | The boy *looks longingly.* |
| The perfume *smells bewitching.* | The mouse *smells suspiciously.* |
| The customer *seems embarrassed.* | (*Seems* never takes an adverb.) |
| The news *appears true.* | The doctor *appears suddenly.* |
| The soldiers *felt unhappy.* | The doctor's hand *felt cautiously.* |

Careful attention should be paid to the distinctions in meaning among *good, bad, ill,* and *well.*

I feel *good.* (In spirit or in health.)
I feel *well.* (In health.)

I feel *bad.* (In spirits or in health.)
I feel *ill.* (In health.)

Do not say "I feel badly" unless you mean that there is something wrong with your sense of touch.

# AVOIDING COMMON SENTENCE ERRORS

## The Sentence

A sentence is a group of related words, or sometimes a single word, which expresses a complete thought. A correct sentence may make a statement, ask a question, express a command or request, or utter an exclamation. Examples of these are as follows:

Our merchandise is sold everywhere.
Do you plan to attend the convention?
Select your gift today.
Please select your gift today.
How pleasant to hear from you!

Common sentence errors include the omission of essential words, vagueness of meaning, and the running together of two unrelated thoughts.

The sentence may be divided into two parts: the *subject* and the *predicate.* The subject is the word or words naming the person or thing about which something is asserted. The predicate is the word or words which express what is said about the subject.

In the sentence "We trust our employees," *we* is the subject and *trust our employees* the predicate. *We* is what is spoken about; *trust our employees* is what is said about *we.* In the sentence "Our proposal was defeated," *our proposal* is the subject because that is what is spoken about and *was defeated* is the predicate because that tells what happened to *our proposal.*

### CLAUSES

A clause is a group of words within a sentence which contains a subject and a predicate, but is not itself a sentence. In the sentence *"Since my subscription has expired,* please renew it," although *since my subscription has expired* contains a subject, *subscription,* and a verb, *has expired,* it is not a sentence because it would not be clear if written alone. Similarly in the sentence "This will introduce Mr. Carter, who represents our firm," *who represents our firm* contains a subject, *who,* and a predicate, *represents our firm,* but is not a sentence because it does not make a complete statement when standing alone. The same is true of the clause in the sentence "We never doubted *that you had good intentions.*"

These examples represent the three different types of clauses. The first is really an adverbial clause because it answers the question *why?* and modifies the verb *renew.* The second is an adjective clause because it describes a noun, *Mr. Carter.* The third is used as a noun because it stands for the thing the writer did not doubt.

### PHRASES

Phrases are combinations of related words made by adding nouns to prepositions, participles, or infinitives. They have neither subject nor predicate.

on the desk, to take a trip, producing steadily, to negotiate

Phrases act *as if* they were nouns, adjectives, or adverbs.

The ledger *on the desk* is mine. (*On the desk* describes a specific ledger and is introduced by a preposition; it is therefore a prepositional adjectival phrase.)

I would like *to take a trip.* (*To take a trip* states the object of the speaker's desire and is an infinitive phrase used as a noun.)

*Producing steadily,* the company prospered. (*Producing steadily* gives meaning to the verb, *prospered,* and is therefore a participial adverbial phrase.)

### Run-on Sentence

A run-on or run-together sentence is a sentence error that is made by writing two or more statements together as though they were one sentence. This is a run-on sentence:

All prices are net, we hope to serve you in the future.

This run-on sentence may be corrected by placing a period after the first complete thought, as follows:

All prices are net. We hope to serve you in the future.

Sometimes run-on sentences may be corrected by placing a conjunction immediately after the first complete thought.

RUN-ON: The orchestra began to play we got up to dance.

CORRECT: The orchestra began to play and we got up to dance.

### Sentence Fragment

A sentence fragment is the reverse of a run-on sentence. It is an error that is made by setting off a part of a sentence, generally a dependent element, as a complete sentence. These are examples of sentence fragments:

Having placed our order last month. We expected shipment this week.

We shall be glad to place an order. If you cut your price.

Sentence fragments may be corrected either by joining the fragment to the complete sentence to which it logically belongs or by making it into a complete sentence.

JOINING TO A SENTENCE: Having placed our order last month, we expected shipment this week.

We shall be glad to place an order if you cut your price.

MAKING INTO A COMPLETE SENTENCE: We placed our order last month. Consequently, we expected shipment this week.

We shall be glad to place an order. However, we can do this only if you cut your price.

### Dangling Expressions

If a participle or adjectival expression begins a sentence, it should clearly relate to the subject of the sentence. Otherwise, it is said to *dangle,* that is, to be unattached. Notice this sentence:

Opening the window, the plane's noise became louder.

Actually this sentence states that the plane's noise opened the window. Obviously this is not what the writer meant. Therefore, we may revise it as follows:

Opening the window, I heard the plane's noise become louder.

Similarly this sentence does not express the writer's meaning clearly:

At the age of two, Ted's father died.

What this says is that Ted's father was two years old when he died. This sentence can be reworded as follows:

At the age of two, Ted lost his father.

### Misplaced Modifiers

As far as possible, modifying words should be placed near the words they modify to insure clarity of meaning. Notice how a shift in the position of *today* in these sentences changes the meaning:

He told me *today* that I had done well.

He told me that I had done well *today.*

One word in particular which gives rise to confusion because it is frequently misplaced is the word *only.* The meaning of each of the following sentences is different because of the placement of *only:*

He *only* wrote to me. (He did nothing else.)
*Only* he wrote me. (Nobody else wrote.)
He wrote *only* to me. (He wrote to nobody else.)

## Double Negatives

One negative word (*no* or *not*) is enough to express an idea of negation. A second negative acts to cancel the first, therefore we say two negatives make a positive.

INCORRECT: I *don't* have *no* time today.
CORRECT: I *don't* have any time *or* I have no time today.
INCORRECT: We *haven't hardly* heard of her. (Hardly contains the idea of negation.)
CORRECT: We have *hardly* heard of her.
INCORRECT: There *wasn't scarcely* room. (*Scarcely* contains the idea of negation.)
CORRECT: There was *scarcely* room.

## The Proper Case before Verbal Nouns

Words derived from verbs that end in *ing* are often used as nouns. When they are so used they are called *verbal nouns* or *gerunds*. Since these words have the functions of nouns it is incorrect to use nouns or pronouns in any but the possessive case before them. Consider this sentence:

What do you think of him joining our party?

This sentence is incorrect as it stands. The object of the verb *think* is not *him*, as would be indicated by its present wording, but *joining*. Whose joining? *His* joining. Compare similarly the following pairs of sentences:

INCORRECT: I don't like *him* interfering in my affairs.
CORRECT: I don't like *his* interfering in my affairs.
INCORRECT: I enjoyed the sight of *them* pulling out of the factory gate.
CORRECT: I enjoyed the sight of *their* pulling out of the factory gate.

In some sentences, however, the verbal noun is not the direct object of the verb, and so does not require a noun or pronoun in the possessive case before it. The following sentences are correct:

We saw *him* coming.
I heard *Sam* breathing.
Ella found *Grace* cleaning out her desk.

In these sentences the direct objects of the verbs are *her*, *Sam*, and *Grace*, and not *coming*, *breathing*, and *cleaning*. Therefore the words preceding the verbal nouns should be in the objective rather than the possessive case.

## Shift of Tense

Be consistent in your use of tenses. If you are describing successive acts that take place at the same time, use the same tense.

INCORRECT: He *enters* the room and *took* a seat.
CORRECT: He *enters* the room and *takes* a seat.
INCORRECT: We *received* your letter and *have* pleasure reading it.
CORRECT: We *received* your letter and *had* pleasure reading it.

## Parallel Structure

Parallel ideas should be expressed in parallel forms. If you use a noun form in one part of a sentence, do not express a parallel idea in verbal form. If you make the first part of a statement in the active voice (the subject acts) do not express the second part in passive voice (the subject is acted upon).

INCORRECT: You will gain not only profit **but** you will have an enjoyable time.
CORRECT: You will gain not only profit **but** also enjoyment.
INCORRECT: You will either pay the bill **or** we shall bring suit.
CORRECT: You will either pay the bill **or** face a suit.
INCORRECT: Being embarrassed and since I **was** alone, I went away.
CORRECT: Being embarrassed and alone, I went away.
INCORRECT: The clerk sorted the goods **and** they were shipped by noon.
CORRECT: The clerk sorted the goods and by **noon** had shipped them.

## Mistakes of Repetition

Here are the most common of these errors:

INCORRECT: Mr. Jones, my neighbor, he called on me today.
CORRECT: Mr. Jones, my neighbor, called on me today.
INCORRECT: He is employed by a great company and which we have all heard of.
CORRECT: He is employed by a great company which we have all heard of.
INCORRECT: The condition in which the patient was in warranted attention.
CORRECT: The condition in which the patient was warranted attention.
INCORRECT: Don't you think the length of this room is too long?
CORRECT: Don't you think the length of this room is too great? OR: Don't you think this room is too long?
INCORRECT: Let us look ahead into the future.
CORRECT: Let us look ahead.
INCORRECT: These are the true facts.
CORRECT: These are the facts.
INCORRECT: In my opinion, I think it an excellent idea.
CORRECT: In my opinion, it is an excellent idea. OR: I think it is an excellent idea.
INCORRECT: Here is a new beginner.
CORRECT: Here is a beginner.

## The "Where" Habit

Do not use *where* to stand for a noun or pronoun.

INCORRECT: A contract is where two persons make an agreement.
CORRECT: A contract is an agreement between two persons.

## Split Infinitives

A split infinitive is not a serious fault; but we should try as far as possible to keep words from interrupting infinitives.

INCORRECT: He would like *to* very much *come*
CORRECT: He would like very much *to come*
OR: *to come* very much.

## Spelling Rules

The spelling of many words is facilitated by learning a few spelling rules. The rules are relatively simple to remember if you keep in mind the basic idea of each rule rather than the exact wording given here. It is also helpful to keep in mind an example of each rule.

### WHEN TO DOUBLE CONSONANTS

When to double a consonant is a common dilemma for writers. Is the word *benefited* or *benefitted*, *regreted* or *regretted*? When words of one syllable end in a single consonant which is preceded by a single vowel, we double the final consonant when adding a suffix that begins with a vowel, as follows:

| | |
|---|---|
| plan, planned | sin, sinning |
| mad, madder | man, mannish |
| pen, penning | rob, robbed |
| clan, clannish | rub, rubber |
| grab, grabbed | let, letting |
| get, getter | Scot, Scottish |

The purpose in doubling the consonant is to retain the sound of the vowel in the original word. If we did not double the consonant, the vowel sounds in the above words would be changed. Thus, if we wrote *planed* instead of *planned*, the vowel sound of *a* in *plan* would take on the sound of *a* as in *late*.

When words of more than one syllable end in a consonant, the doubling of the consonant will depend on the accent. If the last syllable of the word is accented, we double the final consonant, as follows:

| | |
|---|---|
| infer', inferred | refer', referred |
| rebel', rebelled | instil', instilled |
| transfer', transferred | inter', interred |

If the last syllable of the word ending in a single consonant is *not* accented, we do *not* double the final consonant:

| | |
|---|---|
| ben'efit, benefited | inhab'it, inhabited |
| en'ter, entered | prof'it, profited |

When words end in more than one consonant or in one consonant which is preceded by a diphthong, we do *not* double the final consonant:

| | |
|---|---|
| boil, boiled | read, reading |
| beat, beaten | react, reacted |
| fail, failed, failure | dial, dialed |

When the accent of a word moves away from the last syllable, the final consonant is *not* doubled:

infer', infer'ring, *but* in'ference
refer', referred', *but* ref'erence

The following words, all ending in *l*, do not have the accent on the last syllable, and yet it is considered correct either to double the final consonant or not. The sensible course to pursue is to follow the rule given above and not double the consonant.

apparel, appareled, or apparelled
cancel, canceled, or cancelled, *but only* cancellation
*Also:* cavil, bevel, counsel, enamel, equal, label, level, marvel, model, parcel, quarrel, rival, travel

### WORDS ENDING WITH A SILENT *e*

In the case of words ending with a silent *e*, the question arises when to keep and when to drop the *e* when adding a suffix.

If the suffix begins with a consonant, the silent *e* is usually retained.

time, timely; late, lateness; excite, excitement; fate, fateful; advertise, advertisement

The silent *e* before a suffix beginning with a consonant will be dropped if the *e* is preceded by another vowel:

true, truly; due, duly

The silent *e* after *dg*, as in *judge*, is dropped before the suffix *ment*.

judge, judgment; abridge, abridgment

If the suffix begins with a vowel, the silent *e* is usually dropped.

blue, bluish; sale, salable; time, timing; move, movable; define, definite; use, usage

There are certain exceptions to this rule which are not really exceptions, because the spelling of the words depends obviously on the necessity of distinguishing between certain sounds. Thus it is necessary to retain the *e* in *noticeable* because otherwise the sound of the *c* would change to a *k* sound. Other such words are: *peaceable, manageable, changeable, advantageous, outrageous.*

### *ie* OR *ei*

Most of the confusion between *ie* and *ei* may be cleared up by remembering the simple rhyme:

*I* before *e*
Except after *c*
Or when sounded like *eigh*,
As in *neighbor* and *weigh*.

Thus:

believe, chief niece (*i* before *e*)
receive, ceiling, deceit (*e* before *i* after *c*)

Exceptions to this rule are:
either, neither, financier, leisure, seize, weird

### WORDS ENDING IN *cede, sede,* AND *ceed*

These three endings can easily be differentiated. There is only one word ending in *sede*: *supersede*. There are only three words ending in *ceed*: *succeed, exceed, proceed*. The rest end in *cede*: *accede, precede, intercede, secede, concede.*

### WORDS IN WHICH *c* HAS A *k* SOUND

When the *c* at the end of a word is pronounced like *k*, we must add a *k* to the *c* before adding suffixes that begin with vowels.

picnic, picnicked, picnicking
panic, panicked, panicky
shellac, shellacked

### WORDS ENDING IN *able* AND *ible*

Often in writing, we pause before an adjective like *indispensable* and ask, is it *able* or *ible*? If you can form a noun ending in *ation* from the word, then the proper ending is *able*. If you can form a noun with *ion, tion,* or *ive,* then the proper spelling is usually *ible*.

| NOUN | ADJECTIVE |
|---|---|
| dispensation | dispensable. indispensable |
| duration | durable |
| irritation | irritable |
| habitation | habitable |
| navigation | navigable |

| NOUN | ADJECTIVE |
|------|-----------|
| audition | audible |
| collection | collectible |
| diversion | divertible |
| defensive | defensible |

## WHEN TO USE CAPITAL LETTERS

An initial capital letter in a word raises the importance of that word. There are a number of regular occasions when words are given more importance than others by capitalization. These occasions are discussed below.

In the first word of a sentence.

> We have received your letter.

In the first word of a quotation.

> Lincoln said, "With malice toward none. . . ."

In all words of titles except conjunctions, prepositions, and articles. However, if the conjunction, preposition, or article begins or ends the title, it is capitalized.

> *The Cask of Amontillado*
> *An Introduction to Business Law*

In all proper names.

> Edgar Allan Poe, The Campbell Company, Arkansas, Erie Railroad, Red River, Lincoln High School, Tuesday, Decoration Day

All expressions of the Deity, including all pronouns which refer to the Deity.

> God, the Almighty, created in His image

In titles of persons.

> Mr., the Prime Minister, the President

In the names of languages, religions, nationalities, races.

> French, Mohammedanism, Englishman, Indians, Negroes

In the first and last words of salutations, and in the first word only of the complimentary close in business letters.

| | |
|---|---|
| Dear Sir: | Yours truly, |
| My dear Sir: | Yours very truly, |
| My very dear Sir: | Very sincerely yours, |

## PUNCTUATION

Punctuation is a device for making the act of reading as simple and as clear as possible. Any punctuation which interferes with reading ease is bad punctuation. While it is almost impossible to make a general rule, it is safe to say that too little punctuation is preferable to too much.

### The Comma

The comma (,) is the most frequently used punctuation mark in the English language, and also the most troublesome. It has more uses than any other punctuation mark. The most common uses are:

**Comma in a Series.** A sequence of three or more expressions (words, phrases, or clauses) is punctuated by a comma after each.

> The peddler sold needles, nails, knives, and scissors.

Placing the final comma before *and* is optional. In a long series or a long sentence, or whenever it helps speed up the reading, it is definitely preferable.

> He worked hard, came early, and left late.
> Our furnaces save fuel, cost little, and last for many years.

**Comma after Introductory Expressions.** When a sentence begins with a phrase or clause, place a comma after it.

> Having delivered the note, the boy left.
> If you wish to succeed, keep up with the latest developments in your field.

**Comma in Direct Address.** When addressing a person by name or title, we separate the name or title from the rest of the sentence by commas.

> We have read your article, Mr. Smith, and think it excellent.
> We cannot accept, my dear Mr. Allen.
> Friends, Romans, countrymen, lend me your ears.
> I thank you, gentlemen, with all my heart.

**Comma with Words in Apposition.** An expression which is added to a sentence as being equivalent to a preceding one is said to be in apposition with it. Such an expression is set off by commas.

> Our product, the result of years of experiment, is now ready for market.
> Robert Lincoln, son of the President, was connected with the Pullman Company.

**Comma to Set Off Parenthetical Expressions.** Sometimes an expression is inserted for reasons of emphasis between words which ordinarily follow one another. This insertion is called a parenthetical expression, and is set off by commas.

> Your letter was, to tell the truth, unfortunate.
> I hope, if all goes well, to finish in a week.

**Comma to Separate One Independent Clause from Another.** When a sentence contains two or more clauses, each of which would convey a clear meaning when standing alone, the clauses are said to be independent. A comma must be placed after each clause, unless the clause ends the sentence.

> I reported the conversation to Mr. Jones, and his secretary wrote it down. (If there were no comma after *Mr. Jones*, it would seem at first reading that the conversation was reported to both Mr. Jones and his secretary. The comma speeds up reading time.)

**Comma to Set Off Non-essential Clauses.** A clause whose omission would not materially change the meaning of the sentence is a non-essential clause. It is usually present in the sentence to add emphasis, interest, or color. It is always separated from the rest of the sentence by commas.

> Our type of toaster, which is guaranteed for a year, is economically priced.
> Business letters, thousands of which are written daily, are not always written correctly.

A clause which, when omitted, would vitally affect the meaning of the sentence is obviously an essential clause, and therefore is not set off by commas.

> A copy of the book that has been autographed by the author is worth a hundred dollars.

**Comma to Separate a Quotation from the Rest of the Sentence.** A quotation is an expression containing the actual words uttered by a person. Commas surround the words which introduce or explain the quotation.

> Napoleon said, "An army travels on its stomach."
> "Our charge," he wrote, "is quite low."

**Comma to Take the Place of an Omitted Word.**
A comma may be used to indicate that a word has been omitted.

> One businessman may be alert; another, asleep. (The comma takes the place of *may be*.)

**Special Uses of the Comma.** There are certain standard uses of the comma in letters and other forms.

> AFTER THE COMPLIMENTARY CLOSE:
> Sincerely yours,
> Yours truly,
>
> IN ADDRESSES AND DATES:
> December 7, 1947
> Brooklyn, New York

## The Period

A period (.) marks the end of a sentence (unless the sentence is a question or exclamation) and usually follows an abbreviation.

> Our diary is in convenient pocket form.
> i.e.; e.g.; A.M.

## The Colon

A colon (:) introduces a quotation (instead of a comma); precedes an example or a list; follows the salutation in business correspondence; appears in expressions of time.

> Our Constitution begins: "We, the people. . . ."
> Our branch offices are nation-wide: New York, Seattle, New Orleans, and Chicago.
> Dear Sirs:  Gentlemen:
> 5:15 A.M., 4:00 P.M.

## The Semicolon

A semicolon (;) may be used to knit ideas closely together; it is therefore a substitute for the conjunction *and*. Since it tends to produce long sentences, which are not desirable in business letters, it should be used infrequently. Its specific uses are as follows:

To tie two thoughts together.

> I hope to see you when you come to town; I missed the pleasure last time.
> I am not sure of my facts; so I am writing to you. (A common mistake is to use a comma before *so*.)

To separate the clauses of a long compound sentence, that is, a sentence with two or more independent clauses.

> Having reached the decision, I decided to communicate with him by mail; but my client, who was careless in such matters, had gone away without leaving a forwarding address.

To separate items in series, where commas would not be clear.

> On this trip I shall visit our plants at Kenosha, Wisconsin; Sauk Center, Minnesota; and Moline, Illinois.

## The Question Mark

A question mark (?) follows an actual question, and also is used in certain cases to convey sarcasm.

> Are you still interested in the house?
> Will you visit New York this summer?
> The letter contained a gentle (?) hint to pay the bill.

Do not use a question mark after a statement which declares that a question has been asked.

> I asked Mr. Clay whether he was still interested.

## Exclamation Point

The exclamation point (!) is used after expressions of strong feeling.

> Ouch! That hurt.
> Run for your lives!

## The Apostrophe

An apostrophe (') represents an omitted letter; shows possession; shows the plural of figures, words, and letters.

> haven't; isn't; wouldn't; it's; they're; o'clock
> lady's maid; ladies' tailor; women's wear; Mr. Jones's desk
> Do not use too many *and*'s in your letter.
> How many p's in Mississippi?
> Write your 8's legibly.

## The Hyphen

A hyphen (-) is used in the following instances:

In compound adjectives which precede nouns:
> a well-thought-out plan, a half-hearted smile

With certain prefixes:
> An ex-congressman, self-conscious

When the same vowels come together with certain prefixes:
> Re-educate, anti-intellectual

## The Dash

A dash (—) is used as follows:

Instead of commas when setting off parenthetical expressions.
> You have heard—you must have—of our wonderful work.

To precede a summary of a previous statement.
> His property, his honor, his name—all these went in the crash.

To show a change in idea.
> "I shall prove to you, gentlemen—listen carefully—that my client was in his home that night."

As a substitute for a colon.
> One thing is necessary—faith.

The indiscriminate use of the dash as a substitute for the comma is to be avoided since it tends to interrupt the flow of a sentence.

## Quotation Marks

Quotation marks (". . .") have the following uses:

To enclose actual words spoken or written.
> People say, "Carson's is the best buy!"
> "Do you know," asked Mr. Frey, "where I could find a record of the transaction?"
> The referee asked, "What are your assets? I would like a list."

To enclose titles of books when italics are not used.
> Charles Beard wrote "The Rise of American Civilization."

To enclose well-known sayings or slang expressions.

> Franklin D. Roosevelt is identified with "The New Deal."
> Do you "jitterbug"?

Single quotation marks ('. . .') are used for a quotation within a quotation.

> Mr. Collins went on, "Then he said to me, 'I will meet you halfway.'"

Among the common errors in the use of quotation marks are the following:

Enclosing words not directly spoken.

> INCORRECT: He said "that he was in agreement."
> CORRECT: He said that he was in agreement.

Omitting quotation marks when the quotation is interrupted.

> INCORRECT: "Why don't you write, he asked, to your client?"
> CORRECT: "Why don't you write," he asked, "to your client?"

## WORDS OFTEN CONFUSED

The following list contains words and expressions which are often used incorrectly or are confused with each other. A mastery of these words will help to give a writer a command of good diction or usage.

**Accept—Except.** *Accept* is a verb, meaning "to take"; *except* is a preposition. It is also used as a verb, meaning "to omit."

> Will you *accept* my offer?
> We all attended *except* him.

**Act as—Act like.** The first means "to take the part of"; the second means "in imitation of" or "in the manner of."

> John *acts as* shipping clerk during Henry's vacation.
> You're *acting like* a stranger.

**Adapt—Adept—Adopt.** *Adapt* means "to make suitable"; *adept* means "expert"; *adopt* means "to make one's property."

> The immigrants *adapt* themselves to the new world.
> They are *adept* in finding new occupations.
> They *adopt* the customs of the new world.

**Adverse—Averse.** *Adverse* means "harmful"; *averse* means "unwilling."

> His business failed because of *adverse* conditions.
> We are *averse* to investing in stocks at this time.

**Advice—Advise.** The first is the noun; the second is the verb.

> Follow your employer's *advice*.
> The doctor *advised* him to take a trip.

**Affect—Effect.** *Affect* is a verb and means "to influence"; *effect* is used as a noun, meaning "result," or as a verb, meaning "to achieve."

> This bad weather will *affect* our business.
> His rudeness is the *effect* of poor upbringing.
> General Johnson *effected* a retreat.

**Aggravate—Annoy.** The first means "to make a bad condition worse"; it should never be used as a synonym for annoying or teasing.

> A financial depression can be *aggravated* by worry.
> The carpenter's hammering was *annoying* the stenographers.

**Agree on—Agree to—Agree with.** People agree *on* a plan; *to* a proposition or suggestion; and *with* each other.

> The governors *agreed on* the program for combatting poverty.
> The rivals *agreed to* arbitrate their differences.
> I am inclined to *agree with* Mr. Jones.

**Allusion—Delusion—Illusion.** *Allusion* is a verbal reference to something; *delusion* is a false, even insane belief; *illusion* is a deceptive picture.

> The speaker's mention of sour grapes was an *allusion* to the old story of the fox and the grapes.
> He is suffering from a *delusion* that he is royalty.
> The magician did not actually put the coin into his pocket; it was merely an *illusion*.

**Almost—Most.** *Almost* is an adverb; *most* is an adjective or a noun.

> We have *almost* reached our goal.
> *Most* men would agree with you.
> *Most* of us are present.
> (Do NOT SAY: *Most* all men would agree with you.)

**Already—All Ready.** *Already* is an adverb, meaning "by this time." *All ready* (note the spelling) is an adjective, meaning "prepared."

> We have *already* eaten.
> We are *all ready* to leave.

**Alternative—Choice.** The first is a choice between two objects or courses of action; the second applies to three or more.

**Altogether—All Together.** The first is an adverb, meaning "completely." The second, also an adverb, means "as a group."

> I believe you are *altogether* mistaken.
> Let us attend the theater *all together*.

**Amount—Number—Quantity.** *Amount* as a verb means "to add up to"; as a noun, it means "the aggregate of sums or quantities." *Number* as a noun means "a collection of individuals"; as a verb it means "to count or enumerate." *Quantity* is a noun and means "an indefinite amount."

> Our profit *amounts* to $50,000.
> He has a large *amount* of money in the bank.
> The teller has stacked a great *number* of dollar bills.
> The clerk *numbered* each crate.
> We shipped a huge *quantity* of food to Europe.

**Angry—Mad.** *Mad* means "insane" and should not be used for *angry*.

**Angry about—Angry with.** We are angry *about* something, and *with* somebody. Do not say angry *at*.

**Antagonist—Protagonist.** An *antagonist* is a rival; a *protagonist* is the hero or main character in a drama or story.

> The two lawyers, who had long been friends, became *antagonists* in court.
> Philip Carey is the *protagonist* of "Of Human Bondage."

**Anxious—Desirous.** *Anxious* means "worried." Do not use *anxious* as a synonym for *desirous*.

> We are *anxious* to know the results of the laboratory test. (We fear that the results may not be to our liking.)
> I am *desirous* of knowing the results. (I am curious.)

**Apt—Liable—Likely.** *Apt* means "habitually suited"; *liable* implies trouble; *likely* refers to ordinary probability.

> He is *apt* to lose his position.
> He is *liable* to dismissal from the firm.
> It is *likely* to rain.

**As . . . As—So . . . As.** We use the expression *as . . . as* after a positive statement, and the expression *so . . . as* after a negative one.

> We are *as* lucky *as* we expected to be.
> We are not *so* lucky *as* we expected to be.

**As—Like—Such as.** *As* is a conjunction; *like* is a preposition (in comparisons) and may not introduce a clause; *such as* is a substitute for *like* but not for *as*.

> She still sings *as* she always did.
> She sings *like* a bird.
> I prefer serious books *such as* biographies.

**Assure—Promise.** *Assure* means "to give confidence to, to guarantee, to state with confidence." It does not mean "to promise."

> The orders in the morning mail *assured* the sales manager.
> The general's precautions *assured* the army's safety.
> He *assured* her that there was nothing to fear.
> I *promise* to be there on time.

**Balance—Remainder.** *Balance* is an accounting term, meaning the difference between the two sides of an account. *Remainder* is anything which remains.

**Beat—Win.** *Beat* means "to defeat an opponent"; *win* means "to be victorious." We cannot *win* an opponent.

> This week's production *beat* our previous record.
> The company *won* its lawsuit.

**Because—That.** *Because* should be used only after verbs of action, not of being. After verbs of being, use *that*.

> He gave himself up *because* there was no chance.
> The reason he gave himself up was *that* there was no chance.

**Beside—Besides.** *Beside* is a preposition meaning "next to"; *besides* is an adverb, meaning "moreover," and a preposition, meaning "in addition to."

> I mean the desk which is *beside* that large chair.

> I have other reasons *besides* those I have mentioned.
> The employees are considering a strike for higher wages; *besides,* they may ask for a shorter work week.

**Biannual — Biennial — Biweekly — Bimonthly —Semiannual.** *Biannual* and *semiannual* mean half-yearly; *biennial* means every two years; *biweekly* means every two weeks; *bimonthly* means every two months.

**Bound—Determined.** *Bound* means "under legal or moral restraint"; *determined* means "self-decided."

> Under the terms of the contract, you are *bound* to do it.
> He was *determined* to make that sale.

**Bring—Take—Carry.** We use *bring* when we mean motion toward the speaker; *take* applies to motion away from the speaker; *carry* means motion in general.

> Please *bring* me the auditor's report.
> Please *take* this report to the auditor.
> I've *carried* this report all day.

**By—At.** *By* means motion past; it should not be confused with *at*.

> When I go to Philadelphia, I stay *at* the Benjamin Franklin. (NOT: *by* the Benjamin Franklin.)

**Can—Could.** *Could* is the past tense of *can*. In complex sentences, we use the future tense in the independent clause with *can* in the dependent clause; we use the conditional *should* or *would* in the independent clause, and *could* in the dependent clause.

> If you *can* build this machine, I shall invest the money.
> If you *could* build this machine, I should invest the money.

**Can—May.** *Can* shows ability; *may* shows permission.

> I *can* write shorthand.
> *May* I take you to luncheon?

**Capital—Capitol.** The *capital* is the city; the *capitol* is the government building.

> Washington, D. C., is the *capital* of the United States.
> The legislature meets in the *Capitol*.

**Childish—Childlike.** *Childish* is a term of criticism meaning "silly or immature"; *childlike* means "like a child."

> His attitude toward the entire affair is *childish*.
> He sees the world with *childlike* wonder.

**Common—Mutual.** *Common* means "shared by many"; *mutual* means "exchanged."

> Misspelling is a *common* weakness.
> Their feeling of friendship was *mutual*.

**Compare to—Compare with.** Two objects in the same category are compared *with* each other; in different categories, *to* each other.

> Please *compare* this watch *with* the one in the window.
> "Shall I *compare* thee *to* a summer's day?"

**Complement—Compliment.** A *complement* is something which completes; a *compliment* is an expression of praise. Both are either nouns or verbs.

> This dress will *complement* your wardrobe.
> Her dress excited *compliments* from observers.

**Consul—Council—Counsel.** *Consul* is a governmental commercial representative; *council* is a deliberative body; *counsel* means "advice," "the person advising" or, as a verb, "to advise."

> When I was in Paris, I visited the American *consul*.
> The nobleman was heard by the Privy *Council*.
> Mr. Smith will give you expert *counsel*.
> Mr. Smith will *counsel* you.
> Mr. Smith will act as *counsel*.

**Continual—Continuous.** *Continual* means "frequently but with interruptions"; *continuous* means "without interruption."

> You are guilty of *continual* bad behavior.
> The theater has a *continuous* performance.

**Corespondent—Correspondent.** *Corespondent* is a person involved in divorce proceedings; *correspondent* is a person writing and receiving letters.

> The plaintiff named an unknown person as *corespondent*.
> His *correspondent* was a fluent writer.

**Correspond to—Correspond with.** The first means to suit or match; the second means to write.

> That hill *corresponds to* point A on the map.
> I have *corresponded with* a famous author.

**Credible — Creditable — Credulous — Incredulous — Incredible.** *Credible* means "worthy of belief"; *incredible* means "not worthy of belief"; *creditable* means "deserving praise"; *credulous* means "easily convinced"; *incredulous* means "unbelieving."

> His reputation as a businessman makes his latest success *credible*.
> Our salesman's record is a *creditable* one.
> Our office boy is a *credulous* person.
> He listened to the story with an *incredulous* smile.
> The news of his suicide is *incredible*.

**Custom—Habit.** *Custom* is a consciously practiced act; *habit* is automatic.

> It is our *custom* to give a bonus every Christmas.
> His smoking has become a bad *habit*.

**Data.** *Data* is the plural form of the word *datum*. It should, therefore, correctly take a verb that agrees with a plural subject.

> The *data* on our production are in the top drawer.

**Deduce—Deduct.** *Deduce* means "to arrive at a conclusion on the basis of evidence"; *deduct* means "to take away"; *deduction* means either "that which is deduced" or "that which is taken away."

> The detective *deduced* the height of the criminal from the size of the footprints.
> The customer *deducted* the wrong discount.
> The detective's *deduction* was a shrewd one.
> The customer's *deduction* from his bill was too large.

**Definite—Definitive.** *Definite* means "precise"; *definitive* means "final."

> The witness was *definite* in his answers.
> We are publishing the *definitive* edition of his works.

**Deprecate—Depreciate.** *Deprecate* means "to disapprove of"; *depreciate* means "to lessen in value" or "to belittle."

> The company *deprecated* the employee's conduct.
> Our machines have *depreciated* in the last ten years.
> His fiancée *depreciated* his attempts to please her.

**Differ about—Differ from—Differ with.** People differ *about* a point in dispute and *with* each other; one object differs *from* another.

> The partners *differed about* the new styles.
> The partners *differed with* their wives about styles.
> My invention *differs from* his in many ways.

**Discover—Invent.** That which is brought to light is *discovered*; that which is created is *invented*.

> The scientists *discovered* the secret of the atom.
> The scientists *invented* the atom bomb.

**Diseased—Deceased.** *Diseased* means "unhealthy"; *deceased* means "dead."

> The physician studied the *diseased* tissue.
> Our records reveal Mr. Mann as *deceased*.
> Do Not Say: He *deceased*. Deceased is no longer used as a verb.

**Disinterested—Uninterested.** *Disinterested* means "impartial"; *uninterested* means "indifferent."

> A fair verdict can be rendered only by a judge who is completely *disinterested*.
> The judge was so *uninterested* that he yawned.

**Due to—Because of—Owing to.** *Due to* can be used only after a copulative verb in an adjectival sense. *Because of* and *owing to*, on the other hand, can be used only in an adverbial sense.

> The growth of the business was *due to* Henry's foresight.
> The business grew *because of* (or *owing to*) Henry's foresight.

**Dumb—Stupid.** *Dumb* means "unable to talk." It should not be used in place of *stupid*, which means "ignorant."

He was virtually struck *dumb* by the offer.

Only a *stupid* person would buy such a large quantity of that inferior merchandise.

**Economic—Economical.** *Economic* pertains to business, finance, etc.; *economical* means "thrifty."

Production must be maintained at a high level if the *economic* stability of the country is to be maintained.

She is an *economical* housewife.

**Emigrant—Immigrant—Emigré.** An *emigrant* is a person who leaves a country; an *immigrant* enters a country. An *emigré* is also an emigrant, but particularly one who flees from a country.

Eleven thousand *emigrants* left Canada in 1945.

Carnegie was an *immigrant*.

Following the Russian Revolution many *emigrés* found refuge in Paris.

**Emigration—Immigration.** *Emigration* is the act of leaving a country; *immigration* is the act of entering a country.

What are the statistics on *emigration* from Eire?

There was greater *immigration* to the United States than to any other country.

**Evidence—Proof.** *Evidence* is the material with which we consider a situation; *proof* is the material which produces certainty.

The case was thrown out of court for want of *evidence*.

His *evidence* was satisfactory *proof* to the jury.

**Exceedingly — Excessively.** *Exceedingly* means "very much"; *excessively* means "too much."

We were *exceedingly* happy to receive the news.

He was *excessively* annoyed by the noise in the street.

**Exceptional—Exceptionable.** *Exceptional* means "out of the ordinary, superior"; *exceptionable* means "objectionable, that to which exception may be taken."

My stenographer writes with *exceptional* speed.

The lawyer thought the witness's remarks *exceptionable* and so asked the judge to order them stricken from the record.

**Famous—Notorious.** *Famous* means of good reputation; *notorious*, of bad.

His deeds will always be *famous*.

He is *notorious* for his dishonesty.

**Farther—Further.** *Farther* means more advanced in space; *further*, in degree.

He hiked *farther* than the others.

He went *further* in his research than his rival.

**Few—Less.** *Few* relates to a number of items; *less* refers to a quantity.

I have *few* words to say.

He has *less* energy than I.

**Few—Several.** *Few* means "not many," and emphasizes the idea of a small number; *several* means "more than two but not very many," or "different." It emphasizes the idea of more rather than less.

There were *few* people present when I arrived. (More were expected.)

*Several* people have told me the same story.

They went their *several* ways. (Their different ways.)

**Find—Locate.** *Find* means "to meet with" or "discover"; *locate* means "to establish."

I *found* my ring in the office locker room.

I think we should *locate* our new store in a growing city.

Do Not Say: I *located* him at home.

**Former—Latter.** *Former* refers to the first of two; *latter* refers to the second of two.

I spoke to Mr. Clark and Mr. Field yesterday. The *former* seemed quite willing to listen to my idea, but the *latter* was indifferent.

Do Not Say: I spoke to Messrs. Jones, Brown and Smith. The *latter* seemed most interested. Say: The *last* seemed.

**Formerly—Formally.** *Formerly* means "in the past"; *formally* means "elaborately" or "with ceremony."

I knew him *formerly*, in Paris.

When they met they greeted each other *formally*.

**Good—Well.** *Good* is never an adverb. *Well* is both adverb and adjective.

This is a *good* machine.

I feel *good*.

You look *well*.

He is a *well* man.

He does his work *well*.

**Got—Have.** *Got* is the past tense of get. It should never be used as a synonym for *have*.

I *have* a cold. (Not: I *got* a cold.)

**Guess—Suppose—Think.** *Guess* means "to hazard an opinion"; *suppose* means "to assume the truth of"; *think* means "to form in the mind."

He *guessed* that the defendant would be found guilty.

Do you *suppose* they are at home?

I am *thinking* about the matter.

(Do not use *guess* as a synonym for *think*. For example, do not say, "I *guess* I'll go home now.")

**Hanged—Hung.** *Hanged* is the past tense and past participle of *hang*, and applies to the execution of human beings; *hung* applies to the hanging of objects.

The picture was *hung*. The criminal was *hanged*.

**Healthy—Healthful.** *Healthy* applies to living things; *healthful*, to conditions, surroundings, and activities which are conducive to health.

He has a happy mind and a *healthy* body.

Drinking milk is a *healthful* practice.

A windowless room is not a *healthful* place.

Do Not Say: This resort is a *healthy* place.

68

**Hire—Lease—Let.** *Hire* is "to pay for the use of"; *lease* is "to allow the use of," usually with a contract, and also "to take temporary ownership of"; *let* is "to allow the use of."

> These automobiles are for *hire*.
> He *hired* the car.
> He *leased* the apartment to her for six months.
> We *leased* the apartment from the agent.
> These rooms are to *let*.
> He *lets* the typewriters by the month.

**Human—Humane.** *Human* means "pertaining to mankind"; *humane* means "kind."

> Reasoning is a *human* trait.
> He is a *humane* person.

**Hypercritical—Hypocritical.** *Hypercritical* means "overcritical"; *hypocritical* means "false."

> Your judgment of the display is *hypercritical* and unfair.
> Her tears were *hypocritical,* for she really was not saddened.

**If—Whether—That.** *If* implies conditions. After verbs of wondering and asking, we should use *whether* and not *if*; after doubt, use *that*.

> *If* payment is made in ten days, you may take a two per cent discount.
> I wonder *whether* he will come.
> I asked him *whether* he preferred a book or a picture.
> I doubt *that* he would arrive today.

**In—Into.** *In* refers to the inside or being within; *into* refers to the idea of motion from the outside.

> This is the sunniest room *in* the office.
> Carmichael strode *into* the office and slammed the door.
> He entered *into* a contract.

**Infer—Imply.** *Infer* means "to conclude from evidence"; *imply* means "to convey indirectly."

> They *inferred* from his tone that he was not pleased.
> He *implied* by his manner that he agreed with us.

**Its—It's.** *Its* means "belonging to it"; *it's* is a contraction for "it is."

> *It's* time for the dog to have *its* bath.

**Kind of—Rather.** *Kind of* means "a species of"; *rather* means "somewhat." Do not say *kind of a.*

> A sphere is a *kind of* ball.
> I feel *rather* tired.

**Lady—Woman.** *Lady* is an expression of respect; *woman* refers to sex.

> Act like a *lady*.
> She is an unmarried *woman*.

**Lay—Lie.** *Lay* is a verb that takes an object, and means "to place." *Lie* does not take an object, and means "to recline."

> He *lays* his cards on the table. (Present tense)
> He *laid* his cards on the table. (Past tense)
> He *has laid* his proposal before you. (Present perfect tense)
> The man *lies* on the couch. (Present)
> The man is *lying* down. (Present)
> The man *lay* down on the couch yesterday. (Past)
> He *has lain* there a long time. (Present perfect)

**Leave—Let.** *Leave* means "to go away"; *let* means "to permit." Confusion arises because there is a noun, *leave,* meaning "permission":

> Please *let* me go.
> He gave me *leave* to go.
> He has a five-day *leave*.
> I shall *leave* tomorrow.

**Lend—Loan—Borrow.** *Lend* is "to permit the temporary use of"; *loan* is a verb meaning "to permit the temporary use of," or a noun meaning "the thing lent"; *borrow* means "to take temporarily with permission."

> I shall *lend* you my typewriter tomorrow.
> The bank granted me the *loan*. (Noun)
> The bank *loaned* him the money. (Verb)
> He *borrowed* the machine for a few days.

**Madam—Madame.** *Madam* is used in addressing a lady or in the salutation of a letter. *Madame* is used as part of a person's title, and also in the salutation of a letter to a person with that title.

> May I help you, *madam*.
> Let me present *Madame* Tosca, the well-known soprano.

**Majority—Plurality.** A *majority* is more than half; a *plurality* is the difference between the highest and next highest number of votes cast in an election.

> Twenty, a *majority* of the thirty stockholders, voted for the motion.
> Although the candidate did not receive a *majority* of the six thousand votes, he received two thousand, a plurality of five hundred.

**Much—Many.** *Much* refers to bulk or mass; *many,* to number.

> The fireman displayed *much* courage.
> He is a man of *much* wealth.
> He shows *many* signs of cowardice.
> There are *many* bills of large denomination in the safe.

**Near—Nearly.** *Near* is an adjective, a preposition, or an adverb; *nearly,* an adverb.

> He took the *near* seat.
> My office is *near* yours.
> Our train is getting *near*.
> We are *nearly* done. (Adverb)

**Negotiate—Transact.** *Negotiate* means "to discuss a specific matter or to arrange a matter"; *transact* means "to carry on business in general."

> The lawyers are still *negotiating* for a settlement.
> He *negotiated* a loan from the bank.
> We *transact* business at our warehouse.

**Obtain—Sustain.** *Obtain* means "to procure or acquire"; it implies effort. *Sustain* means "to endure or suffer."

69

After many years, he *obtained* control of the company.

As a result of the accident, he *sustained* a broken hand.

**Of—Have.** These words are often confused because of the similarity of sound.

We could *have* bought the house had we tried harder. (NOT: could *of*)

**Oral—Verbal.** *Oral* means "spoken"; *verbal* means "pertaining to words."

I am studying *oral* English.

We have an *oral* agreement.

The Egyptians did not use a *verbal* form of communication, but instead used signs called hieroglyphics.

He made some *verbal* changes in the document.

**Part from—Part with.** *Part from* means "to leave"; *part with* means "to give up."

The friends *parted from* each other at the station.

The merchant *parted with* the garment at a loss.

**Party—Person.** *Party* means "celebration"; it is used as a synonym for person only in legal phraseology.

Please attend the *party* I am giving tonight.

Mr. Smith is hereinafter referred to as *party* of the first part.

NEVER SAY: I met a certain *party* last night.

**Persecute—Prosecute.** *Persecute* means "to treat unfairly"; *prosecute* means "to bring legal action against" or "to follow to the end."

Five hundred members of the *persecuted* minority sought shelter in the United States.

The district attorney *prosecuted* the two embezzlers.

We *prosecuted* the war successfully.

**Plausible—Probable.** *Plausible* means "reasonable" or "seemingly trustworthy"; *probable* means "likely to happen" or "supported by evidence."

He told a *plausible* story.

Reorganization of the company is, of course, possible, but not *probable* this year.

**Practical—Practicable.** *Practical* is the opposite of *theoretical*; *practicable* means "capable of being accomplished."

**Precedence—Precedents.** *Precedence* means "priority in sequence"; *precedents* are events which establish a standard of judgment.

In the seating arrangement, the ambassador has *precedence* over the others.

The judge based his decision on several *precedents*.

**Presently—At Present.** *Presently* means "soon"; *at present* means "now."

We expect Mr. Vane *presently*.

We are *at present* in the market for these items.

**Principal—Principle.** *Principal* is a noun meaning "leader," and an adjective meaning "outstanding"; *principle* means either "a sum of money" or "a fundamental truth, a basic law."

Mr. Smith is the *principal* of the training institute.

I have stated the *principal* reasons for my resignation.

I intend to invest the *principle* in government bonds.

Do you understand the *principle* of the atomic bomb?

**Provided—Providing.** *Provided* can mean "if" or "with the understanding" or "with the proviso that"; *providing* is the present participle of *provide*.

I shall mail the check, *provided* you keep your promise.

Your job is to *provide* the factory with material.

**Raise—Rear—Rise.** *Raise* means "to lift or make grow"; *rear* means "to foster"; *rise* means "to move upward."

The workmen *raised* the fallen tree.

The farmer *raises* corn.

His father *reared* three children.

The temperature is *rising*.

**Real—Really.** *Real* is the adjective; *really*, the adverb.

These flowers are *real*.

He is *really* afraid.

DO NOT SAY: He is *real* afraid.

**Remit—Send.** *Remit* means "to send back," as payment for goods.

He *remitted* a check in payment of the account.

**Respectfully—Respectively.** *Respectfully* means "with respect"; *respectively* means "in the same order." DO NOT SAY: *Respectively* yours.

He arose and bowed *respectfully*.

The winning candidates for the offices of president, vice-president, and secretary were, *respectively*, Mr. Price, Mr. Leigh, and Mr. Ball.

**Rob—Steal.** *Rob* means "to seal from"; *steal* refers to the object taken.

The thief, in *robbing* the bank, *stole* cash and bonds.

**Set—Sit.** *Set* means "to place"; *sit* means "to occupy a seat." *Set* takes an object; *sit* never does.

He *set* the glass on the tray.

He *sat* in the armchair.

**Sick of—Sick with.** *Sick of* means "tired of"; *sick with* means "ill with."

I am *sick of* this rainy weather.

He is *sick with* the mumps.

**Specie—Species.** *Specie* means "metal money"; *species* means "a classification."

The government mints *specie*.

The crocodile is a *species* of reptile.

**Spill—Pour.** *Spill* refers to an accident; *pour* refers to deliberate action.

The waiter, in *pouring* the coffee, *spilled* some on the cloth.

**Stay—Stand.** *Stand* means "to remain erect"; *stay* means "to remain."

I am tired because I have to *stand* all day.

I should have *stayed* in bed.

**Stay—Stop.** *Stay* means "to remain"; *stop* means "to come to a halt."

70

He is *staying* at the same hotel.
The car *stopped* just in time.

**Suitable for—Suitable to.** Actions are *suitable to* an occasion; objects are *suitable for.*

His language is *suitable to* the gutter.
This garment is *suitable for* afternoon wear.

**Suspect—Expect.** We *suspect* something wrong; we *expect* the probable.

The bank examiner *suspected* that there would be a shortage.
We are *expecting* a visit from the manager.

**Teach—Learn.** *Teach* means "to impart knowledge"; *learn*, "to acquire knowledge."

When Mr. Brown *taught*, the students *learned* quickly.

**Than—Then.** *Than* expresses a degree of comparison; *then* expresses time.

He is poorer *than* he used to be.
We were friends *then*.

**Them—Those.** *Them* is a pronoun; *those* is used as an adjective.

We manufacture *those* bags.
Do you find *them* a profitable item?

**There—Their—They're.** *There* means "in that place"; *their* means "belonging to them"; *they're* is a contraction for "they are."

*There* is my car.
The employees presented *their* demands to the board of directors.
*They're* five cents each.

**Therefore—Therefor.** *Therefore* means "for that reason"; *therefor*, "for it."

The machinist was careless; *therefore* he was injured.
Spitting being a misdemeanor, the penalty *therefor* is $20.

**To—Too—Two.** *To* is the preposition; *too*, the adverb; *two*, the number.

Please write *to* all our customers.
This cloth is *too* heavy.
I owe him *two* dollars.

**Transpire—Occur.** *Transpire* means "to become known"; *occur*, "to take place."

At the hearing it *transpired* that the witness had been lying.
The event *occurred* exactly as I described it.

**Unless—Without.** *Unless* means "if not" or "except that"; *without*, "lacking."

*Unless* you join us, I fear nobody will.
Why did you leave *without* your hat?

**Until—To.** *Until* refers to time; *to*, to space.

He waited *until* four o'clock.
Let me drive you *to* the park.

**Valuable—Invaluable.** Valuable means "having value"; invaluable, "priceless."

This is a *valuable* piece of property.
The President's services were *invaluable* to the country.

**Venal—Venial.** *Venal* means "corrupt, bribable"; *venial* means "forgivable."

He is a *venal* journalist.
This was a *venial* sin.

**Very—Quite.** *Very* means "to a great extent"; *quite*, "altogether."

He made me a *very* attractive offer.
This style is *quite* charming.

**Vocation—Avocation.** A *vocation* is a calling or occupation; an *avocation* is a hobby.

Haberdashery is my *vocation,* and stamp-collecting is an *avocation* of mine.

**Who—Whom.** *Who* is the performer of action, the subject of the verb; *whom* is the receiver of action, the object of verb, preposition, or participle.

*Who* was your visitor?
*Whom* do you wish to see?
*Whom* did they toast at the dinner?
To *whom* were you talking?

**Whose—Who's.** *Whose* means "belonging to whom"; *who's* means "who is."

I want to know *whose* purse this is.
I want to know *who's* calling.

**Your—You're.** *Your* means "belonging to you"; *you're*, "you are."

It's *your* turn, I believe.
*You're* always in my thoughts.

## PREFERRED WORDS AND EXPRESSIONS

The following list contains words and expressions that are often incorrectly used. The first word or expression given is the correct form.

**Accuse,** not *Blame It On.*

SAY: He *accused* the clerk of stealing the package.
NOT: He *blamed* the loss of the package *on* the clerk.

**Attention,** not *Mind.*

SAY: Pay him no *attention.*
NOT: Pay him no *mind.*

**Better, Gladder, etc.,** not *More Better, More Gladder, etc.*

SAY: I believe his suggestion is *better* than any other.
NOT: I believe his suggestion is *more better* than any other.

**Complexioned,** not *Complected.*

SAY: He is a light-*complexioned* man.
NOT: He is a light-*complected* man.

**Deal With,** not *Deal On.*

SAY: This report *deals with* the question.
NOT: This report *deals on* the question of immigration.

**Doubt That,** not *Doubt But.*

SAY: We do not *doubt that* his work is efficient.
NOT: We do not *doubt but* what his work is efficient.

**Each . . . His,** not *Each . . . Their.*

SAY: *Each* candidate did *his* best.
NOT: *Each* candidate did *their* best.

**Enthusiastic,** not *Enthused.*

SAY: We are *enthusiastic* about your idea.
NOT: We are *enthused* about your idea.

**Everywhere, Somewhere,** not *Every Place, Some Place.*

SAY: I looked *everywhere.* I lost it *somewhere.*
NOT: I looked *every place.* I lost it *some place.*

71

**First**, not *Firstly*.

SAY: We had several reasons: first,
. . . ; secondly, . . .

NOT: We had several reasons: firstly,
. . . ; secondly, . .

**Graduate From**, not *Graduate*.

SAY: I *graduated from* Northwestern
University.

I *was graduated from* Northwestern
University.

NOT: I *graduated* Northwestern University.

**Had Better, Ought, Should**, not *Had Ought*.

SAY: If we want to catch the train,
we *had better* leave now.

If we want to catch the train, we
*ought to* leave now.

If we want to catch the train, we
*should* leave now.

NOT: If we want to catch the train,
we *had ought* to leave now.

**If I Were**, not *If I Was*.

SAY: *If I were* in your place, I should
take the chance.

*If he were* here, he would tell me
what to do.

NOT: *If I was* in your place, I should
take the chance.

*If he was* here, he would tell me what
to do.

**In My Opinion**, not *To My Opinion*.

SAY: *In my opinion*, the risks are too
great.

NOT: *To my opinion*, the risks are too
great.

**It**, not *Same*.

SAY: Your order was received this
morning; we shall attend to *it* immediately.

NOT: Your order was received this
morning; we shall attend to *same*
immediately.

**Last Night**, not *Yesterday Night*.

SAY: He received the message *last
night*.

NOT: He received the message *yesterday night*.

**Many or Much**, not *Lots Of*.

SAY: You have *many* styles to choose
from.

We have *much* time.

NOT: You have *lots of* styles to choose
from.

You have *lots of* time.

**Operate On**, not *Operate*.

SAY: The doctor *operated on* him last
week.

NOT: The doctor *operated* him last
week.

**Since**, not *Being That*.

SAY: *Since* your bid was entered late,
you lost out.

NOT: *Being* that your bid was entered
late, you lost out.

**So That**, not *So*.

SAY: Please inform us of change of
address *so that* we can keep our
files correct.

NOT: Please inform us of change of
address *so* we can keep our files correct.

**Sure To**, not *Sure And*.

SAY: Please be *sure to* visit us when
you arrive.

NOT: Please be *sure and* visit us when
you arrive.

**The United States**, not *United States*.

SAY: Mr. Dubois visited the United
States.

NOT: Mr. Dubois visited United
States.

**Think**, not *Allow*.

SAY: I *think* I'll take a vacation this
year.

NOT: I *allow* I'll take a vacation this
year.

**This Kind**, not *These Kind*.

SAY: I have always smoked *this kind*
of cigarette.

NOT: I have always smoked *these
kind* of cigarette.

**This, That**, not *This Here, That There*.

SAY: I want to write to *this* buyer.
Where did you buy *that* merchandise?

NOT: I want to write to *this here*
buyer.
Where did you buy *that there* merchandise?

**Try To**, not *Try And*.

SAY: We shall *try to* get the cloth for
you.

NOT: We shall *try and* get the cloth
for you.

**Very**, not *Plenty*.

SAY: He was *very* angry.

NOT: He was *plenty* angry.

**Very Much Pleased**, not *Very Pleased*.

SAY: We were *very much pleased* to
hear the good news.
They were *very much discouraged* at
the poor results.

NOT: We were *very pleased* to hear
the good news.
They were *very discouraged* at the
poor results.

# WORDS TO BE AVOIDED

## Non-Existent Words

There are many words that are commonly used but
which have no recognized standing and should therefore be avoided. These include the following:

anywheres, somewheres, everywheres, nowheres,
ascared, disremember, irregardless, gents,
prophesize, hisself

## Overworked Words

There is a group of words in English that have
been used so often and on so many occasions that
they have lost a great deal of the specific meaning
which they once had. Among these are the following:

get, nice, awful, terrible, cute, lovely, wonderful, fine, dreadful

In place of these words, use synonyms which will
express your meaning more exactly and which will,
at the same time, give your language a sense of
freshness.

## IDIOMATIC USAGE WITH PREPOSITIONS

There are certain expressions which have to be learned through observation and memory. These expressions belong to the category called *idioms*. We list here idioms which are composed of particular prepositions. For the sake of clearness, they are used in sentences:

Although in the minority, he **acquiesced in** our plans.
Why are you **angry with** us?
My interpretation is **at variance with** yours.
This car has been **adapted for** farm work.
We shall be glad to **adapt** this car **to** your specifications.
He **adapted** that style **from** an older one.
The prisoner was **accused of** forging a check.
The defendant was **acquitted of** the crime.
The truck **collided with** the lighter car.
We shall be delighted to **comply with** your request.
You neglected to **charge** me **for** the brush.
This man is **charged with** negligence.
Mr. Jones is a **dealer in** rayons.
No man shall be **deprived of** life, liberty, or the pursuit of happiness without due process of law.
We watched the **destruction of** the warehouse by fire.
I was **disappointed in** the performance.
You are **forbidden to** transact business under that name.
He wishes to be **independent of** any supervision.
I have acted **in accordance with** the rules.
My product is **identical with** the sample I sent you.
We are still **in search of** the kind of lathe you are interested in.
This cloth is **inferior to** the one I saw.
Please do not **inflict** your bad manners **upon us.**
I cannot help being **impatient with** him.
I desire to speak to him **with reference to** insurance.
How long have you **lived in** Omaha?
How long have you **lived at** this address?
This company has a **monopoly of** the fur trade.
They are still **in need of** help.
You seemed **oblivious to** what I was saying.
He came to us **of his own accord.**
He died **on the eve of** success.
This material is **preferable to** the other.
My article **treats of** marketing and distribution.

# Guide to Effective Speaking

### THE IMPORTANCE OF EFFECTIVE SPEAKING IN BUSINESS

An ability to speak effectively is just as valuable for a businessman as is the ability to write letters which accomplish the purpose which the writer has in mind. In the course of a single day a person in the business world might find that there were any number of occasions in which effectiveness in speaking would be of importance to him. Thus he might want to persuade a customer to buy his product; to interview a prospective employer; to induce a manufacturer to extend him credit; to make a reservation, over the telephone, for a train trip; to dictate a letter to a secretary; to conduct a sales conference; to make a report to a board of directors' meeting; to entertain a buyer at lunch; to address a convention of businessmen. Each of these speech situations requires a different kind of speech approach. The businessman must variously convince, explain, and entertain, and he must adapt his speech to each of these objectives. If he does not convince, explain clearly, or entertain, his speech activity may be said to have failed in its purpose.

Our concern in these pages is with the means by which persons in the field of business can improve their ability to speak, and, consequently, to communicate their ideas and so enhance their standing in business. In our study of ways of speaking effectively, we shall be concerned mainly with the use of speech in business. However, the general instructions which we present will hold true for all types of speaking.

The problem of effective speaking will be studied under the three headings into which the subject may be naturally divided: correctness, power, and style. *Correctness* deals with accepted norms of speaking and includes grammatical correctness as well as matters of accent and vowel and consonant values which we group under the heading of correctness of pronunciation. *Power* is that quality in a speaker which makes his speech carry conviction, put over an idea, and touch the listeners' emotions. *Style* is the charm of personality, indefinable, perhaps, but real enough. It is made up partly of the speaker's voice quality, his sense of humor, his speed of thought, his repartee, his vivacity, his intensity, and his enthusiasm.

These last two qualities, power and style, are the magnets which attract people to a speaker, leaving out, for the moment, such attractions as reputation and business or social position. But a powerful speech delivered by a person with a pleasing personality will be injured by incorrectness of grammar or pronunciation. Most listeners expect correctness in speech as a matter of course; it is when a speaker departs from accepted standards that he is penalized, often unconsciously, by the audience. Certainly the radio and motion pictures have sharpened listening faculties to such a point that the speaker must speak correctly habitually lest he lose the favor and support of his hearers.

## CORRECTNESS IN SPEAKING

Correctness in speech is a matter of habit. It cannot be achieved overnight, but it can quite certainly be achieved by making a point of being correct and learning what is and what is not correct in speech over a period of time. We have already covered some of the principles of grammatical correctness; we present here a number of additional pointers that should help you achieve correctness in speech.

### AIDS FOR THE SPEAKER

**Using a Dictionary.** First of all, make a habit of referring to a good dictionary whenever you are uncertain about the meaning or pronunciation of a word. Then, when you have learned the meaning of a word, try to incorporate it into your conversation at your earliest opportunity, making sure to pronounce it as indicated in the dictionary. Every dictionary makes use of a system of diacritical marks to communicate the sounds of words; these must be understood if the dictionary is to be used with profit.

**Listening to Professional Speakers.** Secondly, study the manner of speaking of radio announcers and motion picture and stage actors. You can learn much by making up your mind, in listening to a radio program, for example, to concentrate merely on the speech of the performers. Since these people are professional speakers, they have a serious approach to the whole question of the articulation of sounds, of pitch and stress, and intonation. The advantage of listening to these people is that they serve as models for us; they set a kind of standard, and in this way help us to help ourselves.

**Reading Aloud.** Thirdly, practice reading aloud from all kinds of printed matter: poetry, plays, short stories, financial reports, newspaper editorials. The advantage of reading aloud is that it forces us to listen to ourselves and be critical of ourselves; if we are honest with ourselves, we quickly spot many if not all of our weaknesses. It would, of course, be a good thing to have an audience of a relative or a friend while we read aloud, but most often we will have to be our own audiences.

In line with the preceding thought, we should, if possible, make a recording of our speech, both of conversation and of a reading of a selected passage. For most people, listening to the play-back of the record is an eye-opening and ear-opening experience, and sometimes an unnerving one, for you actually hear yourself as others do; you become aware of faults that you were never aware of and which you may be able to correct very easily.

### PRONUNCIATION LISTS

**Studying Word Lists.** One of the systematic aids in attaining correctness is the study of lists of selected words of special difficulty. We present below three word lists, each of which presents a particular kind of speech problem.

In the first list are words which are often mispronounced because of the addition or subtraction of a sound, e.g. saying "chiminey" instead of "chimney." In the second list are words the pronunciation of which involves the proper choice of vowel or consonant sound, e.g. saying "bring-ging" instead of "bringing." In the third list are words often accented or stressed wrongly, e.g. saying "CIGarette" instead of "cigaRETTE."

## Words Often Incorrectly Pronounced by Adding or Omitting Sounds

**asked** (sound the *k*)
**athletics** (not *atheletics*)
**Brooklyn** (not *Brookalyn*)
**champion** (not *champeen*)
**chimney** (not *chiminey*)
**columnist** (not *colyumnist*)
**diamond** (not *dighmond*)
**different** (not *diffrent*)
**drawing** (not *drawring*)
**elm** (not *elum*)
**environment** (not *enviroment*)
**escape** (not *ecscape*)
**February** (not *Febuary*)
**film** (not *fillum*)
**geography** (not *jography*)
**government** (not *goverment*)
**grievous** (not *grievious*)

**history** (not *histry*)
**idea** (not *idear*)
**identify** (not *indentify*)
**innocent** (not *innercent*)
**intellectual** (not *interlectual*)
**laboratory** (not *labratory*)
**library** (not *libary*)
**licorice** (not *licorish*)
**length** (not *lenth*)
**mischievous** (not *mischievious*)
**modern** (not *modenn* or *modren*)
**often** (do not pronounce the *t*)
**parliament** (not *parlyament*)
**particular** (not *particlar*)
**plenty** (not *plenny*)
**poem** (not *pome*)
**probably** (not *probally*)
**production** (not *perduction*)
**really** (not *reely*)
**recognize** (not *reconize*)
**shouldn't** (not *shoont*)
**strength** (not *strenth*)
**surprise** (not *supprise*)
**temperature** (not *tempature*)
**twenty** (not *twenny*)
**umbrella** (not *umberella*)
**vacuum** (three syllables; not *vacyoom*)
**window** (not *winder*)

## Words Often Incorrectly Pronounced Because of Vowel or Consonant Difficulties

The following are the symbols and marks used to indicate pronunciation in this list:

ā, as in fate; ă, as in fat; â, as in fare; *a*, as in comma and normal; ah, as in father; aw, as in call; ē, as in bead; ĕ, as in bet; *e*, as in dozen and river; ī, as in file; ĭ, as in sit; *i*, as in habit and satin; ō, as in note; ŏ, as in hot; *o*, as in actor and random; ōō, as in soon and food; ŏŏ, as in good, wool; oi, as in toil; ow, as in now; ū, as in cue, union; ŭ, as in cut; û, as in cur and turn; *u*, as in lettuce and circus; N, as in the French words bien and bon; zh, like the z in azure and the s in vision. The accent mark ' follows the syllable which receives the primary stress. The accent mark ' indicates secondary stress.

**absorb** (ab·sôrb')
**adobe** (*a*·dō'bĭ)
**alias** (ā'lĭ·*as*)
**almond** (ah'mŭnd)
**amateur** (ăm'*a*·tur' or ăm'*a*·tūr')
**appreciate** (*a*·prē'shĭ·āt)
**arctic** (ahrk'tĭk)
**aviation** (ā·vĭ·ā'shon)
**banquet** (băng'kwĕt)
**because** (bĭ·kâz')
**bestial** (bĕst'yal)
**bestow** (bē·stō')
**blackguard** (blăg'ahrd)
**bona fide** (bō'na fī'dē)
**bouquet** (bōō·kā')
**bourbon** (bŏŏr'bun)
**bourgeoisie** (bŏŏr'zhwah·zē')
**breadth** (brĕdth)
**cache** (kăsh)
**chaise longue** (shāz lông, not lownj)
**chameleon** (ka·mēl'yun)

Chicago (shĭ·kô'gō or shi·kah'gō)
chiropodist (kī·rŏp'o·dĭst)
clique (clēk)
close (adj.: clōs; verb: clōz)
clothes (clōthz)
comptroller (kŏn·trōl'er)
Coney Island (cō'nĭ, not cōō'nĭ)
congratulate (cŏn·grăt'ū·lāt, not cŏn·grăd'ū·lāt)
coupon (cōō'pŏn)
culinary (cū'lĭ·nĕr'ĭ)
cupola (kū'po·la)
deaf (dĕf)
debt (dĕt)
derisive (di·rī'sĭv)
diaper (dī'a·per)
dilettante (dĭl'e·tăn'tĭ)
diminution (dĭm'ĭn·ū'shun)
diphtheria (dĭf·thĕr'ĭ·a, not dĭp·thĕr'ĭ·a)
docile (dŏs'ĭl)
domicile (dŏm'i·sĭl)
ductile (dŭk'tĭl)
due (dū)
duel (dū'el)
eighth (āt'th)
Eire (âr'e)
electricity (i·lĕk'trĭs'i·tĭ, not i·lĕk'trĭz'i·tĭ)
emaciated (i·mā'shĭ·āt·ed)
English (ĭng·glĭsh)
errata (i·rā'ta)
extraordinary (ĕks·trôr'di·nĕr'i)
fascist (fă'shĭst)
finger (fĭng'ger)
finis (fī'nĭs)
forehead (fŏr'ĕd)
fracas (frā'kas)
fuchsia (fū'sha)
futile (fū'tĭl)
gas (găs, not găz)
gaseous (gas'ĭ·us)
genuine (jĕn'ū·ĭn, not jĕn'ū·īne)
genus (jē'nus)
gesture (jĕs'tūr)
grimace (grĭ·mās')
handkerchief (hăng'ker·chĭf)
heir (âr)
homicide (hŏm'i·sīd)
hostile (hŏs'tĭl)
hundredths (hŭn'dredths)
idea (ī·dē'a)
ignoramus (ig'no·rā'mus)
indict (ĭn·dīt')
initiate (ĭn·ĭ'shĭ·āte)
intelligentsia (in·tĕl·i·jĕnt'sĭ·a)
iron (ī'ern)
Italian (ĭ·tăl'yan)
italics (ĭ·tăl'ĭks)
jodhpurs (jŏd'pōōrs)
laboratory (lăb'o·ra·tō'rĭ)
length (lĕngkth)
libido (lĭ·bĭ'dō)
lichen (lī'ken)
literature (lĭt'er·a·tūr)
longer (lông'ger)
longevity (lŏn·jĕv'i·tĭ)
longing (lông'ĭng)
malinger (ma·lĭng'ger)
maltreat (măl·trēt')
maraschino (măr'a·skē'nō)

mayonnaise (mā'o·nāz)
merchandise (mûr'chan·dīz)
Moscow (mŏs'kō)
multitude (mŭl'tĭ·tūd)
nazi (nah'tsē)
new (nū)
nihilism (nī'i·lĭst or nī'hi·lĭst)
orgy (ôr'jĭ)
our (owr, not ahr)
Parisian (pa·rĭzh'an)
pathos (pā'thŏs)
picture (pĭk'tūr)
posse (pŏs'ĭ)
pretty (prĭt'ĭ, not prĭd'ĭ)
psychiatrist (sī·kī'a·trĭst)
puerile (pū'er·ĭl)
quasi (kwā'sī or kwah'sī)
quay (kē)
query (kwēr'ĭ)
radiator (rā'dĭ·ā'ter)
radio (rā'dĭ·ō)
rationale (răsh'un·ā'lē)
reptile (rĕp'tĭl)
resurrect (rĕz'u·rĕkt')
reveille (rĕv'e·lē')
ribald (rĭb'ald)
Roosevelt (rō'ze·vĕlt, almost rōz'vĕlt)
route (rōōt or rowt)
rout (rowt)
salmon (săm'un)
schism (sĭz'm)
senile (sē'nĭl or sē'nĭl)
servile (sûr'vĭl)
singer (sĭng'er)
slovenly (slŭv'en·lĭ)
solace (sŏl'is)
soot (sōōt or sŏōt)
soviet (sō'vĭ·ĕt' or sō'vĭ·ĕt)
spouse (spowz)
squalid (skwŏl'ĭd)
status (stā'tus)
stipend (stī'pĕnd)
strength (strĕngkth, not strĕnth)
stupid (styoopid) (stū'pĭd)
subtle (sŭt'l)
suede (swād)
suite (swēt)
Thames (tĕmz)
trachea (trā'kē·a)
trauma (trô'ma)
travail (trăv'āl)
Tuesday (tūz'dĭ)
ultimatum (ŭl'·tĭ·mā'tum)
usurp (ū·zûrp')
vagrant (vā'grant)
vase (vās or văz)
vaudeville (vŏd'vĭl or vō'de·vĭl)
verbatim (vûr·bā'tĭm)
vice versa (vī'sē vûr'sa)
virus (vī'rus)
viscid (vĭs'ĭd)
width (wĭd'th)
wizen (wĭzn)
worsted (the cloth, wŏŏs'tĕd; defeated, **wûrst'ed**)
xylophone (zī'lo·fōn or zĭl·o·fōn)
yacht (yŏt)
yeoman (yō'man)
zoology (zō·ŏl'o·jĭ)

## Words Often Mispronounced Because of Accent or Stress Difficulties

To show the accent or stress, the syllable receiving the stress is capitalized. Try covering the right-hand column to test your correct pronunciation of these words.

| WORD | PRONUNCIATION |
|---|---|
| abdomen | abDOEmen |
| address | adDRESS |
| admirable | ADmirable |
| adobe | aDOEbe |
| albumen | alBYOOmen |
| alloy | alLOY |
| ally | alLIE |
| anathema | anATHema |
| applicable | APlicable |
| august | auGUST (adj.); AUgust (noun) |
| automobile | autoMOEbile |
| baptize | bapTIZE |
| bombardier | bombarDEER |
| bouquet | booKAY |
| cerebral | SERebral |
| cerebrum | SERebrum |
| chastise | chasTIZE |
| chastisement | CHAStisement |
| cigarette | cigaRETTE |
| combatant | COMbatant |
| commandant | comanDANT |
| communal | COMmunal |
| comparable | COMparable |
| condolence | conDOElence |
| contrary | CONtrary |
| decoy | deCOY |
| definitive | deFINitive |
| despicable | DESpicable |
| Detroit | DeTROIT |
| dilate | diLATE |
| dilute | diLYOOT |
| dirigible | DIRigible |
| discharge | disCHARGE |
| distribute | disTRIBute |
| duodenum | duoDEEnum |
| eczema | EXzema |
| entire | enTIRE |
| exquisite | EXquisite |
| formidable | FORmidable |
| gondola | GONdola |
| granary | GRANary or GRAYnary |
| grimace | griMACE |
| herculean | herKYOOlean |
| illustrate | ILustrate or ilLUStrate |
| impious | IMpious |
| impotent | IMpotent |
| incognito | inCOGnito |
| inexorable | inEXorable |
| infamous | INfamous |
| influence | INfluence |
| inquiry | inKWIGHry |
| insane | inSANE |
| interesting | INteresting (not interESTing) |
| irremediable | irreMEEdiable |
| irreparable | irREParable |
| irrevocable | irREVocable |
| lamentable | LAMentable |

| | |
|---|---|
| madras | maDRAS |
| magistracy | MAJistracy |
| mankind | manKIND |
| material | maTERial |
| materiel | materiEL |
| mausoleum | mausoLEEum |
| mischievous | MISchievous |
| municipal | myuNISipal |
| object | OBject (noun); obJECT (verb) |
| obligatory | OBligatory or obLIGatory |
| omnipotent | omNIPotent |
| orchestra | ORchestra |
| perfume | PERfume or perFUME (noun); perFUME (verb) |
| personnel | personNEL |
| pianist | piANist or PEEanist |
| positively | POZitively |
| precedence | preSEEDence |
| precedent | PRESSedent |
| president | PREZident |
| quintuplets | QUINtuplets |
| recess | reSESS or REEsess (noun); reSESS (verb) |
| recitative | recitaTEEVE |
| relapse | reLAPSE |
| reputable | REPutable |
| research | reSEARCH or REEsearch |
| robust | roBUST |
| romance | roMANCE |
| sacrilege | SACrilege |
| sacrilegious | sacriLEEjus or sacriLIJus |
| secretary | SECretary |
| secretive | seCREEtive |
| sonorous | soNOrous |
| syringe | SIRinge |
| telegrapher | teLEGrapher |
| theater | THEEater |

## POWER IN SPEAKING

Every speaker wants to use his voice not only correctly but impressively, especially if he has a specific goal in mind, such as convincing a customer to place a large order or trying to persuade a banker to make him a loan. Just as a lawyer in a courtroom, for example, would be useless to his client if he depended only on good grammar and diction, so would the salesman fail if he tried only to be correct. The effective lawyer uses every possible art of voice and intellect to make the needed impressions. While few of us are ever called upon to speak in such critical situations as lawyers are, it is true that speech is a daily activity which can be an asset or a liability in business and social life, depending on the skill with which we are able to speak.

Let us assume that the reader is facing a definite task involving speech; perhaps it is as big a job as making a formal public address before an audience at a business convention; perhaps it is a smaller assignment, comparatively, such as speaking to a group of salesmen on your company's sales plans. What can the reader do to insure effectiveness, to make sure that when the talk is over he will be filled not with a sense of failure but rather with a sense of pride of achievement? The suggestions given below should prove helpful to the reader in achieving this aim.

76

## PREPARING THE SPEECH

**Knowing the Subject.** The mere acquisition of information, facts, statistics, and details strengthens a speaker's morale. His stock of knowledge permits him to think on his feet with confidence, especially in a question period. His obvious familiarity with the topic leads his hearers to feel they are not wasting their time listening. Many a listener has sat patiently through a talk, only to remark at the close, "I learned nothing new from the speaker." Knowledge of the subject, therefore, is basic to effective speaking. No oratorical skill can compensate for ignorance.

In order to obtain the necessary information which will enrich his talk, the speaker must become acquainted with the various sources of information and reference material.

These sources will vary, depending on the nature of the topic to be discussed. Very often, a speaker's own experience will provide him with sufficient material. But even in such cases he might bolster his talk with data obtained from outside sources. If he is talking to a convention, for example, and is reviewing the progress of the trade within the past five years, he might know enough from his own experience in the trade to talk generally on the topic, but his speech would be more impressive if he could provide definite facts and figures which he could get from consulting trade journals, newspapers, and magazines. These might be found at the local library; the library, it should be emphasized, is a good source of information on most topics that the speaker will want to discuss. Additional information might well be obtained from experts in the field—other businessmen, college professors, editors, and research specialists.

**Organizing the Material.** Assuming that the speaker has secured the necessary facts and data for his talk, he must now undertake to shape his material effectively. This matter of organization of material is highly important and deserves the most careful consideration.

First of all, the speaker should jot down on paper whatever information seems to him to be relevant to the topic in hand. At this point he should not concern himself with sequence or comparative importance. His job is to put down everything that comes to mind, to see it on paper before his eyes.

Then he should put the material through a sifting process, eliminating the extraneous and distinguishing the more from the less important ideas and information. Having sifted his material, he can now divide his data into major thoughts and supporting illustrative points.

As he goes over his list of important ideas and subordinate material, he cannot help seeing his speech dynamically, that is, as having a logical progression from idea to idea. This derives of necessity from the fact that he has determined that certain ideas are more important than others. The actual decision about importance helps to decide the relative values or degrees of importance. And this measuring of values helps him decide the order in which he is going to present his material to the audience.

The kind of talk the speaker is going to make will help him answer the question, "Where shall I place my most important idea?"

In one kind of talk, a speaker may find it effective to begin with his most important idea and support it with various examples, reasons, anecdotes, and so on. Secondary or subordinate ideas will then be brought in to complete or round out his picture. Suppose, for example, he is addressing a luncheon meeting of business executives on the topic "What's in Store for Our Trade?" He might, at the beginning, state that the major problem of the trade is finding ways of reaching a wider body of consumers. The rest of the talk would then be an expansion of this idea and the speaker might proceed to suggest specific methods of achieving that objective.

On the other hand, he may find it more effective to withhold his most important idea until the middle or latter part of his talk. This second technique is more effective in some topics because it is more dramatic. When an audience has something to look forward to in a speech, it is being kept in suspense. This is a basic method that most public speakers use, because it guarantees attention from the audience.

If the speaker is addressing a sales conference, for example, his ultimate purpose might be to outline methods for increasing sales and to assign quotas for the individual salesman. He could begin by criticizing the methods used in the past and save for the middle portion of the talk the proposed methods, and close with the assignment of quotas, encouraging his salesmen to strive to reach them with an offer of extra commissions. With this plan his listeners would come away from the talk with the last and most effective point (as far as they are concerned) fresh in their minds.

We can generalize about the organization of one's material as follows: let your most important idea, if possible, be made known dramatically, that is to say, after a period of suspense, or as the answer to a mystifying question, or as the solution of a puzzle or riddle.

## INTERESTING THE AUDIENCE

**Projecting Emotion.** Discover the quality of emotion or excitement in your topic, and try to convey that emotion or excitement to your audience.

Many people like to think that there are interesting and uninteresting subjects, in themselves. It would be truer to say that there are interesting and uninteresting speakers. Once the speaker feels the excitement of his subject, he has a good chance of communicating that excitement to his audience. And once that communication takes place, the speaker is a success. In the sales conference mentioned above, the speaker should be able to spur his salesmen on to greater success by the very tone which he uses in speaking to them.

The question arises, how is the speaker to discover the emotional side of his topic, especially when on the face of it the subject seems completely devoid of emotion. Wherever human beings come into contact with an idea or a thing or an institution or a custom, the emotional aspect is present.

Any speaker who has a feeling for resemblances and differences between things will be able to communicate the emotional aspect of a topic to his audience. That is one of the reasons a joke can be useful to a speaker, because a joke, in addition to arousing a laugh and creating good will, has a subtle intellectual and emotional appeal in the *contrast* which is basic to humor.

**Capture the Audience's Interest.** The speaker

should capture the audience's interest as quickly as possible. The fact that people are listening to a speaker is no guarantee that they are interested or are going to be interested for long. The speaker's job is to draw his listeners into a net of attentiveness, making them hang onto his words, afraid to miss a single thought.

One of the methods of accomplishing this is to change a statement into a question. Instead of saying, for example, that there are a certain number of business machines in the offices of America, the speaker might easily ask whether anyone knows how many business machines are in use. The tendency on the part of people to be interested by questions should be exploited in making a speech. Even the rhetorical question, the question which the speaker himself will answer, brings the listener a little closer. From time to time in the course of a talk, a speaker should see to it that he asks his listeners a question, sometimes humorously, sometimes seriously, but enough to make them *active* listeners. When an audience gets the feeling that it is contributing to the speech, it quite naturally becomes more interested in the speech.

Another way of making contact with the audience is to make reference to things with which they are already familiar. This arouses a certain trust in the speaker who seems to talk their language. If the speaker can make a logical transition from the familiar to the unfamiliar, he will find that his audience comes along with him. On the other hand, for the speaker to plunge into the new topic, the unfamiliar subject, without first having laid the groundwork by dealing with what is already known, is to guarantee disaster.

**Beginning the Speech.** The speaker should consider the method of beginning his talk to be of primary importance. He owes it to his listeners to let them know within a reasonable time what his general drift is going to be. This is only fair to the audience. With this qualification in mind, that the audience should know in general what the speaker's thesis is, his method of beginning should be decided by his subject matter, the kind of audience, and even its mood. A conference on a firm's advertising appropriation might well begin with the mere statement of that purpose. On the other hand, it would be appropriate for a speaker at a dinner honoring an old employee to begin with an anecdote telling of his first meeting with the guest of honor.

**Ending the Speech.** Just as important as the beginning is the way a speaker ends his talk. The ending is important because it is the last thing left in the audience's mind and therefore most likely to be remembered. A speaker therefore should not permit his speech to trail off into something inconsequential but should rather end on the most important idea or a variation of it. He can achieve this purpose by reviewing the highlights of his speech, thus giving the audience an opportunity to fix the main ideas in their minds.

An excellent technique in ending a talk, but one not always feasible, is to elicit some form of action from the audience. Of course, this is always the objective of a sales talk—to get the listener to buy the product—but it might be done on other occasions as well. For example, a speaker might call for a show of hands at the end as an expression of opinion, or have his audience promise to do a certain thing like send him the names of possible users of his product. He may even, just before he concludes, distribute literature among his listeners, so that they may read about his product at their leisure. He may urge his listeners to direct questions at him. This procedure is often the most stimulating part of a talk. The speaker should welcome this period because it gives him an opportunity for a special kind of speaking, to answer all kinds of questions, often unexpected, often irrelevant, and to meet the challenge to his wit, his patience, and his temper.

**Using Other Aids in Speaking.** If he can, the speaker should depend on other aids besides his voice. A wise speaker comes provided with visual material, newspaper clippings, magazine articles, quotations from books and articles, by means of which he can emphasize his points. These little aids are amazingly welcome to audiences. The subject then seems to take on greater dignity and aliveness.

**Rhetorical Devices.** A speaker should avail himself of certain rhetorical devices to hold audience interest. He should make use of the *pause,* the dramatic wait, in which the very silence is a powerful stimulant to thought and feeling; he should make use of *emphasis,* the technique of stressing a thought to make sure it is properly received.

Emphasis is very important. There are several ways of making an idea stand out. One is simply for the speaker to label his thought as paramount and ask his audience to so consider it: "I cannot stress the important of this idea too much." Or: "You may forget everything else I have said, but this thought is essential." A second and a stronger technique is to use illustrations and examples which will throw light on the statement. A formulation of a thought gains in meaning when it is illustrated with incidents and references to already known material. A third technique is to formulate one's thought in different words. This is not the same thing as giving examples of an idea. It means finding general statements to express a truth which will awaken curiosity because of novelty. A fourth method of emphasizing an idea is to use comparisons and contrasts, showing resemblances and differences. When you tell an audience what an idea is and then proceed to tell what it is not, you have done a great deal to put over that idea.

**Anticipating Occasions for Speeches.** A good preparation for speech making is to anticipate occasions when you might be called on to speak by composing speeches for imaginary situations. Thus you might compose a little after-dinner speech for the occasion of a gathering of business colleagues; an address to a meeting of employees; the speech to be made when presenting a gift to an individual on behalf of the firm; the speech of acceptance; a speech introducing a new department head to his subordinates; a speech introducing another speaker; a speech introducing a guest.

In addition to such exercises, a person interested in developing his powers of speaking could well improve his ability as a speaker by retelling a short story he has recently read; this can easily be done at the dinner table to elicit comment, not on the retelling, but on the original story. Likewise, practice defining ideas, customs, and things; this procedure, which serves to sharpen your mental faculties, can be carried out socially in the form of a game.

## STYLE IN SPEAKING

We come now to style, the third ingredient of good or effective speaking. This is the least technical, the most subjective, and, one may say, the most mysterious of the qualities of achievement not only in speaking but in all human accomplishment. It involves the function of the personality in the work at hand. The problem of the speaker is how to communicate the charm of personality in his speech, or, rather, the charm of attractive personality. While we cannot go into the rather involved question of developing an attractive personality at this point, we can offer a number of suggestions which, if put into practice, will enhance the personality which you now possess.

**Having Something to Say.** Perhaps what *not* to do is just as much worth knowing for the speaker as what to do. A person can get a reputation often for virtues merely by knowing the errors not to commit. Thus, for good speaking, let us put down as the first rule not to talk unless you have something to say. This is a very important rule when there are people present who do have something to say. Of course it is another matter when one finds oneself in a gathering in which everybody seems tongue-tied, and the one who breaks the ice becomes a life-saver.

**Being a Good Listener.** The next rule for good speaking is to learn to listen. Most speakers get a profound satisfaction at the sound of their own voices. If we like to hear ourselves talk, then it is most probably true that others also enjoy talking. People who talk want to think that they are not wasting their companions' time, and it is one of the gracious gestures of good behavior to be interested or seem to be interested in what they are saying. When we have listeners enjoying our opinions, our stories, our various contributions to conversation, we are flattered into thinking how intelligent we are. Let us feel this pleasure and let us permit others to feel it. Therefore, listen appreciatively to others, and you will always be considered a good conversationalist.

**Keeping a Conversation Going.** Even when we do have something worth while to say, it is good policy to give the floor to somebody else, by requesting his opinion and implying by manner and tone that that opinion is worth hearing. For whatever good conversation is, it is not monologue, but rather a give and take. A really good conversation requires at least three participants, two to carry the ball and a third to enjoy the sport, even when he is also a participant. This matter of "carrying the ball" means doing one's share to keep a conversation alive. If we are addressed with a remark, even one as matter of fact as that it's been a fine day, the conversation will either progress happily or retrogress miserably if we reply with a grunt or a mere agreement and then say nothing. When people advance an opinion or make a statement, they are in effect encouraging us to do the same thing, and it is discouraging to them to find the remark absorbed like ink into a blotter rather than have that remark serve as a stimulus to further conversation.

A simple trick to keep a conversation going is to tack on a question to a remark; but care should be taken that the remark is brought in naturally and not dragged in just to make talk.

Conversation on certain topics is often likely to develop into a dispute, and the question arises, how far should argument be permitted to go. If we agree that problems are not really solved in argument, that the emotions unloosed are seldom worth the conclusions, if any, arrived at, we shall develop the correct approach to argument. If a disagreement can be handled to permit the speakers to reveal their own expert and special knowledge, then it is worth while to encourage dispute because both sides have something to offer each other and the listeners. But the mere exchange of opinion without a foundation in fact quickly degenerates to personal recrimination and consequently becomes embarrassing.

When there is deep-seated difference of opinion on essentials, then the purpose of argument is not to convince the arguers but rather the listeners. In such cases the natural forum is the debate, with equal time limitations, so that the emotional interruptions of conversation are removed.

The enjoyment of each other's company is the reason people congregate socially. The carrying on of business is the reason they meet commercially. In either case, conversation will be carried on effectively if those participating realize the purpose for which they are gathered.

# How to Write Good Business Letters

IN THIS SECTION we consider ways of writing effective business letters, taking up at the outset the Essentials of Business Correspondence. Here we discuss a number of pointers which should be kept in mind in writing business letters, as well as the accepted forms which should be followed. The second part of this section is given over to Samples of Effective Business Letters. Included here are letters of inquiry and response, letters ordering and acknowledging merchandise, letters of complaint and adjustment, credit letters, collection letters, sales letters, and letters of application.

## Basic Essentials of Business Correspondence

Letters play a much more important part in business than most people realize. They act as ambassadors, stating our case in our absence, and even when making no special point but merely acknowledging a simple fact, they help to form people's opinion of us.

If this fact were realized more widely, fewer letters would go forth badly punctuated, tritely expressed, colorless and impersonal. If more letter writers would look upon their letters as extensions of their own individualities into regions where they cannot project themselves in person, very few letters would be as ineffectual as so many of them frequently are.

### POINTERS IN WRITING GOOD BUSINESS LETTERS

There are a number of helpful hints which will act as guides in mastering the art of writing good business letters, and we shall now take these up in turn. Not every suggestion applies to every letter, but letters do fall more or less into types and you will find that some hints apply to one type more than to another. Although some of these suggestions would apply also to social letters, in this section we shall consider them only in relation to business letters.

### Factors to Keep in Mind

**Use Correct Form.** There are certain forms and styles which with variations are followed in most business letters. Through long usage and through serving their purpose well, these conventions in business letters have established themselves and are accepted as correct form. In speaking of form we refer to the manner of presentation and to the appearance of a letter rather than to its content and mode of expression. The content and expression offer opportunities for individuality, as we shall see; but in the matter of form, unless you have an excellent reason for departing from accepted usage, it is best to follow standard practice.

At first sight, correct form may not seem so very important, but when you stop to think of business letters which you have received, you will recognize that it serves a very real purpose.

With regard to the general appearance of a letter, we all realize how much we are influenced by the first impression. We are likely to pick up a letter with real interest if it is neatly typed, properly spaced, well placed on the sheet, and if the quality of the paper is good and the design of the letterhead appropriate.

It is equally important to have the various parts of the letter placed in one or another of the generally accepted positions on a sheet.

If you should decide to place your signature way to the left in the lower part of the paper, rather than in the usual position to the right, you will achieve an unusual effect, and in so doing may make your letter stand out from other letters and catch your reader's eye. But the effect on your reader may not be favorable; he may find your departure from correct form odd or undignified, in which case you will have done yourself a disservice.

Though there may be penalties for incorrect form, there are no special rewards for being correct, other than the satisfaction of doing what is properly to be expected. Your reader will take good form for granted. Be correct. This is the first law of letter writing.

**Write Courteously.** Every business letter should be phrased in a courteous manner. This is the second law of letter writing. Courtesy, like correct form, is taken for granted by the reader. When it is present, no special applause is forthcoming, but its absence is like a chill wind freezing all warmth out of human relationships. Be courteous even when you are tempted to lose your patience or to use the angry, the biting, the ironical word.

**Avoid Trite Expressions.** It is well to bear in mind that even in the most formal and impersonal letters, extremely rigid and overworked expressions are undesirable. In ordinary conversation a businessman would never say, "I received your esteemed favor of February 5th," but this remark and scores of other trite, colorless bits of jargon are found in business correspondence. They are bad because they are inefficient and take the place of words that have life and make a lasting impression on the reader; because they reveal an indifference to the reader on the writer's part—laziness of expression being a pretty sure sign of indifference; because they actually hide the writer's individuality and personality from the reader and thus lose for the writer one of his most valuable assets.

The following examples of trite expressions, of which some business letter writers are guilty, should be avoided:

> Yours of the 3rd instant received and contents carefully noted.
> We see by your letter
> We beg to advise
> We would state at this time
> We hereby acknowledge
> Your favor at hand and would state
> In answer to your letter would say
> As per your letter
> Awaiting your further orders
> We will forward same
> Please be advised that
> Enclosed please find
> And oblige
> Thanking you in advance, I am *or* remain
> Inst., prox., ult. for *this, next, last*

**Keep the Reader's Viewpoint in Mind.** The manner in which you express yourself in a letter should be governed by what you know about the person to whom you are writing. If your letter is to someone that you have never met, it should be more formal than if it is for someone you know. If it is an answer to an inquiry and is not likely to lead to further correspondence, it should be friendly but impersonal. If the letter is likely to bring about a desired continuity of the relationship with the person to whom it is addressed, the tone would be somewhat more personal. And of course if you are writing to someone you know, the letter should have a personal quality and should reflect your knowledge of the reader and his interests. However, all business letters should devote themselves to the business matter with which they are concerned, and there should be no extended reference to social matters; the degree of personal relationship should rather be indicated by greater naturalness and directness of expression.

**Plan Your Letter Before Writing.** Before you commence writing or dictating a business letter, think over the points which you want to cover. Do not attempt to compose the letter in detail in your mind, but block out the sequence of ideas and topics. If you are writing in answer to a letter from someone else, read over the letter before beginning your reply.

By having your plan in mind you will find that the actual writing or dictating follows along very rapidly and that the choice of phrasing almost takes care of itself. It is when you start without a plan that you find yourself delayed by uncertainty as to the appropriate and logical order and by the necessity of reaching decisions while composing the letter which could have been worked out more satisfactorily in advance. A well-written letter makes its points concisely, and is not cluttered up with statements which are really stages in the writer's thinking while he is arriving at the ideas which he wishes to communicate. Letters which have been planned in advance gain in terseness and effectiveness and consequently make a more forceful impression upon their readers.

**First Sentence.** The first sentence of a letter occupies a strategic position. Make the best possible use of it. The opening sentence should at once convey to the reader what the letter is about and why it is being written. Do not be too abrupt. In a friendly way indicate your subject and purpose so that the reader will see that the letter concerns him; in this way you will have succeeded in capturing and holding his interest. A letter which does not refer to the main idea in the opening sentence runs the risk of emphasizing unimportant details and of developing into greater length than is necessary; furthermore, such a weak opening may fail to attract the reader's interest, and consequently he will give less attention to the later sentences in which the main idea is embedded.

Let us examine some examples of poor first sentences and ways in which they can be improved. The fact that some of these are trite, hackneyed, overworked expressions is not the immediate point. The immediate point is that they are poor openings, failing to come to the main idea quickly, failing to take advantage of the attention-getting value that a first sentence possesses.

> POOR: We are in receipt of your letter regarding the damaged chair.
> BETTER: We are very sorry that the chair reached you in damaged condition.
> POOR: In answer to your letter of the 16th, we believe the following information will be explanatory.
> BETTER: You are certainly entitled to an explanation of the matter which you brought to our attention in your letter dated March 16.
> POOR: The purpose of this letter is to acquaint you with the fact that . . .
> BETTER: We are happy to inform you that . . .
> POOR: I am writing this letter in order to get some information.
> BETTER: Please send me information on the following:

**Closing Sentence.** End your letter with a forceful idea, an idea you want to have remembered by the reader. Too often writers do not take advantage of the psychological opportunity afforded by the closing sentence. The closing sentence should do one or more of the following: *emphasize one thought; repeat the main idea* if several ideas have been discussed; *suggest action,* such as sending the desired information, answering a specific question, getting in touch with someone; *again express appreciation* of a skill, action, or service on the part of the reader.

Like the opening sentence, the closing sentence should avoid trite phrasing; it should aim at original and fresh word combinations. Let us examine various closing sentences which accomplish one or more of the points just mentioned:

*Emphasize One Thought.* "Now that we have told you just how this situation has affected us, we feel sure that you will send in your remittance as soon as possible." In the first sentence of this concluding passage the emphasis is on the need for payment. "We hope that you will let us know whenever we can help you with your decorating problems." In the second sentence the decorating service is emphasized.

*Repeat the Main Idea.* "Because it is so late in the year, we are perhaps more eager than usual to get this information from you." In the body of the letter the information has been requested, and again in the closing sentence the importance of securing this information is repeated.

*Suggest Action.* "As our supplies of this particular article are almost exhausted, we suggest that you let us know at once how many you will want." "A return stamped envelope is enclosed for your convenience in replying." "If it will be easier for you to let me know what you want to do by telephone, please call in the morning between ten and twelve." These and many other "suggest action" closing sentences are effective because usually the recipient does what he is asked to do.

*Again Express Appreciation.* "We always look forward to hearing from you." "Once more accept our congratulations on the skillful way the work was completed." "We are very happy indeed that you found our product satisfactory." "Thank you again for your interest." The letter that ends on an appreciative note is bound to establish good will.

**Vary the Length and Type of Your Sentences.** It is a major fault to introduce monotony into your letters through sameness. Variety can be achieved in a number of ways. You may introduce occasional sentences which are longer than the average; this is possible when a thought consists of two or more intimately related parts which can be combined. You may introduce occasional very short sentences which give an effect of precision and emphasis. Some sentences should be the very simplest statement of fact. Some may be questions, exclamations, or urgent injunctions. And the form may also be varied by having some sentences commence with the grammatical subject, and others have the subject preceded by a phrase or clause.

**Use Short Paragraphs.** A typewritten letter is inviting and readable when it consists of comparatively short paragraphs. A large solid mass of typewritten matter looks very forbidding to most readers. Short paragraphs also make it easier for the reader to absorb your ideas since each paragraph can be devoted to a particular point. Occasionally it is effective to have a one-sentence paragraph, a one-line paragraph, or even a one-word paragraph, provided the topic of such a brief statement is sufficiently important to warrant this emphasis.

**Accentuate Important Parts.** The very fact of dividing a letter into many short paragraphs introduces additional white space which is welcome to the eye and achieves emphasis. You can accentuate points still further by introducing larger amounts of white space between paragraphs. And you can focus attention on a particular word or group of words by underscoring, or by indenting and tabulating items in the form of a list, or by saving a point and introducing it in a postscript where it will stand out.

**Value of Transitional and Connecting Words.** There are words which smooth the progress of the eye and mind from idea to idea. They make it easy for the reader to follow the development of a theme. Chief among these are conjunctions and phrases such as: *moreover, again, furthermore, consequently, secondly, thirdly, but, nevertheless, besides, although, on the other hand, in conclusion, on the contrary.* Not only do such words provide continuity and fluency, but if well chosen they actually indicate precisely the relationship between the thought which precedes and the thought which follows them, in some cases coordinating ideas of equal importance, in other cases subordinating one to another, and in still other cases pointing up the contrast between two ideas.

**Study and Outline Letters You Admire.** Whenever you come across or receive letters which you like, try breaking them down into basic units of individual ideas, and then reorganize their contents to see whether the letters can be improved.

The most famous example of a man who did this sort of analysis was Benjamin Franklin who invented for himself a game of competing with the phrasing of the best writers that he could find. He tells us in his *Autobiography* that often he improved on his models by reorganizing the sequence of their thoughts and in many cases the wording.

## Sales Letters

**Differences between Sales Letters and Daily Business Letters.** Up to this point we have taken up matters which apply to individual business letters written in order to obtain information, or to place an order, or in reply to an inquiry. Such letters are a part of daily business correspondence. Other letters are intended to promote business and may be properly referred to as sales letters. Identical copies of such letters are usually sent out to a large number of persons, and consequently the letter is not personal. In a sales letter it is appropriate to use selling devices and special types of emphasis which would be out of place in an individual business letter.

The points which we have already mentioned about the importance of opening and closing sentences should of course be borne in mind in writing sales letters. In letters of this sort you may use more dramatic phrasing than in individual business letters. Also certain devices to obtain emphasis, such as the setting of some words or phrases in full capitals, are appropriate in sales letters, but undesirable in daily business correspondence.

**Suggestions for Sales Letters.** Here are a few of the ways of commencing sales letters: *asking a question, appealing to the reader's curiosity, making a statement that is of an unusual or startling nature* which serves the purpose of provoking the reader to pause and wonder, *beginning with an anecdote or story or dramatic incident.* This last is probably the most effective of all beginnings.

Throughout the sales letter the reader must feel that you are thoroughly familiar with the product, or service, or organization about which you are writing. Do not overstate or make exaggerated claims, but rather rely on clear-cut facts in order to obtain your reader's confidence. On the other hand, do not make your statements so matter-of-fact as to appear to the reader obvious and uninteresting. Permit yourself to use colorful, striking, and enthusiastic phrases which convey definite information and at the same time get and hold attention.

If a sales letter is to go out to a miscellaneous list of people, there is no way in which you can refer to any individual interests of your reader. But if the letter is sent out to a mailing list of persons associated with some particular activity, it is very desirable to commence the letter by some reference to the known interest of those to whom the letter is being sent, and perhaps to make some further reference to it at some other point in the course of the letter.

In appearance and form a sales letter follows the standard and approved practice for all business letters. The section on The Form of the Business Letter, which follows, therefore applies both to daily business correspondence and to sales letters; and in the later section, Samples of Effective Business Letters, we include a special group of examples of sales letters.

## THE PREFERRED FORM FOR BUSINESS LETTERS

**General Recommendations.** The business letter of average length is single-spaced, with double spaces between paragraphs. The short letter is usually double-spaced.

The margins should be thought of as a frame surrounding the letter. In letters of average length, all margins should be at least an inch in width. Short letters should have wider margins.

Never write on the *back* of a letter. Use a second sheet of the same quality paper without the letterhead; write your correspondent's name at the upper left side, the number of the page in the center, and the date at the upper right side.

### Standard Parts of a Business Letter

**Standard Parts and Optional Details.** Good usage dictates that every business letter contain six standard divisions:

1. Heading
2. Inside Address
3. Salutation
4. Body of the Letter
5. Complimentary Close
6. Signature

In addition, there are five optional details that a writer finds useful at times:

1. Attention Phrase
2. Dictation Data
3. Enclosure Reference
4. File Information Data
5. Postscript.

**Heading.** The contents of the heading depend on whether the paper is printed with a letterhead. If it is, then the heading consists merely of the date. If there is no letterhead, the heading consists of the writer's address (two lines) and the date (one line). The heading usually appears at the upper right side of the paper, about two inches below the letterhead or top of the paper. The margin on the right formed by the heading should be at least one inch in width.

Whether the firm's address is printed or typewritten, the name of the state should be followed by the *ZIP code number*. The *National ZIP Code Directory* lists ZIP codes for all U.S. addresses.

Streets whose names are numbers under ten should be spelled out, such as Ninth Street. Numbered streets over ten should be written as 11th Street, 50th Street, 100th Street. Names of streets and avenues, including the words East, West, North, and South, should *not* be abbreviated. Do not introduce a number with "No." or "#".

Dates are usually written in the order of month, day, and year, and are not abbreviated. Some business firms vary the writing of the date to suit their type of business or style of correspondence. Thus:

| | |
|---|---|
| January 8, 19— | January 8<br>19— |
| January<br>8<br>19— | January<br>Eighth<br>19— |
| Eighth<br>January<br>19— | January the Eighth<br>Nineteen Hundred . . . |

The habit of writing 1/8/— is frowned upon. Many people might read: the first of August, 19—; instead of January 8, 19—.

Heading of a letter with letterhead:

CORNELL CARPET COMPANY
5 East 10th Street
Chicago, Illinois 62521
March 4, 19—

Heading of a letter with letterhead:

1300 Broadway          Box 55
New York, N.Y. 10001   Nashville, Tennessee 37202
February 14, 19—       September 3, 19—
          R.F.D. 5
          Selma, Georgia 31084
          May 1, 19—

**Inside Address.** The name and address of your correspondent makes up the inside address. It usually takes three lines, starts flush with the left margin, and should begin three or four line spaces below the heading. Its purpose is threefold: (1) it makes a record on your carbon copy of the identity of your correspondent, (2) insures against error in mailing, and (3) permits restoration to addressee in case of loss.

Examples of inside addresses follow:

Mr. Fred Grove          Mr. James Blank
39 Court Street         Friendly Insurance Co.
Tucson, Arizona 85702     1452 Main Street
                           Akron, Ohio 44310

Brown Bros., Inc.       The Traffic Agent
25 Franklin Square      Reading Railroad
Philadelphia, Pa. 19123  Reading, Pa. 19603

A married woman should be addressed:

**Mrs. Ellen N. Smith** *or* **Mrs. James Smith**

When in doubt about the marital state of your correspondent, address her as "Miss".

Doctors should be addressed:

Dr. John French  *or*  John French, M.D.
*Never:* Dr. John French, M.D.

Titles such as Chairman, President, Secretary, may be on the same line with the name or on a separate line, depending on length of line and general visual result.

Public officials like mayors and congressmen should be addressed as "Hon." or "The Honorable".

**Salutation.** The salutation is a dignified form of greeting. It should begin at the left margin, two spaces below the inside address. It is always followed by the colon. The most commonly used salutations are:

To a man:

Dear Sir:
Dear Mr. Blake: (more personal in tone)
Sir: (very formal)
My dear Sir: (more formal than "Dear Sir" but less than "Sir")

To a woman:

Dear Madam: (for a married or unmarried woman)
Dear Miss Bright:
Dear Mrs. Gale:
My Dear Miss Conrad: (formal)

To a firm of women:

Ladies:
Mesdames:

To a firm of men, or men and women:

Gentlemen:
Dear Sirs:

When the word "dear" is not the first word of the salutation, it is not capitalized.

The following are considered unacceptable: Dear Mister, Dear Lady, Friend John.

In writing to people of position and prominence, like the President of the United States, members of the cabinet, congressmen, judges, governors, and diplomats, the simplest and wisest course to follow is to use the salutation, "Sir."

**Body of the Letter.** The letter proper is the body of the letter. It may be written in block style, indented style, or modified block style.

Try to have a minimum of three paragraphs, although there is nothing dogmatic about the number. Three are suggested on the theory that they most naturally fit the division of the letter into a beginning, middle, and end.

**Complimentary Close.** All letters should end courteously with a complimentary close, which should be punctuated with a comma.

Usual forms:

Yours truly,
Very truly yours,
Yours very truly,
Faithfully yours.

More personal tone:

Sincerely yours,
Cordially yours,
Yours sincerely,
Very cordially yours,

To a superior, or to a person in a position of dignity:

Respectfully yours,
Yours respectfully,
Very respectfully yours,

Do not use a participial phrase, such as, "Hoping to hear from you soon," or "Hoping to be of further service." Change this construction to read, "We hope to hear from you soon." The complimentary close should begin flush with the date.

**The Signature.** The writer or dictator of a business letter should sign his name in ink about two spaces beneath the complimentary close, and should write out both his first and last names. If he uses a middle initial, he sometimes uses the first initial also. Examples of the correct form for signatures follow: William Black, William A. Black, W. A. Black, William Allen Black.

To protect the reader from the discourtesy of a possibly illegible signature, the writer's name should be typewritten two spaces under the signature.

Never use a stamped signature.

If the writer is signing in the name of his company, he may use the following forms:

Yours truly,
William A. Black, President
CONTINENTAL SHIRT CORPORATION

Yours truly,
CONTINENTAL SHIRT CORPORATION
By William A. Black, President

If the secretary is signing for the dictator, she should sign her own name with the addition of a statement that it is for the dictator, or she should sign his name with her own name or her initials added, for example:

Frances Mann
    for William A. Black

William A. Black
    F.M. (*or* Frances Mann)

**Optional or Supplementary Parts.** In addition to the preceding divisions of a business letter, there are five others which frequently appear.

ATTENTION-CALLING PHRASE. If the writer desires to have his letter brought to one individual's attention, in case the addressee is a firm or corporation, he makes a statement to this effect, usually between the salutation and the body of the letter, or on the same line with the salutation, as follows:

Royal Furniture Company
720 Madison Avenue
New York, N.Y. 10021

Gentlemen:        Attention of Mr. G. H. Regan
                            *or*
Gentlemen:
        Attention of Mr. G. H. Regan

DICTATION DATA. Sometimes the writer of the letter finds it useful to add the initials of the dictator and of the stenographer. This information is placed flush with the left margin on a line with the signature or a space or two below. The initials are not individually punctuated, but the dictator's initials are usually separated from the stenographer's by a colon. Sometimes other separating marks are used. The initials may be written either in capitals or small letters.

MW:IK  sew:jro  AWS,FW  LMC/DW

**Example of dictation data:**

Yours truly,
BROWN SALES COMPANY
JAS:TP          By John A. Sackett, Secretary

ENCLOSURE REFERENCE. If material, such as an accompanying check is enclosed with the letter, the fact is recorded under the dictator's initials with the abbreviations, "Enc." or "Encl.", or the spelled-out word, "Enclosure". If there is more than one enclosure, the number appears: "Two enclosures," "2 enc.", or "Encl. 2". The optional spelling and abbreviations, "inclosure", "inc.", or "incl.", are sometimes used by business houses.

| FLH:GSW | GBS:FH | JWR:ot |
|---------|--------|--------|
| Enc.    | 2 Encl.| Incl.  |
| DC:SC   |        | JK:WS  |
| Enclosure |      | Two Enclosures |

FILE INFORMATION DATA. Sometimes the writer requests his reader in his reply to make reference to a code number or letter which is used by the writer for filing purposes. This request usually appears in the upper left side or other conspicuous part of the letter.

In your reply please refer to File *H224*.

POSTSCRIPT. The postscript, always written "P. S.", is a useful device for adding emphasis or a personal note to a business letter. It is, of course, a natural method of writing an afterthought, but its conspicuous position gives it great strategic value. Its discreet use can be very effective. Using it too frequently, however, destroys its value.

After the postscript, the initials of the writer are added.

## Letter Style

There are three standard ways or styles of arranging a letter on paper: *indented, block,* and *modified block.*

The *indented* style consists of indenting the second and third lines of the heading (when there is no letterhead); and indenting the inside address, the first line flush with the left margin, the second line indented below it, the third indented below the second. The beginning of each paragraph is indented, usually on a line with the indention of the second line of the inside address.

1657 Broadway
New York, N.Y. 10019
January 11, 19—

Johnson Sales Company
14 Maiden Lane
New York, N.Y. 10001

Gentlemen:
(Begin paragraph here)

The indented style is not as popular with businessmen as the block or modified block styles.

The *block* style consists of writing all the lines of the heading directly under the first (if there is no letterhead), without indentions; beginning each line of the inside address and each new paragraph at the left margin. The only departure is found at times in the writing of the complimentary close, which usually appears aligned with the date line. However, many business letters are written with the complimentary close flush at the left margin.

March 4, 19—

Bristol's Department Store
Elm and Bird Streets
Birmingham, Alabama 35213

Gentlemen:
(Begin paragraph here)

Yours truly,          *or*     Yours truly,

One of the advantages of the block style is that it lends itself to the single-spaced style, with double spacing between paragraphs. It is popular also because it produces a neat appearance and saves typing time.

The *modified block* differs from the block style in that the paragraphs are indented:

August 14, 19—

Mr. Frederick Douglas,
Miami Bank,
Miami, Florida 33101

Dear Sir:
(Begin paragraph here)

Whatever style is adopted should be followed consistently. In other words, do not mix styles. The effect is one of carelessness and lack of balance.

## Punctuation

The tendency in modern business letters is to use the *open* form of punctuation rather than the *closed.*

The *open* form results in a minimum of punctuation, which means refraining from abbreviations, since abbreviations have to be punctuated. In writing the date with the open form, a comma is placed between the number of the day of the month and the year. The name of the month should not be abbreviated. In the inside address, the comma is omitted at the end of lines but inserted between city and state. Some writers even omit the colon after the salutation, but this is considered affectation by most writers. Likewise, in the endeavor to be consistent, some writers omit the comma after the complimentary close, but this practice has not become widespread. The punctuation in all preceding examples, save the last, is the open form.

The *closed* form of punctuation consists of placing a comma after the first two lines of the inside address, and making use of abbreviations with the accompanying punctuation. In the case of a letter typed or written without a letterhead, the first two lines of the heading are punctuated with a comma:

10 Shore Blvd.,
Buffalo, N.Y. 14216
Jan. 12, 19—

Gramercy Sales Agency
15 West Park St.,
Chicago, Illinois 60650

Gentlemen:

## The Envelope

The address on the envelope should be identical with that in the inside address. The first line of the address should begin halfway down on the envelope.

The writer's name and address should appear in the upper left corner of the envelope, and not on the reverse side. This is a convenience, not only for the addressee but also for the postal authorities.

The window type of envelope, which permits the inside address to act as the envelope address, is a time-saver, but it is inadvisable to use it when the letter is out of the routine class. It is used mostly for sending bills and statements.

# Samples of Effective Business Letters

## The Principal Types of Business Letters

Most business offices have to write many different kinds of business letters in the handling of their daily routine matters. On the pages which follow we give examples of business letters, which we have classified as: Letters of Inquiry and Response, Orders and Acknowledgments, Letters of Complaint and Adjustment, Letters that Deal with Credit, Collection Letters, Sales Letters, Letters of Application, Miscellaneous Letters. Several suggested letters are given under each classification.

## Letters of Inquiry and Response

Business transactions are often preceded by an exchange of correspondence involving an inquiry and a response.

The inquiry should be *clear* in meaning as an act of courtesy to the reader who wishes to make a satisfactory reply; it should be *brief* to save reading time; and it should be accompanied by a stamped, addressed return envelope when the inquiry is in the nature of asking a favor.

The response to the inquiry should be answered *promptly* because a prompt answer builds good will; it should be a *definite* answer to the question asked; and it should contain a *sales talk*, since inquiries are one of the most likely preludes to a sale.

### LETTERS OF INQUIRY

Academy Book Store
15 Park Row
San Francisco, California 94110

Gentlemen:
I am interested in books dealing with the development of business and industry in the nineteenth century, and in biographies of businessmen of the same period.
Please send me your catalogue of second-hand books which deal with these topics, or a list of titles you have in stock.
I should like to know whether you offer a discount on an order of three or more books.
Yours very truly,

Mr. Theodore Franklin
39 Madison Avenue
Madison, N.J. 07940

Dear Mr. Franklin:
When I passed your store window today I must confess I envied your artistic haberdashery display. Whoever is responsible certainly knew his job.
Would it be too much to ask his name? I wouldn't mind taking a few lessons to improve the appearance of my hardware store window.
I shall be grateful for an opportunity to return the favor.
Cordially yours,

Mr. Henry Schmidt
Consul of the Swiss Republic
50 Broadway
New York, N.Y. 10004

Dear Sir:
As a distributor of high quality prints and reproductions, I should like a list of firms in your country which manufacture these items.
Very truly yours,

Thompson Manufacturing Company
1122 Randolph Boulevard
Chicago, Ill. 60607

Gentlemen:
I am at present engaged in research for a magazine article on the latest methods of merchandising ladies' handbags.
As a manufacturer of fine leather handbags, you may possibly be able to supply me with several useful ideas which retailers of your product have been exploiting profitably.
I enclose a stamped addressed envelope for your reply.
Sincerely yours,

A-Z Exterminating Co.,
15 Circle Place,
Cincinnati, Ohio 45232

Gentlemen:
Please send us information on your low-cost exterminating service which you advertise in this week's Gazette. We have a three-story factory manufacturing mattresses, quilts, and cushions.
If you decide to send a representative, please have him call between two and four in the afternoon.
Very truly yours,

Messrs. Brown and Clark
Hotel Supply Company
Troy, New York 12180

Gentlemen:
I am in the market for fifty new or good second-hand electric refrigerators, not larger than six cubic feet in volume, to be installed in a bungalow colony fifty miles from Albany.
In addition to your quotation of a price, I would like to know whether your company could handle the installation of the refrigerators.
May I have your answer as soon as possible.
Very truly yours,

Alfred Typewriter Service
287 Lawrence Avenue
Baltimore, Md. 21230

Gentlemen:
Your firm has been recommended to us as dependable typewriter repair people.
We would like to know your charge for keeping fifteen typewriters in our offices serviced each month; also the charge for overhauling.
We would prefer a visit from your representative to a written reply.
Sincerely yours,

### RESPONSES TO INQUIRIES

Mr. Richard Roth
28 Riverside Drive
New York, N.Y. 10023

Dear Mr. Roth:
I am enclosing a list of twenty books now on my shelves which deal with the topic you are interested in.
On an order of five or more I shall be glad to offer a discount of ten per cent.
For a complete index of books dealing with the development of business and industry in the nineteenth

century, I suggest you consult the exhaustive card catalogue at the New York Public Library.

In case you wish to purchase books not in stock, I should like to suggest the book searching service of our store—a specialty in which we take pride, and for which there is no charge.

Sincerely yours,

Mr. Vincent Marx
1976 Amsterdam Avenue
New Castle, Ind. 47362

Dear Mr. Marx:

Your inquiry about the latest methods of merchandising ladies' handbags interests us greatly. Although we ourselves cannot supply you with the kind of information you desire, we are glad to enclose a list of our customers, some of whom are in your city, who have created a number of novel techniques of sale and display.

You are at liberty to use our name in approaching them.

We should be most happy to see your article in print.

Very truly yours,

Mr. John Aldershot
35 Market Street
Madison, N. J. 07940

Dear Mr. Aldershot:

Your request for the name of the person responsible for my attractive window is most flattering since it is none other than the writer of this letter.

However, to tell the complete truth, I must confess that the latest issue of *The Retailer's Guide* was the immediate source of the hints I followed in trimming my window. I refer to the article, "Outside Looking In," pages 74–79.

Step in and borrow my copy if you haven't one.

Cordially yours,

Benson Manufacturing Co.,
445 Sterling Street,
Cincinnati, Ohio 45239

Gentlemen:

Thank you for your inquiry about our low-cost exterminating service. As you suggest in your letter, we shall be in a better position to render an estimate after a visit of our representative to your factory.

Mr. Thomas Beer, of our office, will call on you, in accordance with your request, on Thursday of this week, at three in the afternoon.

In addition to the service we perform in ridding establishments of termites, roaches, mice, rats, and beetles, we specialize in safe, scientific fumigations which involve practically no inconvenience to the customer.

Mr. Beer is eminently qualified to answer all your questions.

Sincerely yours,

Mr. Paul Stark
Lakewood Colony
Columbus, Ohio 43216

Dear Sir:

We appreciate your coming to us with your problem of securing a quantity of electric ice boxes for your summer bungalow colony.

If you can possibly delay purchasing these refrigerators until next season, we feel that the supply of good second-hand boxes will be adequate.

In the meantime we can help you by letting you have the temporary use of twenty electric refrigerators at a rental fee of $17.00 each, plus an installation charge of $1.25 a box.

The fact that a good part of your bungalows will be equipped with automatic ice boxes should help build good will and afford a legitimate basis for revising bungalow rentals.

We intend to continue our search for more of these commodities, and shall, of course, inform you immediately of any success.

Sincerely yours,

Lawrence and Clark,
198 Center Street,
Baltimore, Md. 21204

### Attention of Miss Cortney

Gentlemen:

In accordance with your inquiry of February 24, we have instructed Mr. Michael Ring, our representative in your district to call on you to discuss a contract for servicing and overhauling your company's typewriters.

Mr. Ring is authorized to quote a price of $.75 a typewriter for each month of servicing, and an overhauling fee of $22.50 a typewriter, for which we do a complete dismembering, oil bathing, cleaning, and repairing job.

Our service includes the substitution of a typewriter in good condition while your own is being serviced in our shop.

Yours very truly,

The Good Shop
Manchester, N.H. 03101

Gentlemen:

Our desire to grant your request for a distributorship in your area of our nationally advertised all-duty floor mop, for the time being must go unsatisfied because of prior commitments.

If within six months you are still interested in repeating your request, we shall be glad to hear from you again.

Thank you for the good wishes you have shown our company.

Sincerely yours,

## Orders and Acknowledgments

Letters ordering merchandise are considered routine letters. They do not involve the art of persuasion or selling, but call rather for clearness, exactness, and brevity. The following considerations should be borne in mind when writing letters of this type:

Every possible detail pertaining to goods ordered should be specified, such as size, shape, color, style, catalogue number.

Each item should be listed in a separate paragraph.

Method of shipment desired should be stated, such as parcel post, express, truck.

Payment for goods ordered should be referred to, such as enclosed remittance or future payment with terms of discount and date of payment.

State the date desired for receipt of merchandise.

The order should be signed by a responsible official.

If credit has not yet been established, financial references should be given.

If reference is made to a previous order, be specific as to date, order number, and other details.

Keep a carbon copy of your order.

## ORDERING GOODS ENCLOSING REMITTANCE

Brown Shoe Company
Lynn, Massachusetts 01903

Gentlemen:

Please send the following items by express, prepaid:

| | |
|---|---|
| 1 doz. pair Elk leather boots, Size 6, Width D, at $2.00 a pair........ | $24.00 |
| ¼ doz. pair Elk leather boots, Size 8, Width C, at $2.00 a pair........ | 6.00 |
| ½ doz. pair Alligator grain calf oxfords, Size 11, Width D, at $3.00 a pair ......................... | 18.00 |
| Total ................... | $48.00 |

Please deliver these goods no later than two weeks from date of order. I enclose my check for $48.00.

Sincerely yours,

## ORDERING WITHOUT REMITTANCE

Alpha Metals Company
50 West 6th Street
New York, N.Y. 10003

Gentlemen:

Please ship the following merchandise by truck, F.O.B. location, at the earliest possible date:

| WEIGHT | MATERIAL | | PRICE PER LB. | |
|---|---|---|---|---|
| 50 lbs. | Aluminum sheet | .032x48"x144 | .2134 | $10.67 |
| 100 lbs. | " " | .064x48"x144 | .2550 | 25.50 |
| 500 lbs. | " coil | .091x18" | .1852 | 92.60 |
| 75 lbs. | " bar | 5/16x1" | .2053 | 15.40 |
| | | | TOTAL | $144.17 |

Please charge to our account.

Yours truly,

Revere Department Store
Revere, Connecticut 06875

Gentlemen:

Please deliver to the above address one (1) utility steel cabinet, measuring 29" x 21" x 15", costing $19.94, as advertised by you in today's "Express".

I shall make payment on delivery.

Yours truly,

Cross Stationers
Adelphi Square
Minneapolis, Minn. 55422

Gentlemen:

This letter confirms the order I gave you over the telephone yesterday for 500 assorted greeting cards at 3½ cents per card.

Terms of payment: 2% thirty days; net, sixty days.

Very truly yours,

New Products, Inc.
100 Fulton Street
Pittsburgh, Pa. 15233

Gentlemen:

We are interested in making a trial order of your new plastic paint. Please send us the following by express prepaid:

| | | |
|---|---|---|
| Five Pints Plastic Paint | $.90 a pint...... | $4.50 |
| Five Quarts " " | $1.75 a quart..... | 8.75 |

Please send us information about your best discount terms.

For credit rating, you may consult The Third National Bank, Toledo, Ohio; and Hamlin and Hamlin, Builders, in your city.

Very truly yours,

## ACKNOWLEDGING ORDERS

It goes without saying that orders should be acknowledged as soon as possible, regardless of when the order is filled. The acknowledgment not only informs the writer of the order that it has been received (an act of courtesy), but it helps to prevent misunderstandings. The best time to send out an acknowledgment is the day the order is received.

All corrections of data in the order and all points of disagreement or doubt should appear in the letter of acknowledgment, since their omission will imply an acceptance of the terms of the order, such as price, discount, shipping method, and quantities.

If the order is identified by a number or departmental letter, the acknowledgment should refer to this number or letter.

The Friendly Radio Shop
15 Queens Street
Little Rock, Arkansas 72204

Gentlemen:

Thank you for your order dated March 15, 1946, for five electric phonographs, model number 3007, covered with two-tone simulated rawhide leather, at $22.50 each.

Discount terms of 2% ten days are quite satisfactory.

We shall ship these phonographs by express, insured, not later than two weeks from this writing.

Yours very truly,

Mr. William Post, Electric Appliances
457 Pembroke Road
Rochester, New York 14620

Dear Sir:

We shall be happy to send you the two infra-red ray lamps which you ordered in your letter of April 21st as soon as we receive a confirmation from you of the new price of $19.50 a lamp.

The former price of $17.80 has been amended because of increased costs.

The usual discount terms will, of course, be in effect.

Sincerely yours,

Majestic Hardware Company
Baton Rouge, Louisiana 70821

Gentlemen:

We are glad to acknowledge your order of January 12 for 1½ dozen cleavers, 2 dozen ice picks, and 4 dozen oyster and clam knives, and also thank you for the accompanying remittance of $71.00.

We are sending you the ice picks and knives by express within the next two days. The cleavers should reach you not more than a week later.

We hope the delay in the arrival of the cleavers will not inconvenience you.

Very truly yours,

Under certain conditions, the acknowledgment of an order may at the same time be a goodwill-building letter or a sales letter. For example, it may be the response to a first order or to an increase on previous orders. If the writer of the acknowledgment thinks that some kind of encouragement or congratulation is due the orderer, he should say so, but always with moderation and dignity.

Bon Ton Shop
575 Main Street
Greensboro, N. C. 27410

Gentlemen:

May we say welcome to a growing family of friends as an acknowledgment of your order for one dozen of our Feelwarm Blankets. We know you will find special sales appeal in our guarantee against moth damage and in the extra tuck-in length, as our blankets are longer than any others on the market.

When the time to re-order arrives, we suggest you

consider our luxurious percale sheets, described in the enclosed booklet.

Please let us know what your customers say about Feelwarm Blankets.

If you are interested in some new and effective merchandising ideas, we have a brochure you may find useful. Just drop us a line.

Sincerely yours,

In acknowledging an order which is not clear, the first requirement is courtesy.

Mr. Wilfrid Williams
58 Corlears Street
Andersonville, S. C. 29621
Dear Sir:

Thank you for your order of March 15, for one dozen Put-away Service Tables.

Before we can fill your order, we shall need further information on the sizes you desire. The enclosed descriptive circular gives you all the relevant figures.

We shall be ready to ship these sturdy articles just as soon as your answer reaches us.

Very truly yours,

## Letters of Complaint and Adjustment

Every businessman finds it necessary at times to write letters of complaint and answers to complaints.

Naturally, in the course of business many misunderstandings may arise. One should be prepared, human nature being what it is, to find errors creeping into bills, shipments, services, and materials. The businessman who discounts unpleasant situations in advance fortifies himself. He learns to accept calmly, if not cheerfully, occurrences which annoy him. He learns that he can turn them to his advantage by building good will. The wise businessman benefits from handling complaints.

While it is perfectly true that many a complaint is unjustified, that many a customer is exasperatingly difficult to satisfy, it still remains a good general rule that the customer is right because most customers, when making a complaint, are making an honest one.

Likewise, when writing a letter of grievance, a businessman should in all courtesy assume the good intentions of the firm to which he is complaining. Such an assumption will result in a letter making an easier adjustment.

The letter of complaint should be courteous and specific. Sarcasm, innuendo, or outright insult defeat their own purpose. In addition to mentioning all relevant data, such as order number, date of shipment, quantities, etc., the claimant should state definitely the kind of adjustment he would like to have, such as a refund of money, a deduction from a bill, a substitution of merchandise, and so on. If the situation calls for serious action, like canceling an order or severing business relations, the writer should say so as directly as possible, and with courtesy.

The response to the letter of complaint, the letter of adjustment, is a challenge to the diplomacy of the writer. It requires tact, self-respect, consideration of the correspondent in the spirit of fairness, courtesy, and good cheer. A letter of adjustment which convinces the reader that every effort is being made to see his point of view is a successful business letter. It promotes a friendly feeling on the part of the correspondent for the writer.

The letter of adjustment should explain the background of the situation, merely refer to the claimant's grievance rather than specify its contents, show the willingness of the writer to cooperate with his correspondent, and state specifically the steps to be taken in meeting the problem.

### LETTERS OF COMPLAINT
### About Defective Merchandise

Gentlemen:

The last lot of doll cribs, retailing at $3.00, which I received from you before the Christmas and New Year seasons have been a great disappointment to me. The demand for them was strong, and I could have disposed of all of them, but the flimsiness of construction, the fragility of the wood, and such minor omissions as the requisite number of nails, resulted in the return of most cribs purchased or no sales at all.

I have therefore decided to send back to you all unsold as well as returned cribs, and request that you credit my account accordingly.

Most people felt, and I agreed, that when they paid $3.00 for a doll crib, they should get a good one.

Very truly yours,

### About Damage in Moving

Gentlemen:

After your men moved my household goods into my new apartment yesterday and left the premises, I discovered the following injuries which were not present prior to moving and which could have been caused only by the act of moving:

A large chip in my hall mirror and a weakening in the mounting
A partly crushed and battered lamp shade
A large sliver removed from one of the legs of my bedstead

I think I am entitled to compensation for these damages, but will not specify a sum until your representative comes here and sees for himself.

Sincerely yours,

### About Damages in Shipping or Packing

Gentlemen:

When I opened your shipment of neckties which I received today, I found eight of the ties very badly creased; so badly, in fact, that their being offered for sale is out of the question. I am returning them to you by parcel post.

It seems a pity that such really beautiful merchandise cannot be displayed after all the care that went into its manufacture just because it was carelessly packed. I have no doubt that you will make the appropriate financial adjustment, but I do feel that any unnecessary annoyance should be guarded against.

Very truly yours,

### About a Shortage in Shipment

Gentlemen:

In checking the shipment of 1 gross #10 loose-leaf binders which arrived today, we find a shortage of 1/12 gross.

We suggest that when you bill us you charge us for 11/12 gross or send us the missing binders within the week.

Very truly yours,

### About Inefficient Service

Gentlemen:

Yesterday I visited your store to examine, with a view to purchasing, the seconds in boys' underwear advertised in the newspapers. Perhaps because the merchandise was seconds, your sales girl was quite inattentive to my presence at the counter for at least five minutes while she carried on a conversation with the girl at the next counter; and when she did give me her attention, she seemed quite indifferent to the questions I asked. At any rate, I got the impression she was not interested in serving me. You will have to take my word for it that ordinarily I am not a fussy person with an extra-sensitive skin.

When she dropped me to pay attention to another customer who wanted to look at some merchandise, I walked away without having bought the two sets of underwear I was considering.

I think I am entitled to some explanation of a reception I have never yet encountered in your store.

Very truly yours,

### About an Error in Filling an Order

Dear Sir:

I find that instead of receiving 3 dozen rolls of outdoor color film, and 1 dozen rolls of indoor, as my order called for, I have been shipped the reverse, 3 dozen of indoor and 1 dozen of outdoor.

Could you send a special messenger this week to make the necessary changes?

Very truly yours,

### About Delays in Shipment

Gentlemen:

We cannot help observing that with practically every order we have given you in the past six months, in contrast with previous months, we have had to prod you for timely deliveries. This is the first time we have called your attention to the annoyances and sometimes embarrassments caused us by these late shipments.

Since we do not intend to call this matter to your attention again, we hope that merchandise will hereafter be delivered by the date promised.

Sincerely yours,

### About Defects Discovered after Delivery

Gentlemen:

About a week ago, on March 18, your delivery men brought the 12x20 carpet and mat which I had ordered a month before.

Two days ago what I can describe only as an invasion of moths took place in my home. On turning up the carpet I discovered literally a score of moth nests distributed all over the mat.

I was able to call in the superintendent of the apartment house I live in who, with the help of his assistant, wrapped carpet and rug in two individual sturdy brown paper parcels. They are now waiting in the cellar to be picked up by your men.

I have spent quite some time, and been put to some expense, fumigating all my closets and sending all woolen garments to be cleaned.

Please let me know what course you intend to follow. While I would prefer another carpet and another mat, I will accept the ones you originally sent if you have them cleaned.

Sincerely yours,

### LETTERS OF ADJUSTMENT
### Admitting Blame

Dear Mr. Ferguson:

Like any other business firm, we do not want to see our customers inconvenienced as you were in the matter of the doll cribs, especially during the holiday season.

We shall, of course, credit your account as you request.

We are taking the liberty of sending you a duplicate shipment of cribs of superior quality, and in consideration of the inconvenience to which you were put, we

are quoting a price very little above those which disappointed you.

Should you desire to re-order on those we are now shipping, the price will be $2.00 each. The special price we are asking in this case is $1.70.

Very truly yours,

### Giving the Customer the Benefit of the Doubt

Dear Mrs. Fiske:

Mr. James Mann of our company has been instructed to call on you with reference to the articles damaged in moving.

Although we employ moving men who are specially trained to be careful in moving household effects, it is not always possible to guarantee a perfect job; and when accidents occur, we are more than glad to make good the damage done.

May we point out that often an inefficient packing job will cause injuries to furniture and effects in moving which would not otherwise occur; and in the long run a house owner saves trouble and money in having the moving people do the packing also.

We are certain that Mr. Mann will do everything necessary to give you satisfaction.

Very truly yours,

Dear Sir:

We are sending you eight ties to take the place of the ones you returned, and want to thank you for the compliment you paid their quality.

The only explanation we can make for the faulty packaging of the creased neckties is carelessness on the part of a clerk who is no longer with us.

Thank you again for the spirit in which you communicated with us.

Sincerely yours,

Gentlemen:

We are at a loss to explain how the shortage you mention could have occurred as the containers in which we ship are specially designed for quantities of one gross.

May we ask that you check once more in your receiving department on the number of binders you received. If your re-examination still shows a shortage, we shall deduct the charge from your bill.

Very truly yours,

### Soothing Hurt Feelings

Dear Mrs. Pine,

We like to think that every member of our sales staff is always courteous, and well-informed about our merchandise. From time to time, however, incidents such as the one your described in your letter reveal either that we have not always made the wisest choice in personnel, or that an otherwise capable sales girl is committing an error, or that we ourselves are not doing everything in our power to understand the personal problems of our staff. We are grateful, indeed, for such a reminder as your letter furnished.

In the meantime we see no reason why you should continue to be deprived of the opportunity to secure the two sets of boys' underwear you wanted. We enclose an order blank and a stamped return envelope which we hope you will use.

Sincerely yours,

### Denying Blame

Gentlemen:

We must confess to a feeling of disappointment when we read your protest about our late deliveries, when all this time we were complimenting ourselves on the way in which we were hastening your orders in these days of scarcity of materials and poverty in man power.

We admit that we should have been more explicit

in the matter of the delivery date which we were promising; but we rather took for granted that you were experiencing the same difficulties that we were.

We can promise that we shall continue to pay every attention to the matter of getting orders out on time.
Very truly yours,

## Admitting Responsibility

Dear Mrs. Wright:

Your letter about a carpet and mat has been referred to me as general manager of the Simon Department Store.

There is always a possibility, though rare, that incubating moths may be present in a carpet or mat, although at the moment we have no way of knowing whether it was so in your case.

We shall have the items picked up in a day or two, and if examination reveals the presence of the nests prior to shipment, we shall send you a new carpet and mat.

We notice that while you refer to the expense incurred in fumigating and cleaning garments, you do not request that we reimburse you. Should our examination of the merchandise reveal us as being at fault, we shall insist on paying any expenses incurred by you.
Sincerely yours,

## Letters That Deal with Credit

When we consider that at least 75 per cent of all business transactions take place on a credit basis, the importance of correct credit procedures becomes apparent.

The following situations are the most common which occur in ordinary business life: applying for credit; granting credit; denying credit; inquiring about an applicant's business standing; replying to such inquiries; making adjustments in credit ratings.

Of all these activities, the greatest responsibility falls on the person who has to decide to grant or deny credit. There is an element of risk which is unavoidable in extending credit to a customer. The commonsense safeguards are to find out as much as possible about his financial status, his business reputation and past performances, and his personal reputation or character.

Whoever grants the credit must first of all think of protecting his own company from financial loss in extending credit to an inefficient businessman whose poor business methods may result in inability to pay his bills; at the same time, he must in granting credit be able to set a limit which will actually be a protection of the customer, since it helps prevent him from over-committing himself.

Writing letters dealing with credit requires tact. Successful credit letters result in improved customer relations and enlarged business activity, since a customer who operates on credit is more likely to order everything from the same house rather than spread his business among several firms as is the case when paying cash.

The person who grants credit should guard against a state of mind in which he feels he is bestowing a favor on the customer. Credit does not originate in a mood of generosity in the person supplying goods or services. It originates in the ability of the purchaser to keep his promise to pay for goods or services. Without this promise to pay, business would be demoralized. If, therefore, a credit manager overlooks this fact, he is unwittingly fighting the trend of business itself.

## Applying for Credit

When a businessman places an order with a firm with which he has no previous credit rating, he should either accompany the order with such a request or precede the order with one. To help his correspondent make the correct decisions, he should provide a financial statement or give suitable references; and he should convey an idea of his business experiences and plans as they bear on the question of establishing credit or confidence.

Gentlemen:

As a retailer of ladies' clothing accessories, I am interested in setting up a special counter devoted to perfumes and cosmetics.

I am interested in securing an attractive line of merchandise, and would like to have an account established with you for this purpose.

You may get in touch with the Third National Bank for information on my financial condition; and with the following firms with whom I have been doing business for periods of one to six years: Bird and Harmon, handbags, Paterson, N. J.; Ward, Light and Prentiss, manufacturers of novelty jewelry, 45 Flatbush Avenue, Brooklyn, N. Y.; and Mr. Francis A. Cary, jobber, of your city.

If you have any descriptive material pertaining to your products, I should be very glad to receive it.
Sincerely yours,

Gentlemen:

After investigation of the samples on display in your outdoor garden, I am placing the following order:

    3 Artificial Stone Benches, 6'x11/12' $17.50 $52.50
    2 Bird Baths .................. 15.00 30.00

I enclose my check for $82.50. Please deliver to the home of Mr. Frederick Clayton, 45 Laurel Drive, Tulsa, Oklahoma, and inform me when shipment takes place.

Since I would prefer to place future orders on a credit basis, I refer you to Howe and Howe, builders, Oklahoma City, and to C. Lincoln Bradford, contractors and builders, Kansas City, Missouri, for information about me.
Very truly yours,

## Withholding Credit for Further Information

Dear Sir:

We appreciate the confidence in our product represented by your first order with us for six dozen freshmen caps.

While we are in the process of filling your order, will you please fill out the enclosed questionnaire and return as quickly as possible. Prompt attention to this will help us establish the satisfactory credit relations you desire.

The enclosed circular gives a complete picture of the various hat and cap styles we offer.
Very truly yours,

## Inquiring of References about Applicant

Gentlemen:

In making application with us to open an account, Mr. Vincent Clark has given your name as reference.

Any information pertaining to his business dealings with you, financial status, and personal character will be most welcome. We shall, of course, hold this information in strict confidence.
Sincerely yours,

## Replying Favorably to a Credit Inquiry

Gentlemen:

In our dealings with the firm of Richards and Robbins, about whom you inquired in your letter of February 5, we have always found them prompt and scrupulous in the payment of their bills.

As far as we ourselves are concerned, they can be considered a good credit risk, and we are happy to inform you to this effect.

Very truly yours,

## Replying Unfavorably to a Credit Inquiry

Whenever a businessman finds it necessary to comment negatively on the credit rating of another, a wise policy to follow is to refer to him not by name but indirectly.

Gentlemen:

In our relations with the person of whom you recently wrote us, we can say very little that can be considered favorable. We have had to mark several statements "past due" a little too often, and are inclined to permit only cash transactions in the future.

Sincerely yours,

Gentlemen:

We think you can safely extend credit to the firm about which you recently inquired, but would suggest that the sum of $300.00 as a limit is out of bounds. Cutting it in half would save annoyances in the long run.

Very truly yours,

## Granting Credit to an Applicant

Dear Sir:

We are extending the credit terms you inquired about in your letter of March 15.

The excellent reports we have of you encourage us to expect only pleasant relations in business, which we hope will extend to the personal.

Your order should reach you the middle of next week. Please write us about the reception our merchandise receives among your customers and do not hesitate to ask us any questions which may arise.

Cordially yours,

## Asking for Further Information

Gentlemen:

Thank you for your order for two dozen stapling machines which we received today.

In the case of first orders not accompanied by a remittance, we usually request that the enclosed form be filled out. This practice helps us to make the quickest and most satisfactory completion of orders.

We are looking forward to pleasant business relations.

Very truly yours,

## Denying Credit to an Applicant

Dear Sir:

Because of the state of business in general, and the conditions prevailing in our field in particular, we are compelled to withhold the shipment of goods except on a basis of remittance accompanying order.

As soon as circumstances permit, we shall be glad to extend credit, with discount terms of 2% 10 days, net 30.

Until then we are willing to permit a cash discount of 2% with the remittance.

We shall be glad to give your order our immediate attention as soon as we hear from you.

Very truly yours,

## Collection Letters

Collection letters are annoying to read or write. They represent one of the unpleasant aspects of business relations. Nevertheless, the alert business-man will utilize the opportunity presented by collection letters to extract whatever good he can by selling good will.

As the name implies, a collection letter is written for the purpose of collecting a debt. The fact that such a letter is written means that a promise to pay for goods or services received has not been kept. The most common method in business of collecting debts whose payment is past due is the letter. There are, of course, other ways of collecting debts, such as the personal visit or recourse to law; but in the long run the letter does the job, provided the writer of collection letters has patience, persistence, and persuasiveness.

From one point of view, the procedure to follow in the case of a bad payer is short and simple: sue and collect.

The reasons for not following such a policy are obvious and strong. First of all, it is expensive, the cost sometimes out of proportion to the size of the debt; secondly, it loses a customer unnecessarily, since experience has shown that most past due accounts are straightened out if the debtor is given a chance; and thirdly, it tends to lay emphasis on the wrong place, on the collection of debts (important as that is) rather than on the service which a businessman can give and which is at the foundation of his career and success.

Therefore a businessman wisely reconciles himself to the necessity of collection letters, profiting to the extent that he tries to make corrections where they belong in his credit policies.

Once a businessman has to send out a collection letter, he usually finds that he has merely begun a series of such letters. Inertia of the pocketbook is not usually overcome by a first collection letter. There comes a second, then a third. When is one to stop? And is each letter to be a parroting of the preceding one?

Each businessman is the best judge of how to answer the first question. As to the second, each letter in a collection series must be built on the preceding, differing in tone and building up to the point where the writer decides to use methods other than letter writing.

Collection letters usually go through the following steps: First, the *reminder* that an account is still open; this may be expressed in one or more letters. Second, the *persuasive* period, in which one or more letters explain the need of the creditor to be paid; or overcome the debtor's resistance by appealing to his pride, his sense of fairness, his friendship, his self-interest; or give advice to the debtor on how to arrange his affairs to the point where he can pay his bills; or insist, with varying degrees of politeness, that the debt be paid. And third, the final stage, the period of *projected action*, in which the debtor is informed that certain steps, such as placing the matter in the hands of an attorney, are to be taken if the debt is not paid.

The threat of action should never be made unless it is to be acted on.

There are certain threats which make a businessman legally liable and which should be guarded against: he should not threaten to expose a debtor to other creditors or write collection letters on post cards, since such writing tends to make public knowledge of the debt and thus tends to injure the debtor's credit.

The following letters represent various stages in the process of collecting unpaid bills.

STEP ONE—REMINDERS

Dear Mr. Blank:
The enclosed statement shows that your account is past due. We hope there is no implied criticism of our service in your omission to send us a remittance, and we look forward to hearing from you shortly.
Very truly yours,

Dear Sir:
We respectfully call your attention to an unpaid balance of $30.00 on your account. We are looking forward to a settlement of this bill at your earliest convenience.
Very truly yours,

Sometimes a reminder is sent in the shape of a printed form with blank spaces for appropriate information. This gives a highly impersonal quality to the correspondence which is desirable in collection situations. The preceding letters could easily be used as printed forms. Here is another:

Gentlemen:
The pressure of business matters has undoubtedly diverted your attention from your account with us of ............ for the period of ................
We shall appreciate prompt attention.
Yours very truly,

Gentlemen:
Merchandise sold to you more than thirty days ago is still not paid for. We do not have to point out what an inconvenience it is to wait for a past due account to be settled. May we have your check?
Very truly yours,

STEP TWO—PERSUASIVE LETTERS

Dear Sir:
You will agree it is a bother to get reminders to pay for goods received. We assure you it is a bother to have to write them. Why not save both of us a great deal of trouble by sending us your remittance in the enclosed envelope?
Very truly yours,

Dear Sir:
Certain as we are that the merchandise we sent you has proved satisfactory, we cannot be equally certain about other things, such as how easily we shall be able to meet our own obligations. We cannot be certain of that because your tardiness in sending us a check for past shipments contributes to a confusing situation as far as we're concerned.
We feel sure you do not want your negligence in this matter to proceed any further.
Very truly yours,

Gentlemen:
We have an idea that our past letters of reminder about your unpaid account have gone unanswered because of sheer embarrassment. We assure you that if that is the situation, you can depend on our perfect sympathy and understanding. You can gather that we ourselves have been in similar situations, and, for all we know, may be again.
Why don't you drop your reserve and let us know a few things? We may be able to give you advice; or if it is a matter of extending the time of credit, we shall be interested in doing that. The point is that unless you let us know, we have to do a mind-reading act.
Sincerely yours,

Dear Sir:
We were wondering whether your recent inactivity as regards your unpaid account of $.......... was not due simply to the awkwardness of having to meet the full payment. If that is the case, we suggest that you send us part now, say a half or two-thirds, and the balance next month.
The enclosed informative booklet should give you some idea of what you're missing in not having ordered from our recent line.
Cordially yours,

Dear Mr. Blank:
While we would naturally have been pleased to receive a check from you in answer to our last two letters reminding you of your unpaid debt of $......, we expected at least a word of explanation from you. We are most curious to know why you have not sent us your remittance.
Is there anything in our past relations which entitles us to a "silent" treatment?
Very truly yours,

Dear Sir:
We do not want you to feel that because we are writing to you once more about your unpaid bill, that our interest in you is solely financial. We feel, somehow, that you would have paid your bill long ago (it is now three months past due) if it were not for something involving us but which you are reluctant to mention. In all fairness to us, we think we deserve to know why we have not heard your reason for omitting payment. If it is simple dilatoriness, please don't ask us to prod you further. Send your check and let's get on with new business.
Very truly yours,

Dear Sir:
Do you like riddles?
There's one we can't answer but which you can, the riddle of why you don't want our good will.
We want yours. We want to serve you to the best of our ability, resources, talent. But you're turning us down.
Don't you think it's time your account with us was settled?
The amount is $............
"It's been a long, long time."
Very truly yours,

Dear Sir:
There's a certain thrill in the unknown, the mysterious. But there can't be any thrill of that kind for you because every time you see a letter from us, you don't have to open it to know that we want to be paid for the goods we sold you . . . months ago.
Well, we hate the thought of being unwelcome correspondents. We would like instead to write such things as, "Yesterday your order for . . . went out on time," or "Thank you for your check".
And come to think of it, we're entitled to such pleasures.
Very truly yours,

STEP THREE—ACTION THREATENED
OR IMPLIED

Dear Madam:
Four letters about your account long past due have been sent to you without even the courtesy of a reply from you.
We therefore inform you that this is the last request we are making before proceeding to other forms of action which will be made necessary by your continued silence.
We regret that we have had to send you this letter by registered mail, but you have given us no choice.
Very truly yours,

Dear Sir:

We don't like to lose money; and we cheerfully assure you that we intend to see your account on our books satisfactorily settled.

And we then intend to give business service as we have in the past, even though you may not like having to pay the bill *via* a collection agency.

But there's one thing especially we don't like; we don't like to see our confidence in people misplaced.

Do you?

Very truly yours,

Dear Sir:

You are hereby informed that your account, unpaid since the 15th of February of this year, has been placed in our attorney's hands. We have instructed him to proceed if within the next two weeks you have not made satisfactory settlement.

Yours truly,

Dear Sir:

Before we draw a draft against you on the first of next month (two weeks away), I suggest you give serious attention to the matter about which we have seemingly so far failed to interest you. Is it worth the embarrassment that usually accompanies a draft presentation? I assure you it is not our intention to embarrass you. We simply want fair treatment. Is there anything in our past relations which will permit you to say we have not given you fair treatment?

Why not settle this account at once, and send us your remittance by return mail?

Sincerely yours,

Dear Mr. Blank:

We can honestly say that we regret having to alter our method of securing payment for goods we have sold. Your continued inexplicable refusal to meet your obligations is making it necessary for us to start suit for collection.

You are probably saying that this is going to be a nuisance. It is! We're saying the same thing. But we're going through with it.

Today is Monday. Friday is the deadline.

We hope you make it.

Sincerely yours,

Dear Sir:

You cannot expect our patience to go on forever. We think we have shown more than average willingness to give you time to pay your bill of $...... due several months ago.

This is our final notice.

Very truly yours,

Gentlemen:

You will observe this is a registered letter. Such a letter is a prelude to further action when a customer shows an unreasonable attitude to his legitimate obligations.

We don't know the reason for your mysterious reluctance, and we sincerely would like to know.

But soon, to be quite frank, the reason won't interest us.

Why not let us in on the secret?

Very truly yours,

## Sales Letters

The sales letter deserves careful thinking because it is most directly related to the actual commodity the businessman is selling. In such a letter the businessman is being challenged to find a substitute for his own personal presence, enthusiasm, and sincerity.

Perhaps it would be better to call sales letters *persuasion letters*, for they have one aim, to bring the customer to the counter and make him say, "I want that."

Such letters have several hurdles to jump: the reader's resistance, indifference, antagonism, and inertia. To accomplish these minor miracles, sales or persuasion letters try to do the following: *capture attention, excite desire,* and *encourage action.*

Sales-persuasion letters fall into two classes usually—the individual letter aimed at a specific person, and the circular aimed at a group or class. It is obvious that the writer of this type of letter must know not only what a definite individual will respond to, but what people in general like and dislike.

In either the individual or circular type of letter, a businessman cannot say he has made satisfactory contact with his prospect after one letter. In a sense the sales letter writer woos the customer with a sequence of letters. Resistance is the kind of thing that falls before persistence. One must not be discouraged by a lack of response to a first sales letter. There must be a follow-up of one or more letters.

The following sales letters are offered as examples of the kinds various businesses and professions have found effective.

Dear Neighbor:

Every once in a while, we succeed in obtaining an item of merchandise that we want to shout about. We don't want to wait for our customers to come upon it on display. We want to tell the world. You've had the feeling more than once, so you know what we mean.

Have you seen our new "Sponge Mop"?

Well, we'll first take a deep breath: you can clean hardwood floors, bathroom floors, kitchen floors, merely by rubbing the long handled mop and pressing it as required in the special device which fits into the rim of your pail. And the same clever "Sponge Mop" will wax your floors in two minutes or less, guaranteeing a cleaner, neater, and longer lasting job than you've ever seen.

Price? $1.19.

Why not give it a try?

As ever,

Dear Sir:

We appreciate the fact that having a choice of some nine competing camera stores in the Fair Street and Main Street areas, you chose to try ours and make your purchase of an 8mm camera and projector, together with a portable screen.

Your yourself gave us part of the reason when you mentioned that we were willing to explain things and give you the time and attention you wanted. We know, sir, that in our business a customer almost always needs talking to rather than convincing. He needs an understanding salesman behind the counter.

We intend to continue this policy because we like it personally, and because it is good business.

So we want to thank you for confirming our own impressions; and want to sign off with a wish that you get the most wonderful kick out of the movies you've taken and are going to take.

The enclosed circular will give you further insight into the pleasures awaiting a movie camera owner.

Very truly yours,

Dear Madam:

We know that you are planning to decorate your home.

No one told us. We just know.

And we have made it our business to give you all the advice and assistance you are looking for in

*Decoration Days*, a new book by Katherine Blake, well-known editor and interior decorator.

Just to show that you don't have to take our word for it, we enclose the table of contents (exciting, isn't it?) and a sample page on Color and Light.

We have your copy set aside for you. There's a stub at the bottom of the table of contents you can fill out. When shall we send it?

Very truly yours,

**Dear Homeowner:**

Cheer up! We bring you good news.

About a warm bedroom on a winter morning . . . a cozily heated bathroom for that cold shower . . . a floor without ankle-high draughts . . .

Whatever automatic heating system you happen to be using, our system of evenly distributed warmth where you want it, when you want it, is yours to test, yours to enjoy, adaptable with ease and surprisingly inexpensive!

We invite you to a demonstration. The enclosed card is your free ticket.

Your good news messenger,

**Dear Madam:**

We think you're going to like reading this letter. It's an invitation, an invitation to stay at home!

Yes, ma'am, an unexpected opportunity to do so many of those little things you've been postponing because you can't delay going downtown to shop for—what was it?—curtains, table mats, extra saucers, linen dish towels . . . you know better than we.

Very few women enjoy the wear and tear of competing, jostling, choosing, rejecting, being jammed into elevators, fretting on escalators, carrying bundles, standing on one's feet—three, four, five hours. And come to think of it, if somebody is willing to do it for you, it's pretty silly not taking advantage, isn't it?

That is our service. We know what people want, the details as well as the general idea. We do the competing, jostling, choosing, rejecting; we get jammed into the elevators, carry the bundles, stand on our feet —for you.

Our fee is absurdly little. You'll scold us for not making it more expensive, but we're interested primarily in your good will.

Just tell us your shopping needs. A post card will serve. The phone is quicker.

If you have a charge account, we arrange to have your purchases recorded there. If you want a charge account with us, we do that too!

What does madam wish?

Very willingly yours,

**Dear Mr. and Mrs. Blank:**

May we add our congratulations on the recent birth of your son, Robert.

From the moment of his birth, your pride was flavored with that desire to protect the little fellow which every parent feels. You intend to keep him from harm, to guide him in the ways of truth. Everything love can do for a child will be done for your child.

We are not presuming when we say you intend to give him the best education you can. But are we far from wrong in making a guess that you've done nothing about it yet?

Very few parents are in a position, when their son or daughter graduates from high school, to finance a four-year college education. But when one sees that it's merely a matter of planning when the child is born, that it is merely a routine affair to be taken for granted just as an amortization or the monthly telephone bill, we wonder why every parent hasn't followed the plan.

What plan?

**Why, our Education Insurance Plan**—a natural, eas-

ily carried method of guaranteeing a sum of money in eighteen years to permit your boy to go to any college in the country; to pay his tuition; buy his books; pay his laboratory, library, and other fees; feed him; house him; yes, and keep him in pocket money too!

You owe it to your boy to investigate our Plan. You have only to call Midway 4-8765 or fill out the enclosed card to receive the best advice you ever got.

Very truly yours,

**Dear Madam:**

Your credit is perfectly good at our establishment for securing an attractive fur coat or jacket on our banking plan. For enjoying the privilege of spreading the cost of your fur garment over 12 to 15 months, you pay 4% a year, as you would if you borrowed from a bank.

But there's another enticing feature—the special marked-down price. That is our traditional way, at this time, of securing a number of new customers whose business permits us to keep our employees on a year-time basis.

We make a practice of deducting liberally from the cost of the purchase when a customer decides to turn in her old fur coat.

We have the permission of several pleased customers to use their names; and if you want to know any, we shall supply them gladly.

Very truly yours,

**Dear Mrs. Foley:**

We hope your plans for the coming summer include a visit to the Southwest, for we want to extend to you a most cordial invitation to enjoy our hostelry, "The Lodge."

Most guests like our accommodations on a monthly basis, but those who cannot stay longer than a week or two find the rates quite reasonable.

New Mexico sunshine defies description. Easterners literally fall in love with it. They love a morning ride in the hills on a sure-footed pony, accompanied by the best cowboy guides in the state. And enough said when we say that you can't get better eating anywhere between the Rio Grande and St. Louis.

We prefer reservations. We hate turning guests away who have been too careless to write in advance and find the "filled up" sign when they arrive.

Cordially yours,

P.S. You don't have to come all dressed-up. Dungarees make good riding breeches.

**Dear Building Owner:**

If you have a low pressure steam boiler that needs cleaning, you have only to call on us to do the job.

Attention to this chore now can save you hundreds of dollars in fuel costs. We do not set a financial price on the good will earned among your tenants.

We offer you the following service: supply of cleaning materials; installation of materials into boiler; leaving complete instructions with your superintendent for draining, flushing, and refilling boiler; collecting water samples for laboratory check-up; full report.

We undertake to clean out mud, rust, and all foreign matter which accumulates during a heating season.

Our charge for this service is $7.50, a mighty small sum for the good we do.

We suggest you call us up before the heating season starts.

Very truly yours,

**Dear Madam:**

May we send you, with our compliments, a free copy of Mary Burton's *Cooking Quiz*? Just sign and mail the enclosed card. No stamp is required.

This fascinating booklet will test your ability to

meet the challenges of modern kitchen life. It will show you what your weaknesses are. It will help you turn out a better meal today.

Your returned card will also bring you, without obligation to buy, a free-examination copy of Mrs. Burton's *Modern Cooking*. This is a comprehensive guide to the best cooking practices which will help you prepare dishes designed to create a reputation over night, and make you the most popular hostess in your set.

If you decide within a seven-day period that *Modern Cooking* has a message for you, send $3.00 in full payment. Otherwise, we shall accept its return with pleasure.

In any case, we hope you enjoy the quiz and benefit by it.

Very truly yours,

Dear Madam:

Were you glad when you saw that the new place being opened in your neighborhood was to be a laundry?

If you've been getting the kind of service so many people have been complaining about, you bet you were. We want your patronage, so we're going to make a few promises and we're going to keep them.

We promise a speedy three-day delivery service.

We promise the cleanest and neatest delivery wagon and representative.

We promise painstaking and neat ironing.

We promise careful packaging.

We promise efficient mending, darning, and button sewing.

We promise longer life to your sheets, pillow cases, shirts, handkerchiefs, and curtains.

We promise to starch or not to starch according to taste.

Will you promise to give us a try?

Please expect us within the next few days.

Very truly yours,

Dear Mr. Jones:

Now that you have signed a five-year lease for half the third floor of the Towers Building, you would be seizing a real chance to design your space layout if you consulted our facilities first.

First impressions are important in offices, reception rooms, show rooms. You do not do your business justice, you do not convey the best idea to the public, by haphazardly furnishing and decorating your new establishment. First impressions must be planned.

Whoever takes on the mission, let us urge that it be one all-designing, planning mind. Let the person who selects your floor covering select your chairs, think of the walls, the ceilings, the doors, the windows. When the floors merge their meaning with the walls, you are letting things and space talk for you.

Don't you think we have something for you? We know we have.

Yours very truly,

Dear Friend:

The world seems to be waking out of a long sleep and rarin' to go places. All those far-away spots with the glamorous names are beginning to beckon us. Today, with a two weeks' vacation, South America, Cuba, the West Coast are no longer merely a wish, but a real possibility.

Perhaps you don't intend to go any further than that mountain resort where you played tennis and canoed.

In either case, how's your luggage?

Do you want to take advantage of 60 years of rich experience in the field? We can give you the soundest advice for your trunk and suitcase need. Don't ask us about hats or coats; we'd be kidding you if we said we knew about them.

But we KNOW luggage.

We're not boasting, just saying.

You're welcome to come in, look around, ask questions. You'll probably find what you're looking for. Most people do.

Cordially yours,

Dear Folks:

Over fifty years of dependable storage and warehouse experience are at your disposal.

Competent, careful men are ready to manage every detail of your household removals.

Separate rooms to store your furniture and merchandise are yours for the asking.

Do you desire packing and crating? We can do it for you.

We mothproof and fumigate as a free service.

Of course you want our telephone number. It's Main 4-1786.

Yours very truly,

Dear House Owner:

We can sell your property!

More—we can sell your property quickly and efficiently, without those small annoyances and delays that often crop up in real estate transactions.

You can also get intelligent, confidential handling of your real estate and mortgages merely by asking. There is no phase of real estate activity that we neglect.

We appraise, sell, manage, advise.

We are ready to serve you.

Very truly yours,

Dear Music Lover:

It's amazing how quickly our youngsters grow up. It seems only yesterday we were saying that when Junior was ten, we'd get him a piano.

Well, have you bought that piano?

We're here to do a little prodding. You know you're going to get that piano eventually, and we don't see why we should wait until some more energetic piano firm takes you by the hand and says, "Here's your instrument!"

No, we're the most energetic piano firm in these parts. We can beat anybody's prices and there's hardly a piano wish we can't grant. Whether new or used, spinet type, baby grand, we have them all.

We're not going to let this suggestion stop here. Please expect to hear from us again if we don't find you dropping in to look over our pianos. And when you do come, please bring Junior.

Very truly yours,

Dear Mr. Brown:

Have you ever been "stood up" by a date? Remember the disappointment when she failed to appear? That was a long time ago, when we were both younger.

But, frankly, that's the way I felt when you didn't act on my invitation to come a-visiting. I actually felt you would want to see for yourself what I have to offer the discriminating buyer of men's wear. When you see my stock of materials for shirts, you'll agree with me that it's a date worth keeping.

I haven't mentioned handkerchiefs, mufflers, or men's jewelry, but they're all ready for inspection. You're in for an exciting time.

Cordially yours,

Dear Mrs. Blank:

Thank you for the confidence you showed in our service by giving us the trial we requested. We do not want you to think that because we moved your be longings to your new home and were paid for the job, we no longer have an interest in your affairs.

First of all, are we correct in assuming you were satisfied with our performance? We would indeed be grateful for any suggestion or criticism which would help us do a better job for the next fellow.

Secondly, we hope you will remember us when your next moving or storing problem arises.

And finally, may we wish you a happy life in your new house.

Sincerely yours,

## Letters of Application

The letter of application for a job or position is in reality a sales letter, since its purpose is to sell the services of the writer of the letter to the reader. However, it presents such special problems that it deserves a section all to itself.

In the first place, the letter of application is probably the one letter everybody has to write at sometime in his life, whether he is just beginning his career as a high school or college graduate, or is an experienced and mature businessman seeking greener pastures.

In the second place, while the letter of application is so very important, it happens to be a comparatively rare letter, composed only at special moments; it is therefore a type of letter with which the writer is not likely to be familiar. The chances are that instead of taking special pains—it being the most important letter he will ever be called on to write—his very unfamiliarity with the problem will cause him to produce a hastily written, poorly organized, de-personalized and unpersuasive letter which is sure to be lost in the shuffle.

It would also seem a silly afterthought to remind the reader that certain practices are taboo, such as sloppy appearance, poor spelling and grammatical construction, but too many employers have testified to this incredible phenomenon not to make the warning worthwhile.

There is no feature of letter writing which the applicant for a position can afford to ignore. It would be wise here to review the section entitled Pointers for Good Business Letters, which begins on an earlier page. Quite often a modest and neatly written letter will make a favorable impression out of sheer contrast to the run-of-the-mill applications.

The *immediate objective* of the letter of application is to obtain an interview for the writer. Letters of application are not or rather should not be called applications for positions but applications for interviews. If we bear this in mind, we will slant our letters with the thought uppermost that we must get our prospective employer *interested* in meeting us.

How can you make a person interested in you? The best way undoubtedly is to show that you are interested in him. This does not mean, in writing letters of application, that you must be fawning, hypocritical, flattering. It does mean that you must present your qualifications in such a manner as to convince the prospective employer that you would be useful to him. Therefore you should not plead economic need or desire for experience as your reason for applying; nor should you point out the advantages to yourself only that would result if you landed the job. You should emphasize the advantages that would result to the employer. This is not easy. Let the reader sense or feel the desirability

of employing you or of meeting you as a result of the effective way in which you present your qualifications.

Would an employer be impressed favorably with a candidate who wrote illegibly or in pencil or in poorly constructed sentences? Without a word about his qualifications, such a candidate has described himself sufficiently well to make the employer think, "This applicant would not be an asset in *my* business." Simple neatness and good English enable the employer to see at once that the applicant is careful, neat, self-respecting. These virtues may not be enough, but they are a great help. This simple point is mentioned only to emphasize the main idea that a letter of application is a sales letter intended to excite the reader's desire to meet the applicant for the purpose of considering him as an employee.

The following details are important in the successful composition of a well-thought-out letter of application:

> Give a statement of experience, listing the skills you have learned through association with people in business.
> Give a statement of education, emphasizing that part which bears on the job you are seeking.
> Give references.
> Omit specific amount in discussion of salary if possible.
> Do not send originals of letters of recommendation or legal documents like birth certificates; use copies or photostats.
> Be neat.
> Use many and brief paragraphs.
> Ask for an interview.
> Throughout the letter bear one thought uppermost, "What good will it do the employer to hire *me*?"

There are two kinds of letters of application, the solicited and unsolicited. Most applicants are in the habit of writing only the first type, overlooking the interesting possibilities of the other.

Usually an applicant looks into the help wanted columns or through personal association becomes aware of a businessman's need of an employee. He then writes his letter in response to the solicitation of the advertisement or the individual. One of the handicaps he is up against is the inevitable competition of many other applicants all of whom have seen the same advertisement, and are writing letters in response. The applicant is thus placing himself in a position where he is being compared with others —a rigorous and severe test. From the employer's point of view, it is the best kind of test. From the applicant's point of view, it may seem unnecessarily severe, and if he can do something to place himself in a more advantageous position, he should try. He can do this by writing the unsolicited letter of application.

The unsolicited letter undertakes to convince an employer that the applicant would be a valuable individual to employ even though the employer at the moment has not acknowledged his need of assistance. Such a letter reveals to the employer that the writer has a certain amount of initiative, a quality any employer likes to see in the people around him. Just as the employer often goes into action on his own to get business, so the applicant for a position need not wait for the job to announce itself, but should go out looking for it.

In addition to revealing an inner useful initiative, the unsolicited letter of application also places the writer in a unique position. He is not competing with other applicants, many of whom may have greater experience, better education, and other desirable qualities.

All the applicant has to do in order to find out to whom to write this type of letter is to decide on the kind of job he wants, and next to examine the business sections of newspapers or the trade papers in the field in which he is interested to discover what changes are taking place in management, plans, and other business activities. As a matter of fact, many executives in the business world, well placed as they may be, keep posted about developments of all kinds in their own and allied fields, and when they see an opportunity present itself, often write the unsolicited letter, the first step in an ambitious man's career.

### SOLICITED LETTERS OF APPLICATION

W 18
The Evening Bulletin
New York, N.Y. 10036
Gentlemen:

I am interested in your advertisement for a man with general steamship experience who also has a knowledge of Spanish and Portuguese. My training and background qualify me, I believe, to serve your needs.

Before I graduated from college, I was fortunate in being sent to Central America during summers as the representative of the Beaver Work Clothes Company, traveling by burro into the interior, and picking up a great deal of Spanish to supplement my high school and college studies. My marks in this language, by the way, averaged 85 to 90 over a four-year period.

While I have never had occasion to speak Portuguese in the course of business, I did take a six months' special course at the Recophone Language School to prepare myself for just such a situation as your advertisement presents. My reading knowledge of Portuguese definitely excels my speaking ability.

Through my Latin American associations, I became quite interested in foreign trade in general. As a result, I served as assistant bookkeeper for the Argent Company, 56 Broad Street, Philadelphia; statistician in the office of the Superior Shipping Company, 60 Perry Street, New York; and spent a year acting as guide for tourists in the Traveler's Conducted Tours, 500 Boylston Street, Boston.

Since your advertisement is not specific about the duties I would be expected to fulfil, I shall not add other information about my experience which might enlighten you further about my ability to serve you. This information I shall be glad to give you in a personal interview.

Other facts about myself: I am 28 years of age; American; five feet, eight inches tall; weigh 145 pounds; a graduate, ranking in the upper third, of the Boys High School and of the State University.

My telephone number is Main 4-8795.

Respectfully yours,

Gentlemen:

Your advertisement for a sales manager is a challenge. You even announce a special bonus for the right man.

Who can resist this kind of dare? Especially if deep down he really is convinced he is the right man?

I would not be writing this if I thought that by hiring me your company would be obtaining simply a tried and true sales manager, a follower in accustomed paths. You would not want me then.

I must warn you that I try experiments, and sometimes they don't work out, and sometimes they even cost more than one would like. But this experimentation has brought me from ledger clerk with the General Tool & Die Manufacturing Company, of Spokane, Washington, to my present position of sales manager with the Frost Electric Plating Company, of Delaware, the most enterprising concern in the field.

Since I was given this position, three years ago, our sales have increased 44%.

I sincerely believe I have talents that a firm as large as yours can use. If you think so too—or are curious enough to have a talk—I can arrange to meet you a day after I hear from you.

Sincerely yours,

Gentlemen:

This is the first letter I have ever written as an applicant for a position. That is because I have never worked in a business office, having spent my time up to now teaching in the elementary and high schools of our city.

In your advertisement for a young man who will begin as assistant bookkeeper, you ask the applicant to mention experience in his letter. While I cannot claim to have had business experience, I feel that the following activities can be called "experience".

1. I have kept the financial account of a neighborhood social and athletic club for the past year as the club's treasurer.
2. Among my extracurricular activities at the Spencer Avenue High School, I assisted one period a day in the Accounting Department office, learning many useful practices of office procedure.
3. My school ratings in business subjects, namely, Gregg Shorthand, bookkeeping and accounting, business law, office practice, and commercial arithmetic averaged 90%.
4. I was one of the founders of a new club in our school, the Business Club, which met weekly and discussed various problems arising out of magazine and newspaper articles, especially those on the financial pages of our city's newspapers.

If you think that I sound like the kind of person you want in your employ, please call me in for an interview in which I can answer all your questions at length.

Very truly yours,

Dear Mr. Tracy:

Following Mr. Brown's suggestion, I am writing to offer my time, willingness to work, skill and experience to your company as secretary to the president.

Since I was graduated from Fairmead College where I majored in Business Administration, I have held a variety of positions so that I could get the feel of our many-sided business world. For example, I sold floor mops, waxes, and cleaning materials in Harris's Department Store, in Rochester, for three months; and I was office manager of TransFilms, a company importing foreign motion pictures, for one year.

Some vital statistics: 28 years old; married; speak good and clear English; can take and execute orders: quick and accurate with shorthand and the typewriter.

I shall look forward to hearing from you.

Very truly yours,

Dear Sir:

Subject: Your advertisement for a Sales Correspondent.

I believe that my training and experience qualify me for this position.

Training: After graduation from high school, I took

special courses at the Lehigh Business School to supplement my academic education. There I studied stenography, bookkeeping, business correspondence, and business law.

Experience: My first position in business was that of saleswoman in the Grand Store, Cleveland. There, in addition to valuable information about department store management, I learned consumer-psychology. I think this experience has given me the kind of insight sales correspondents need.

My second position, and my present one, is that of secretary to Mr. Robbins, vice-president of The Turner Company, furniture manufacturers. As secretary, I have done the practical work of composing many types of letters, have gained in fluency and ease of expression.

Personal Data: I am 24 years old, American, born in Cleveland, educated there, and am in excellent health.

May I have an interview?

Very truly yours,

### UNSOLICITED LETTERS OF APPLICATION

Dear Sirs:

### Attention of Mr. Bell, Vice-president

With the rapid expansion of world trade, business houses everywhere are making inquiries about possible fields of new activities.

The many recent changes in both foreign and domestic commerce are not easily visible to the casual observer. One has to know how to look under the surface to estimate the potentialities of new markets.

Over a period of more than 20 years, in association with American and British manufacturers, I have been able to reach an understanding of the world picture in a variety of business activities which I can justifiably claim to be equaled by very few. I contend that the firm which utilizes my knowledge of foreign trade must benefit to a great extent from that knowledge.

May I be given an opportunity to show you how I can immediately increase your business in both the European and Latin American markets?

This is my bid for entry into your export department. Am I correct in assuming you have a place for a person who can serve you as I can?

Respectfully yours,

Gentlemen:

### Attention of Personnel Manager

My name is Walter Robbins, and I am a lawyer with six years' experience in the general practice of law.

I am 37 years old; and married; received my A.B. degree from Franklin University in 19—, and my LL.B. degree in 19—.

I am curious to know whether your company will be interested in utilizing the skills of a legally trained, business-minded executive who would rather apply his knowledge to manufacturing and business than limit himself solely to litigations and consultations.

In preparation for the interview which I hope you will grant me, I have tabulated several aspects of your company's activities in which I believe my type of service would be useful. Are you curious enough to hear my suggestions for increasing your firm's commercial and industrial radius?

May I add that certain other skills may be of interest to you—an ability to speak in public, enriched by several years of experience in that field; a developed knack of rhetorical composition; and a working knowledge of French, German, Greek, and Italian.

Sincerely yours,

Dear Mr. Price:

Let me begin by making a confession. This letter is being written to four other businessmen. I am making each one the same offer. In fairness to all, I shall give each one every consideration before I make my decision.

I am offering you the services of Philip Black, construction engineer.

He is 33 years old with 11 years of construction experience on residential and commercial buildings; thoroughly conversant with contract work, estimating costs, supervising all phases of construction, and the qualities of materials, as well as with the intricacies, pitfalls and problems of labor relations.

He can be especially valuable for situations requiring construction liaison.

He asks a salary of $10,000 a year.

Of the possible business firms to which I could have written, I have chosen five as most likely to profit by his talents. The question is which one will secure those services?

An early interview is my best suggestion.

Very truly yours,

*Philip Black*

Dear Mr. Jones:

If I were a businessman hiring people, I would look for the kind of person who intends to advance his own career with the advancement of the company he works for.

In less than a month, I am being graduated from the Commercial Training High School. I have already made up my mind about what I want. I want to get into a business which, first of all, is engaged in the kind of work I think I would like. Then, after I secure a position with that company, I intend to invest part of my evenings in supplementary study to make up for the fact that I am not going to attend college.

If I give service that my employer values, I expect to receive consistent salary increases and promotions to positions of greater responsibility.

This is my plan. I think your company is the kind I would like to work for. Would your company be interested in hiring me?

To help you come to a decision, I am listing the names of several people who know me and whom you may wish to consult about my intelligence, reputation, and character.

Mr. Randolph Ginn, Dean, Commercial High School

Mrs. Ida Chester, Teacher of English, C. H. S.

Miss Beatrice Williams, Teacher of Bookkeeping, C. H. S.

Mr. Adolph Marcus, Pharmacist, 45 Main Street.

I have not specified the kind of job I am looking for, because I am not looking for any one kind of work. I am anxious to do the various tasks necessary for the carrying on of a successful business, and I intend to fill many positions in the firm I work for.

Respectfully yours,

## Miscellaneous Letters

Under the heading of "Miscellaneous Letters" are those which may not be classified under previous headings but which occur frequently in business and should not be overlooked.

For example, consider the "thank you" letter. It is usually short and expressive of the writer's appreciation for a service rendered. There is nothing compulsory about it, and it is something not ordinarily expected of the writer. That is why the recipient of such a letter may be encouraged to continued good effort or get the thrill of knowing that other people are aware of his existence and his contributions.

Then there are letters such as inter-office communications, secretary's letters, and others. Several examples follow.

### Deferring a Final Answer

Dear Mr. Franklin:

We should have had an immediate answer to your question about tire shipments but for the fact that our reorganization has not yet been completed.

We feel certain that we shall be able to send you specific information not later than a week from now.

Yours sincerely,

### A Secretary's Letter

Dear Mr. Jones:

The matter about which you wrote to Mr. Carson last week will be brought to his attention as soon as he returns from a trip to Seattle. He is expected back within ten days.

If you consider the matter urgent enough, I can either let you have his Seattle address or telephone number.

Very truly yours,

### Making an Appointment

Dear Mr. Smith:

Mr. Jackson has asked me to write you that he cannot meet you, as you request, next Monday at 2:00.

If it is convenient for you, he will be glad to keep next Wednesday at 3:30 open for you.

Very truly yours,

*Alice Williams*

Secretary to Mr. Jackson

### The Season's Greetings

Gentlemen:

With a pleasant look backwards and a cheery look ahead, may we at this time of the year wish you the merriest Christmas and the happiest New Year!

Cordially yours,

Dear Mr. Brown:

We thank you for remembering us in your season's greetings and heartily wish the same to you!

Cordially yours,

### Congratulations

Dear Mr. Harris:

We here in the home office think you have done a splendid job this past year managing the branch in Akron.

If this should spur you on to greater achievements, more power to you!

Sincerely yours,

Dear Mr. Hill:

May I, as a business associate, add my congratulations to those of your personal friends on your recent marriage, about which I learned through the local press.

Sincerely yours,

### A Letter of Introduction

Dear Mr. Wilson:

I hope this letter will take my place in introducing to you the bearer, Fred Bates.

Fred is a young man whom I have watched grow up through high school and college. Right now he needs to enlarge his acquaintance, to meet the kind of people whom he could copy to advantage. I am sending him to you because I think you could help him. I am sure the advice you give him will be worth following.

Sincerely yours,

Dear Mr. Watson:

The bearer of this letter, Miss Irene Ember, is a competent young lady whom I have known many years. She has several questions to ask you; and I took the liberty to assure her she would find you an attentive listener.

Sincerely yours,

### A Letter of Recommendation

Dear Mr. Standish:

If it will help you to form an opinion of Mr. William Fisher, who has applied to you for the position of office manager, I shall be glad to tell you what I know about him.

Mr. Fisher first came to our office about five years ago as a ledger clerk. After eight months he was promoted to assistant bookkeeper. A year later he won another promotion, that of full bookkeeper, which position he has filled to our complete satisfaction.

Since he desires to progress further in business and there is no immediate opening in our office, I want to emphasize that he is fully capable of running a modern office and, in my opinion, would be an asset to the firm which employs him.

Sincerely yours,

### Reply to an Applicant

Dear Mr. Custer:

Your letter describing yourself has aroused our interest. We shall be glad to have you call on us Friday morning, at 10 o'clock.

Yours very truly,

Dear Mr. Phillips:

Please call for an interview in reference to the position of statistician, about which you wrote to us last week.

Mr. Hill, our personnel manager, will expect you any morning before eleven, next week, in Room 756.

Very truly yours,

### Letter to a Person Named as Reference

Dear Sir:

Miss Wilhelmina Jones has applied to us for a position in our accounting department and has given your name as a business reference.

May me have information from you about the applicant's personality and record which would help us form an opinion?

We need hardly say that all information of this kind is considered as altogether confidential.

Very truly yours,

### A Thank You Letter

Dear Mr. Bridges:

When I look back on my recent trip to San Antonio, I find myself recalling most pleasurably the hospitality I enjoyed at your hands. Of many happy experiences, those associated with your kindness seem happiest. May I, in expressing my thanks, urge that you soon allow me to show my appreciation of your generosity in a more tangible manner when you visit our city?

Sincerely yours,

# Useful Business Facts
# and Figures

---

IN THIS SECTION we take up various specific facts and figures which will be useful both in business and everyday affairs. First we give Postal Information and Rates. Here all the classes of mail are described and rates for each class are given. Next we discuss the various kinds of Telegrams and Cablegrams, as well as the comparative rates for each type. Under Tables of Weights and Measures we present the various units used in measuring distance, area, volume, and weight. The units commonly used in this country and the units of the metric system are both given, with their approximate equivalents indicated. Finally, we list the meanings of Abbreviations which are commonly used in business and the professions.

## Postal Information
## and Rates

### Domestic Mail

The term *domestic mail* is used to include all matter that is placed in the mails to be delivered locally, or to be sent from one part of the United States to another. It also includes mail to, from, or between the possessions of the United States. Domestic mail is divided into four classes as follows:

#### FIRST-CLASS MAIL

First-class mail, which is limited to 70 pounds and 100 inches, length and girth combined, and consists of written and sealed matter such as letters; it also includes post cards. The rate for first-class mail other than post cards is 8 cents for each ounce or fraction of an ounce. Government post cards as well as private mailing post cards are mailed at the rate 6 cents each. Reply (double) post cards are 12 cents each (6 cents each half).

*Domestic Air Mail.* The rate for air mail to be delivered in the United States or in any of its possessions is 11 cents for each ounce or fraction of an ounce, up to 8 ounces. For matter weighing more than 8 ounces, consult the Air Parcel Post Service rates. In order that air mail be recognized and identified as quickly as possible, the sender should use special air-mail stamps and air-mail envelopes. Air-

mail stamps may not be used on other than air mail. Air mail may be sent special delivery, it may be registered, insured, or sent C.O.D. Do not send by air mail any article that is subject to damage by freezing.

Post cards may be sent air mail at the rate of 9 cents for each card.

When air mail is to be delivered to *Army Post Offices* or *Fleet Post Offices* (in care of the postmaster) beyond the limits of the continental United States, the domestic air mail rates are charged.

#### SECOND-CLASS MAIL

Second-class mail, which has no weight limit, includes magazines, newspapers, and other periodicals which bear a notice indicating that they have been entered as second-class matter. Such mail is sent unsealed; if sealed, it must be sent as first-class mail. The rate for second-class mail is 6 cents for the first 2 ounces and 1 cent for each additional ounce. If it can be sent at a lower rate as fourth-class mail, that classification is used instead.

#### THIRD-CLASS MAIL

Each piece of third-class mail may weigh up to but not including 16 ounces. It includes circulars, proof sheets, other printed material (except second-class publications). The rate is 8 cents for the first 2 ounces or fraction, and 2 cents for each additional ounce or fraction of an ounce.

BULK MAIL. The postal laws allow the cheaper mailing of third-class matter in large quantities at the rate of 23 cents per pound with a minimum charge of 4 cents per piece. Books and catalogues having at least 24 pages (including covers), roots, plant bulbs and plants, cuttings, seeds, and scions may be sent at the third-class bulk rate of 17 cents per pound with a minimum charge of 4 cents per piece.

Addresses on bulk-rate mail must be zip-coded and must be presented in lots of at least 200 identical pieces or 50 pounds, whichever is the lesser.

#### FOURTH-CLASS MAIL (PARCEL POST)

Fourth-class mail or parcel post includes matter weighing 16 ounces or more and not included in first-, second-, or third-class mail. The length and girth combined cannot measure more than 72 inches, and the limit of weight is 40 pounds if for delivery in the local, first or second zone and 20 pounds if for delivery in the third, fourth, fifth, sixth, seventh, or eighth zones. Certain important exceptions to these limits are noted below. If the parcel weighs less than 10 pounds but measures more than 84 inches in length and girth combined, it must be sent at the 10-pound rate but must not exceed 100 inches.

Parcel post rates vary according to the zone in which the parcel is to be delivered. Zones 1 and 2 include a distance up to 150 miles from the sender; Zone 3, between 150 and 300 miles; Zone 4, between 300 and 600 miles; Zone 5, between 600 and 1000 miles; Zone 6, between 1000 and 1400 miles; Zone 7, between 1400 and 1800 miles; Zone 8, over 1800 miles.

The rates for parcel post mail are as follows:

| ZONE | I TO 2 LBS. |
|---|---|
| Local | $ .60 |
| 1-2 | .65 |
| 3 | .70 |
| 4 | .75 |
| 5 | .80 |
| 6 | .90 |
| 7 | 1.00 |
| 8 | 1.05 |

In general, as the weight of the parcel increases, the charge per pound decreases.

The exceptions to the limits in size and weight are that 100 inches length and girth combined and 70 pounds weight are permitted for live plants, trees, shrubs, agricultural commodities, baby fowl, books, appliances for the blind, and for parcels mailed on rural or star routes or to a United States Territory or possession outside continental United States, or to or from Army, Navy, or Air Force post offices. The rates are the same as in the table above.

Parcels for fourth-class matter must be mailed at a regular post office or branch post office, or may be delivered to a rural carrier. They cannot be mailed at railway post office cars. Addresses must include a ZIP code number.

For information regarding the shipment of firearms, live animals, fowl, insects and reptiles, consult your local postmaster.

Meat and meat-food products, parcels of game, and nursery stock may be mailed under certain conditions. Consult your local postmaster for details on such mailings.

### Exceptions to the Above Rates

*Educational Materials.* Books of 24 pages (22 of which are printed) without advertising other than incidental announcements of books; manuscripts; periodical articles; music; objective tests, printed educational reference charts; 16 mm. and narrower width films and their catalogues, and sound recordings may be mailed to all zones for 14 cents for the first pound and 7 cents for each additional pound up to 70 pounds.

*Library Books and Materials.* Up to 70 pounds can be mailed to or from public libraries and other non-profit organizations in all zones at the rate of 6 cents for the first pound and 2 cents for each additional pound.

*Catalogues.* Catalogues and similar printed advertising material can also be mailed at special rates, provided that the matter to be mailed weighs 16 ounces or more but not more than 10 pounds, has 24 or more pages, 22 of which are printed and is in bound form. The catalogues must be individually addressed. The following table shows the approximate rates for catalogues (but does not apply to bulk mail that contains a number of pieces to be delivered to a single address). Any fraction of a cent resulting from computing the total postage is counted as a full cent.

| ZONE | I TO 1½ LBS. | 2 LBS. | EACH ADDTL. LB., APPROX. |
|---|---|---|---|
| Local | $.28 | $.29 | $.02 |
| 1-2 | .34 | .35 | .04 |
| 3 | .34 | .36 | .04 |
| 4 | .36 | .38 | .05 |
| 5 | .38 | .41 | .06 |
| 6 | .40 | .43 | .08 |
| 7 | .42 | .47 | .09 |
| 8 | .46 | .51 | .11 |

### SPECIAL HANDLING

Parcel post (fourth-class mail) and third-class mail do not receive the same quick service as first-class mail; however, by paying a fee for special-handling service, the sender may secure the equivalent of first-class mail privileges for his parcel. These privileges, known as *expeditious dispatch transportation and delivery,* do not include special delivery. (That is, the parcel is transported rapidly, but when it reaches the destination post office it is delivered in the regular delivery schedule.) Special handling fees are paid in addition to the regular postage, as follows:

| | |
|---|---|
| Up to 2 pounds | 25 cents |
| Over 2 pounds up to 10 pounds | 35 cents |
| Over 10 pounds | 50 cents |

### AIR PARCEL POST SERVICE

Mail weighing more than 8 ounces which is to be shipped by air is charged the rates for air parcel post service. All parcels sent via air parcel post should be prominently endorsed "Via Air Mail," not only on the address side but on each end and side. When available, printed labels bearing these words should be affixed to parcels. All parcels must bear the name and address of the sender. Domestic registered, insured, and C.O.D. mail may be sent by air parcel post upon payment of the prescribed fees, which are in addition to the air zone postage, and surcharges when required on registered mail.

Parcels weighing up to and including one pound can be sent to all eight postal zones for $1.00. Charges for additional weight are now computed at half-pound increments and vary with the distance the parcel is sent. Precise costs can be obtained at the post office. Eighth zone airmail rates apply to all air parcels sent from the United States to Puerto Rico, the possessions of the United States, the Canal Zone, and islands of the United States Trust Territory in the Pacific. Parcels weighing less than 10 pounds but exceeding 84 inches in length and girth

# Useful Business Facts and Figures

combined are subject to the 10-pound rate. They must not exceed 100 inches combined.

## DOMESTIC REGISTERED MAIL

All mail of value may be registered to protect the sender from loss. This means that the post office must pay to the sender an amount equal to the declared value of the mail if the latter is lost. Declared value must be the full value. If registered mail is also commercially insured, postal liability has a maximum or is pro-rated. The fees for registered mail are the first-class or air mail rate plus a registry fee based on the value of the mail, as follows:

| VALUE | FEE |
|---|---|
| $.01 to $100.00 | .95 |
| $100.01 to $200.00 | 1.25 |
| $200.01 to $400.00 | 1.55 |
| $400.01 to $600.00 | 1.85 |
| $600.01 to $800.00 | 2.15 |
| $800.01 to $1,000.00 | 2.45 |

The fee for declared value of $1,000-$2,000 is $2.75. For successive thousands the additional cost is 30 cents a thousand up to $10,000 (for which the fee is $5.15). For $10,000 to $1,000,000 the rate is $5.15 plus 20 cents for each additional thousand.

## DOMESTIC INSURED MAIL

Only third- and fourth-class mail can be insured; mail of the first and second classes is usually registered if it is valuable. The schedule of domestic insurance fees is as follows:

| AMOUNT OF INSURANCE | FEE |
|---|---|
| From $.01 to $15.00 | $.20 |
| From $15.01 to $50.00 | .30 |
| From $50.01 to $100.00 | .40 |
| From $100.01 to $150.00 | .50 |
| From $150.01 to $200.00 | .60 |

## RETURN RECEIPTS

The sender may, for an extra fee, request the post office to send him a return receipt signed by the person who will receive the mail. The fee is 15 cents for domestic registered and insured mail if the return receipt is requested at the time of mailing. A fee of 25 cents must be paid if this receipt is requested after the time of mailing. If the return receipt is to show to whom, when, and the address where the mail was delivered, the charge is 35 cents. For restricted delivery the charge is 50 cents.

## CERTIFICATES OF MAILING

If evidence of mailing only is required, a certificate of mailing may be purchased for all classes of mail. The purpose is to certify at the post office that something was mailed. A receipt is not obtained upon delivery of the mail to the addressee. A certificate of mailing does not insure the article against loss or damage. The fee for a certificate of mailing is 5 cents for each individual piece. If identical pieces are mailed in bulk, the fee is 25 cents for up to the first 1,000 pieces and 5 cents for each additional 1,000 pieces or fraction thereof.

## CERTIFIED MAIL

Any first-class mail (including air mail and special delivery) which has no intrinsic value may be accepted as certified mail. This service provides for a receipt to the sender and a record of delivery at the office of address. No record is kept at the office at which mailed. No insurance coverage is provided. The fee for certified mail is 30 cents in addition to postage. The fees for return receipts are the same as those for domestic registered and insured mail return receipts.

## DOMESTIC C.O.D. MAIL, UNREGISTERED

C.O.D. (Collect on Delivery) mail of the third- or fourth-class, and sealed mail that bears postage at the first-class rate may be sent according to the following fees:

| AMOUNT OF C.O.D. CHARGES OR AMOUNT OF INSURANCE DESIRED | FEE C.O.D. |
|---|---|
| From $.01 to $10.00 | .70 |
| From $10.01 to $25.00 | .80 |
| From $25.01 to $50.00 | .90 |
| From $50.01 to $100.00 | 1.00 |
| From $100.01 to $200.00 | 1.10 |

## DOMESTIC C.O.D. MAIL, REGISTERED

C.O.D. (Collect on Delivery) mail that is sealed and registered, and bears postage at the first-class rate, may be sent according to the following formula for computing the fee:

FEE FOR REGISTERED MAIL PLUS FLAT FEE FOR C.O.D.

(Based on declared value of package as shown in above table under "Domestic Registered Mail.")  $.60

Although the limit of collections is $200.00, C.O.D. mail may be registered for larger amounts, as in the regulations for Domestic Registered Mail.

There is a fee of 5 cents for notifying the sender of inability to deliver a C.O.D. article.

## DOMESTIC SPECIAL DELIVERY

The fees for special delivery service (paid in addition to the regular postage) for *first-class* mail are:

Up to 2 pounds..............60 cents
Over 2 pounds up to 10 pounds...75 cents
Over 10 pounds..............90 cents

For *second-, third-,* and *fourth-class* mail, special delivery fees are also paid in addition to the regular postage, as follows:

Up to 2 pounds..............80 cents
Over 2 pounds up to 10 pounds..90 cents
Over 10 pounds..............$1.05

## DOMESTIC MONEY ORDERS

The maximum amount for which a single money order may be issued is $100. When a larger sum is to be sent, additional orders must be obtained; any number of orders may be drawn on any money order office in any one day. The following table lists the fees for money orders drawn on the domestic form (for information on international money orders, see the discussion of foreign mail):

Payable in the United States, including Hawaii, Puerto Rico, and the United States Virgin Islands, or in Guam and Tutuila (Samoa); also for orders payable in Antigua, Bahamas, Barbados, Bermuda, British Honduras, British Virgin Islands, Canada, Canal Zone, Dominica, Grenada, Guyana, Jamaica, Montserrat, Nevis, Newfoundland, Philippine Islands, St. Kitts, St. Lucia, St. Vincent, and Trinidad and Tobago.

| AMOUNT | FEE |
|---|---|
| From $.01 to $10.00 | $.25 |
| From $10.01 to $50.00 | .35 |
| From $50.01 to $100.00 | .40 |

### ZIP CODE SYSTEM

The purpose of the ZIP Code is to achieve greater accuracy and speed in the dispatch and delivery of mail. The ZIP Code is a five-digit system of mail sorting, distribution, and delivery which identifies each post office and delivery unit as well as the sectional center or major office through which mail is routed. The first digit identifies the geographical area; the second and third identify the major city or sectional center, and the fourth and fifth digits identify the post office or other delivery unit. The ZIP Code should appear on the last line of the address of destination and the return address following the city and state. No comma should be inserted between the State name and the ZIP Code, but there should be a space of not less than two-tenths of an inch between the last letter of the State and the first digit of the code. When the State name is abbreviated, the use of a period punctuating the name of the State is optional so long as the space precedes the ZIP Code. For large volume mailers, the ZIP Code may be carried as the bottom line of the address and should be indented not less than two tenths of an inch.

### METERED MAIL

Although most letters are stamped and postmarked (canceled) before they can be delivered, many business concerns prefer to use special machines which make the use of postage stamps unnecessary. Mail that has been postmarked by a machine of this type is known as *metered mail*. These machines are not manufactured by the government, but by private companies. After buying the meter, the purchaser takes it to the post office; there it is set for a certain amount of money or a number of "impressions." The required payment for this service must be made when the meter is set by the post office. An added convenience is the fact that this machine indicates at all times exactly how much postage has been used, and the amount (if any) that remains to the credit of the firm.

### RURAL DELIVERY

In many rural localities throughout the United States, mail is delivered by rural carriers. Any person who wishes to avail himself of this service must erect a mailbox 3½ to 4 feet above the surface of the ground, on the righthand side of the road in the direction of travel of the carrier. Whenever possible, rural mailboxes should be placed in groups.

### UNMAILABLE MATTER

Matter that does not conform to the rules regarding the size or weight of a parcel, legibility of address, or any other regulations cannot be mailed. Unmailable matter also includes revolvers, pistols, or any other type of firearms that can be hidden on the person; poisons; inflammable or explosive articles; dunning post cards; all spirituous and malt liquors; any articles that have a bad odor; indecent matter (written or otherwise); and liquor advertisements to or from localities where the sale of liquor is prohibited by law. Game killed out of season is unmailable, and the mailing of lottery, endless chain, and fraudulent matter is likewise illegal.

### HOW TO RECLAIM MAIL

After mail has been posted, it can be reclaimed by the sender only in case of urgent necessity. The sender must fill out a special form giving complete information in regard to the mail, and he must also furnish satisfactory identification. All expenses which the process of recalling the mail may involve must be paid by the sender; for example, if the mail is already on its way to its destination, the postmaster may send a telegram to have it returned, but the sender must pay for such a telegram.

## Foreign Mail

### FIRST-CLASS MAIL

*Letters.* The rate to Canada and to Mexico is 8 cents for each ounce, just the same as for domestic letters.

For all other countries, including Central and South America, Bermuda and other Atlantic islands, England and all Europe, Asia, and all other foreign destinations, the rate is 13 cents for the first ounce and 8 cents for each additional ounce.

*Letter Packages.* In order to send merchandise to a foreign destination at the letter rate, a customs declaration or invoice must be enclosed, and a green label—obtainable at the post office—must be attached securely to the outside of the wrapper or envelope.

*Weight.* Foreign letters and letter packages are limited to 4 pounds, 6 ounces except to Canada (including Newfoundland) for which it is 60 pounds.

*Post Cards.* The rate to Canada and Mexico is 6 cents for each post card. For post cards to be sent to any other foreign destination, the rate is 8 cents per card. Post cards should not be less than 4¼ inches long and 3 inches wide; and not more than 6 inches long and 4¼ inches wide.

*Air Mail.* The rate for air-mail letters to Canada and Mexico is 11 cents per ounce or fraction of an ounce. For air-mail post cards to Canada or Mexico the rate is 9 cents per card.

Air-mail rates for each half ounce or fraction thereof, to other foreign countries, are as given below:

To Central America, South America (including Guyana, French Guiana, and Dutch Guiana or Surinam), the West Indies, Bermuda, 15 cents.

To any of the countries of Europe (except the U.S.S.R.), as well as all islands (including the Azores) located within the waters that surround the continent of Europe, 20 cents. The rate for all other localities is 25 cents.

In each instance the weight is limited to 4 pounds, 6 ounces, except air mail destined for Canada (including Newfoundland) for which the limit is 60 pounds.

For air mail post cards to all foreign destinations except Canada and Mexico, the rate is 13 cents.

Aerogrammes, or special lightweight letter blanks which fold to form their own envelopes, may be purchased at the post office for 15 cents and sent to all countries. No enclosures are permitted.

### SPECIAL DELIVERY (EXPRES)

Special delivery mail to a foreign country is 60 cents extra up to 2 pounds, 75 cents for 2—10 pounds, and 90 cents for over 10 pounds. However, the domestic special delivery fee is paid for mail to Canada. An exprès label should be attached to the envelope or wrapper; or the word exprès may be marked clearly in red ink directly below the stamps. Only letters and articles at the letter rate may be sent special delivery to Canada (including Newfoundland). In the following countries, ordinary and registered letters, post cards, printed matter, commercial papers, small packets and samples—but not parcel post packages—may be sent exprès: Argentina, Australia, Bahamas, Belgium, Brazil, British Honduras (Belize only), Chile, China (Formosa), Cyprus, Dominican Rep., Ecuador, Egypt, France, Ghana, Gibraltar, Great Britain and Northern Ireland, Guatemala, Guyana, Ireland, Israel, Jordan, Kenya, Mexico, Panama, Portugal, St. Pierre and Miquelon, Sweden, Switzerland, Uganda, and Union of South Africa.

### INTERNATIONAL MONEY ORDERS

From time to time International Money Orders to certain countries are discontinued temporarily. Consequently it is important to consult your post office if there is any doubt as to this service being available for a given country. We give the standard list although service to a few of the countries listed may be found to be discontinued.

The following rates apply when the money order is payable in Argentina, Australia, Austria, Belgium, Brazil, Chile, China (Nationalist), Colombia, Costa Rica, Czechoslovakia, Denmark, Finland, France, West Germany, Great Britain and Northern Ireland, Greece, Guatemala, Hungary, Iceland, Iraq, Ireland, Italy, Japan, Lebanon, Luxemburg, Malaya, Mexico, Morocco, Netherlands, New Zealand, Norway, Peru, Philippines, Poland, Republic of South Africa, Ryukyu Islands, Salvador, Surinam (Dutch Guiana), Sweden, Switzerland, Syria, Thailand, Tunisia, United Arab Republic, Uruguay, and Yugoslavia:

From $.01  to $10.00 . . . . . . . . . . . $.45
From $10.01 to $50.00 . . . . . . . . . . . .65
From $50.01 to $100.00 . . . . . . . . . . . .75

The maximum amount for which a single money order may be drawn in the United States is $100.

### OTHER FOREIGN POSTAL INFORMATION

On account of varying conditions and rates, information in regard to parcel post, registered, C.O.D., and other mail to foreign destinations should be secured at the post office.

# Telegrams and Cablegrams

Domestic rates for Telegraph messages, Day Letters, and Night Letters include United States, Canada (including Newfoundland) and Mexico. Messages to all other countries are considered international communications and are sent as Cablegrams. Rate sheets for domestic and international communications are available at all telegraph offices.

### TELEGRAMS

*Regular Telegrams.* The regular telegram (known as a full-rate expedited service) is the most rapid form of telegraphic service, and it has the right of way over every other type of telegram. Its rates are higher than for the other kinds. The minimum charge made for a regular telegram is for fifteen words, with an additional charge for each word above fifteen. Rates vary according to distance. The name and address of the person to whom the telegram is being sent are not counted or charged for. Also there is no charge for the name, in the signature; but if the sender wishes to include his address, the number of words in the address are counted and charged for (a house number or street number counting as a word).

*Day Letters.* The day letter is a deferred (less rapid) service at lower than the regular telegram rates. Charges for a day letter are made on the basis of 50 words, which can be sent for approximately 1½ times the cost of sending a regular 15-word telegram. The sender may use code language in a day letter if necessary.

*Night Letters.* The night letter is sent at rates considerably lower than the regular telegram or the day letter. It is a deferred service. A night letter may be sent at any time during the day and up to 2 A.M. for delivery not earlier than the following morning. The minimum charge is for 50 words. Additional words are charged for in groups of five words.

*Mailgrams.* Mailgrams can be sent anywhere in the continental United States at a cost of $1.60 for the first 100 words or less, and 80 cents for each additional 100 words or less. The message is transmitted electronically from the city of the sender to the city of the receiver, and then delivered by a postman on the next business day.

*Money Orders.* Money may be sent by telegraph, accompanied by a message, with the same rapidity that a regular telegram is sent. The sender fills out a money order at the telegraph office, giving the clerk the amount of money to be sent; if the sender wants personal identification to be required of the payee, he signs his name on a special line to indicate his wishes and also writes out some information that could be used for a test question.

Domestic money orders (orders for delivery within the United States) will be canceled and a refund made to the sender if the payment cannot be effected within 72 hours after the money order has been received at the paying office. In the case of a foreign order, the foreign equivalent of the amount stated in the order is paid at the current rate of exchange.

*Other Information.* To avoid errors or delays, the sender of a telegram message of any type may ask that it be telegraphed back to the originating office for comparison. For this, one half of the unrepeated message rate must be paid in addition.

It is not necessary to write numbers out; five figures are counted as a single word. A rate of five letters to a word is charged for groups of letters which are not to be found in dictionaries. The sender is allowed to use words from foreign languages, however. Signs which can be transmitted in domestic messages are: $, &, #, ' (for feet), and " (for inches). No charge is made for signatures and ordinary addresses. Abbreviations are considered to be complete words and are charged for accordingly. Normal punctuation marks are not counted.

*Special Services.* Hotel and/or motel reservation service is handled by Western Union. Accommodation in any U.S. locality is assured. The rate is telegraph cost plus a nominal fee.

Congratulations, holiday and birthday greetings, and children's Christmas Santa-grams are delivered on decorated blanks within the United States.

Singing telegrams cost regular rates plus 75 cents.

Fifteen-word Public Opinion Messages may be sent to Washington or to state capitals for $1.00 plus tax.

*Special Handling.* All telegrams can be delivered, if requested, in four different ways: personal delivery only, delivery by messenger only, delivery by telephone, and with report of delivery. "Personal delivery only" telegrams are delivered *only* to the addressee. Telegrams delivered by messengers can be received and signed for by persons other than the addressee.

*Report Delivery.* The time and the address to which a telegram is delivered can be furnished at the cost of a return telegram. The sender should simply mark "Report Delivery" or "Report Delivery and Address" after the addressee's name.

### CABLEGRAMS

The cost of sending a cablegram varies from 23 to 34 cents a word, according to the destination and the type of messages sent. Signatures and addresses are counted and charged for. For frequent users of international communications various forms of code are available or some concerns formulate their own codes. Many users of cable service pay a charge of $25.00 a year or $15.00 for six months to have individual code cable addresses registered at the offices of the cable companies. (In New York City the cost is $15.00 a year and $9.00 for six months.)

*Full-rate Cablegrams.* Full-rate cablegrams are the standard service. This is the most rapid cablegram, and the full rates are charged. The minimum charge is for seven words. Addresses and signatures are counted and charged for. In the address, the name of the destination point, if a compound, should be joined and counted as one word, regardless of length. Groups of letters, figures, signs, or a combination of these are counted in groups of five which equal one word. Single punctuation marks are counted as one word as well as sets of parentheses or quotation marks.

*Code Messages.* These cablegrams consist of five-letter groups, and receive the same service as full-rate cablegrams.

*Letter Cables.* Letter cables are overnight plain-language (not code) messages, and are a deferred service, charged for at one half of the full rate. The minimum charge is for 22 words. In counting the words in a letter cable, the address and signature must be counted, and also one word must be allowed for the telegraph code LT which means "letter cable."

*Ship Radiograms.* The sending of ship radiograms is a service to ships at sea in all parts of the world. Either plain-language or code may be used for these messages. No deferred service is available for sending ship radiograms. The rate is 33¼ cents a word to ships of American registry and 38¼ cents a word to ships of foreign registry.

# Table of Weights and Measures

## Linear Measure

### ENGLISH UNITS

| | |
|---|---|
| 12 inches | = 1 foot |
| 3 feet | = 1 yard |
| 5½ yards | = 1 rod |
| 320 rods | = 1 mile |
| 1760 yards | = 1 mile |
| 5280 feet | = 1 mile |
| 40 rods | = 1 furlong |
| 6080.27 feet | = 1 nautical mile |

### METRIC UNITS

| | |
|---|---|
| 10 millimeters | = 1 centimeter |
| 10 centimeters | = 1 decimeter |
| 10 decimeters | = 1 meter |
| 10 meters | = 1 dekameter |
| 10 dekameters | = 1 hectometer |
| 10 hectometers | = 1 kilometer |
| 10 kilometers | = 1 myriameter |

### APPROXIMATE EQUIVALENTS

| | |
|---|---|
| 1 centimeter | = .39 inch |
| 1 inch | = 2.54 centimeters |
| 1 meter | = 3.28 feet |
| 1 foot | = .31 meter |
| 1 meter | = 1.09 yards |
| 1 yard | = .91 meter |
| 1 kilometer | = .62 mile |
| 1 mile | = 1.61 kilometers |

## Surface Measure

### ENGLISH UNITS

| | |
|---|---|
| 144 square inches | = 1 square foot |
| 9 square feet | = 1 square yard |
| 30¼ square yards | = 1 square rod |
| 160 square rods | = 1 acre |
| 4840 square yards | = 1 acre |
| 640 acres | = 1 square mile |

### METRIC UNITS

| | |
|---|---|
| 1 square millimeter | = .000001 square meter |
| 1 square centimeter | = .0001 square meter |
| 1 square decimeter | = .01 square meter |
| 1 square kilometer | = 1,000,000 square meters |
| 1 square kilometer | = 100 hectares |

### APPROXIMATE EQUIVALENTS

| | |
|---|---|
| 1 square centimeter | = .15 square inch |
| 1 square inch | = 6.45 square centimeters |

| | | |
|---|---|---|
| 1 square foot | = | .09 square meter |
| 1 square meter | = | 10.76 square feet |
| 1 square yard | = | .84 square meter |
| 1 square meter | = | 1.20 square yards |
| 1 square mile | = | 2.60 square kilometers |
| 1 square kilometer | = | .39 square mile |

## Measures of Volume

### ENGLISH UNITS

| | | |
|---|---|---|
| 1728 cubic inches | = | 1 cubic foot |
| 27 cubic feet | = | 1 cubic yard |
| 128 cubic feet | = | 1 cord |

### METRIC UNITS

| | | |
|---|---|---|
| 1 cubic millimeter | = | .000000001 cubic meter |
| 1 cubic centimeter | = | .000001 cubic meter |
| 1 cubic decimeter | = | .001 cubic meter |

### APPROXIMATE EQUIVALENTS

| | | |
|---|---|---|
| 1 cubic inch | = | 16.39 cubic centimeters |
| 1 cubic centimeter | = | .06 cubic inch |
| 1 cubic foot | = | .03 cubic meter |
| 1 cubic meter | = | 36.31 cubic feet |

## Measures of Capacity

### LIQUID MEASURE—U.S.

| | | |
|---|---|---|
| 4 fluid ounces | = | 1 gill |
| 4 gills | = | 1 pint |
| 2 pints | = | 1 quart |
| 4 quarts | = | 1 gallon |

### KITCHEN MEASURE

| | | |
|---|---|---|
| 3 teaspoonfuls | = | 1 tablespoonful |
| ½ fluid ounce | = | 1 tablespoonful |
| 16 tablespoonfuls | = | 1 cupful |
| 2 gills | = | 1 cupful |
| ½ liquid pint | = | 1 cupful |
| 8 fluid ounces | = | 1 cupful |
| 2 cupfuls | = | 1 pint |
| 16 fluid ounces | = | 1 pint |
| 4 cupfuls | = | 1 quart |

### DRY MEASURE—U.S.

| | | |
|---|---|---|
| 2 pints | = | 1 quart |
| 8 quarts | = | 1 peck |
| 4 pecks | = | 1 bushel |

### LIQUID AND DRY MEASURE—METRIC SYSTEM

| | | |
|---|---|---|
| 1000 cubic centimeters | = | 1 liter |
| 1 centiliter | = | .01 liter |
| 1 deciliter | = | .1 liter |
| 1 hektoliter | = | 100 liters |

### APPROXIMATE EQUIVALENTS

#### *Liquid Measure*

| | | |
|---|---|---|
| 1 liquid quart | = | .95 liter |
| 1 liter | = | 1.06 liquid quart |
| 1 gallon | = | 3.79 liters |
| 1 liter | = | .26 gallon |

#### *Dry Measure*

| | | |
|---|---|---|
| 1 dry quart | = | 1.10 liters |
| 1 liter | = | .91 dry quart |
| 1 peck | = | 8.81 liters |
| 1 bushel | = | .35 hektoliter |
| 1 hektoliter | = | 2.84 bushels |

### APOTHECARIES' FLUID MEASURE

| | | |
|---|---|---|
| 60 minims | = | 1 fluid dram |
| 8 fluid drams | = | 1 fluid ounce |
| 16 fluid ounces | = | 1 liquid pint |
| 8 liquid pints | = | 1 gallon |

## Measures of Weight

### AVOIRDUPOIS

| | | |
|---|---|---|
| 27⅓ grams | = | 1 dram |
| 16 drams | = | 1 ounce |
| 16 ounces | = | 1 pound |
| 7000 grams | = | 1 pound |
| 14 pounds | = | 1 stone |
| 100 pounds | = | 1 hundredweight |
| 2000 pounds | = | 1 ton |
| 2240 pounds | = | 1 long ton |

### METRIC

| | | |
|---|---|---|
| 1 centigram | = | .01 gram |
| 1 decigram | = | .1 gram |
| 1 kilogram | = | 1000 grams |
| 1 quintal | = | 100 kilograms |
| 1 tonnean (metric ton) | = | 1000 kilograms |

### APPROXIMATE EQUIVALENTS, AVOIRDUPOIS

| | | |
|---|---|---|
| 1 grain | = | .07 gram |
| 1 gram | = | 15.43 grains |
| 1 ounce | = | 28.35 grams |
| 1 gram | = | .04 ounces |
| 1 pound | = | .45 kilogram |
| 1 kilogram | = | 2.21 pounds |
| 1 ton | = | .91 metric ton |
| 1 metric ton | = | 1.10 tons |

### TROY WEIGHT

| | | |
|---|---|---|
| 24 grains | = | 1 pennyweight |
| 20 pennyweights | = | 1 ounce |
| 12 ounces | = | 1 pound |
| 5760 grains | = | 1 pound troy |

### APOTHECARIES' WEIGHT

| | | |
|---|---|---|
| 20 grains | = | 1 scruple |
| 3 scruples | = | 1 dram |
| 8 drams | = | 1 ounce |
| 12 ounces | = | 1 pound |
| 5760 grains | = | 1 pound |

# Abbreviations Used in Business and Professions

A. acre
A.B. Bachelor of Arts
ABC. American Broadcasting Company
abst. abstract
acc., acct., a/c. account
A.D., A.D. Anno Domini
ad., advt. advertisement
admr. administrator
advp. avoirdupois
AFL-CIO. American Federation of Labor and Congress of Industrial Organizations
agt. agent
AK. Alaska
Ala., AL. Alabama
AMA. American Medical Association

A.M. Master of Arts
A.M., A.M. ante meridiem (before noon)
amt. amount
anon. anonymous
A-1. first class
ans. answer
AP. Associated Press
Apr. April
Ariz., AZ. Arizona
Ark., AR. Arkansas
assn. association
asst. assistant; assorted
Aug. August
&. and
@. at
B.A. Bachelor of Arts
bact., bacterial, bacteriology

# Useful Business Facts and Figures

bal. balance
BBC. British Broadcasting Corporation
bbl. barrel
B.C., b.c. Before Christ
B.D. Bachelor of Divinity
b.l., B/L. bill of lading
bldg. building
b.p., B/P. bills payable
b.r., B/R. bills receivable
Bro. Brother
b.s., B/S. bill of sale
B.S. Bachelor of Science
bu. bushel
c. cent; centigrade; centime; hundred
CAB. Civil Aeronautics Board
c.a.f. cost and freight
Cal., Calif., CA. California
cap. capital; chapter
CBS. Columbia Broadcasting System
c.c. cubic centimeter
C.E. Civil Engineer
cent. hundred; centigrade
cf. compare
Ch. E. Chemical Engineer
c.i.f. cost, insurance, and freight
cm. centimeter
co. company, county
c/o. care of
C.O.D. cash on delivery
Colo., CO. Colorado
Conn., CT. Connecticut
C.P.A. Certified Public Accountant
ctge. cartage
cu. cubic
c.w.o. cash with order
cwt. hundredweight
C.Z. Canal Zone
d. penny; pence
D.C., DC. District of Columbia
D.D. Doctor of Divinity
D.D.S. Doctor of Dental Surgery
Dec. December
Del., DE. Delaware
Dept. Department
div. dividend
D. Lit., D. Litt. Doctor of Literature
doz. dozen
Dr. Doctor; debtor
D.S. Doctor of Science
ea. each
Ed. Editor
e.g. for example
Esq. Esquire
et al. and others
etc. et cetera
exp. export; express
F. Fahrenheit
FBI. Federal Bureau of Investigation
FCC. Federal Communications Commission
FDIC. Federal Deposit Insurance Corporation
Feb. February
ff. following

FHA. Federal Housing Authority
Fig. Figure
Fla., FL. Florida
f.o.b. free on board
Fri. Friday
frt. freight
ft. foot
FTC. Federal Trade Commission
fur. furlong
g. gram
Ga., GA. Georgia
gal. gallon
gm. gram
Gov. Governor
gr. gross
GTC. Good till cancelled
HI. Hawaii
h.p. horsepower
hrs. hours
Ia., IA. Iowa
ib., ibid. ibidem (in the same place)
ICC. Interstate Commerce Commission
id. idem (the same)
Ida., ID. Idaho
i.e. id est (that is)
Ill., IL. Illinois
in. inch
Inc. Incorporated
Ind., IN. Indiana
in re. in regard to
INS. International News Service
ins. insurance
inv. invoice
I.O.U. I owe you
I.Q. Intelligence Quotient
Jan. January
Jr. Junior
k. karat
Kans., Kan., KS. Kansas
kg. kilogram
km. kilometer
kw. kilowatt
Ky., KY. Kentucky
L., £. pound (sterling)
La., LA. Louisiana
lat. latitude
lb. pound
l.c. lower case
l/c. letter of credit
L.H.D. Doctor of Literature
LL.B. Bachelor of Laws
LL.D. Doctor of Laws
LL.M. Master of Laws
lon., long. longitude
L.S. locus sigilli (place of the seal)
l.t. long ton
Ltd. Limited
m. married; masculine; meter
M. Monsieur; Marquis
M. thousand (L)
M.A. Master of Arts
Mar. March
Mass., MA. Massachusetts
MBS. Mutual Broadcasting System
M.C. Member of Congress; master of ceremonies

M.D. Doctor of Medicine
MD. Maryland
mdse. merchandise
M.E. Mechanical Engineer
Me., ME. Maine
memo. memorandum
Messrs., MM. Gentlemen
mfg. manufacturing
mfr. manufacturer
Mgr. Manager, Monsignor
Mich., MI. Michigan
Minn., MN. Minnesota
Miss., MS. Mississippi
mm. millimeters
m.o. money order
Mo., MO. Missouri
Mon. Monday
Mont., MT. Montana
M.P. Member of Parliament; Military Police
Mr. Mister; Master
Mrs. Mistress
M.S. Master of Science
MS., MSS. manuscript; manuscripts
Mt. mount; mountain
N.A.M. National Association of Manufacturers
N.B. Nota bene (Note well; take notice)
NBC. National Broadcasting Company
N.C., NC. North Carolina
N. Dak., N.D., ND. North Dakota
Neb., Nebr., NB. Nebraska
Nev., NV. Nevada
N.H., NH. New Hampshire
N.J., NJ. New Jersey
NLRB. National Labor Relations Board
N. Mex., N.M., NM. New Mexico
no., nos. number, numbers
Nov. November
N.P. Notary Public
N.Y., NY. New York
O., OH. Ohio
o/a. on account
Oct. October
Okla., OK. Oklahoma
OK. all correct
Oreg., Ore., OR. Oregon
Oxon. Oxford; of Oxford
oz. ounce
p. page
Pa., PA. Pennsylvania
p. & l. profit & loss
pd. paid
per cent. by the hundred
pfd. preferred
Ph.D. Doctor of Philosophy
P.M., p.m. post meridiem (afternoon)
P.M. Postmaster; past master
P.O. Post Office
p.p. post paid
pp. pages
pr. pair
PR. Puerto Rico
Pres. President

Prof. Professor
pro tem. pro tempore (for the time being)
P.S. postscript
Q., Qy. query
q.e. quod est (which is)
Q.E.D. Quod erat demonstrandum (which was to be proved)
Qt. Quart
q.v. quod vide (which see)
reg. registered
Rep. Representative
ret. returned
Rev. Reverend
RFC. Reconstruction Finance Corporation
RFD. Rural Free Delivery
R.I., RI. Rhode Island
RR. railroad
R.S.V.P. Répondez, s'il vous plaît (please reply)
Rt. Hon. Right Honorable
Sat. Saturday
S.C., SC. South Carolina
Sc.D. Doctor of Science
S.D., S. Dak., SD. South Dakota
SEC. Securities and Exchange Commission
Sec., secy. secretary
Sen. Senate
Sept. September
sp. gr. specific gravity
sq. square
Sr. Senior
St. Saint; street
S.S. steamship
Str. steamer
Sun. Sunday
Supt. Superintendent
t.b. trial balance
Tenn., TN. Tennessee
Tex., TX. Texas
t.f. till forbidden
Thurs. Thursday
T.N.T. Trinitrotoluene
tr. transpose
treas. treasurer
Tues. Tuesday
TVA. Tennessee Valley Authority
u.c. upper case
UN. United Nations
UPI. United Press International
U.S.A. United States of America
U.S.N. United States Navy
U.S.S. United States Ship
UT. Utah
Va., VA. Virginia
vs., v. against
Vt., VT. Vermont
Wash., WA. Washington
W/B. way bill
Wed. Wednesday
Wis., WI. Wisconsin
wt. weight
W.Va., WV. West Virginia
Wyo., WY. Wyoming
yd. yard
yr. year

108